Office of Vice President
for University Advancement
North Dakota State University
P. O. Box 5753
Fargo, ND 58105

*Where Seldom
Was Heard
A Discouraging
Word ...*

*Bill Guy
Remembers*

Bill Guy

William L. Guy

The North Dakota Institute for Regional Studies
Fargo

© 1992
North Dakota Institute for Regional Studies
North Dakota State University
Fargo

ISBN
0-911-042-42-3
Library of Congress Number
92-6056

I dedicate this book to my wife Jean and our five children, Bill, Jim, Debby, Holly and Nancy. They kept the skies from becoming cloudy all day.

Table of Contents

My Life Before Politics   1

My Early Experiences in Politics   37

A Democratic-NPL Governor is Elected   67

Being Governor (and the Governor's Family)   79

There's a Lot to Being Governor That Doesn't Have
Much to Do with Governing   103

The Presidents I Knew   119

Governing Can Be a Funny Job   159

A Governor Has to (Try to) Relax, Too   171

At Governor's Conferences   183

Off to Vietnam   207

Foreign Customs Abroad and at Home!   221

Famous North Dakotans   235

Representing North Dakota   351

Politics and Politicians   275

Conclusion 285

Acknowledgements

Jean Guy, my wife, who has encouraged me, or should I say prodded me to write this manuscript, and whose memory I could always depend on.

Bonnie Leno Chase, my secretary for many years, who patiently took dictation and recorded many of the incidents.

David Danbom, whose expertise in historical recording kept me on track, on schedule and under budget.

Foreword

Every two years, in this land of the free and home of the brave, election time rolls around. The average Joe and Jane citizen might be surprised to know that probably not many more than one percent of the population of a state or the nation actively engage in organized politics, the lifeblood of our democratic process. And only about ten percent or less of the adult Americans become interested enough in politics to listen to the speeches and contribute money to the politicians to carry out their campaigns. Then to crown it all, usually less than half of the eligible voters cast their votes on election day. That the system works so well is amazing, when, by all odds, it shouldn't work at all.

The one percent of the population actively engaged in organized politics has most of the fun. Oh, I know those in the other nine percent who listen to the speeches, attend the banquets, and write the checks for political contributions are in on it, too. But there's nothing like being a candidate, or a member of the campaign team, or a precinct committee person to savor the joys and sorrows of the American political process.

A political candidate strives to get next to the voters, to gain the confidence of those many people who will talk to one another over a cup of coffee at the local cafe or exchange comments while pushing the shopping cart down the aisle of the local supermarket. A politician must be looked upon as a leader on the one hand, but he also must be regarded as no better than the voters who are listening to him if he is to be successful. Political candidates constantly are trying to relate to the common person, while getting the common person to look to them as a leader. It is a delicate, sensitive process that defies description. Some candidates master it; others don't.

Picture a political rally in a small North Dakota town hall. The chairs, lined up in rows, are old theater seats that creak and groan as people shift their weight. The veneer on the backs has been chipped off, and enough gum has been plastered beneath the folding seats to keep the Russian army chewing for months. The candidate is on the stage, standing before a backdrop of faded and dusty green plush curtains. His knuckles are white as he grips the sides of the old, battered lectern at the edge of the stage. The speaker is a politician. He knows from experience that the microphone angling out from the chromium pipe anchored in the heavy metal base may or may not work, depending on his luck. And, when it doesn't work, the engineer in charge of keeping the microphone working is probably at home eating supper or vacationing in some faraway land. The politician probably pulls that standing microphone nearer to the edge of the lectern because it gets pretty tiresome shouting across a lectern, trying to talk into an ancient microphone.

The candidate hesitantly begins. "You can't blame me for feeling a little scared, standing up here, speaking to a crowd in a big city like Crosby, cause I'm more used to speaking in a little place, like my hometown of Amenia. Yes, I said Amenia—not amnesia, and not anemia—but Amenia. I grew up in that little town back in the depression years of the 1930s. Now, I don't expect any women in this audience to be old enough to remember those depression years of the 1930s, but I'll bet there are a few men in this audience who can remember." The self-conscious titter of the older women in the audience eases the tension and the politician stops gripping the lectern and starts to gently caress its battered sides.

"Amenia was Sanforized when it was established before the turn of the century," the politician says. "It had about 84 people then, and it hasn't shrunk or stretched since. But, back in those dirty depression years of the 1930s, we were terribly poor in Amenia, like everybody else in North Dakota. When I compare it to the problems that we have today, there just isn't any comparison. Today, towns, and even counties, are plagued with where to pile all of their trash and junk—'solid waste disposal,' they call it. We didn't have a solid waste disposal problem when I was a kid, because back in those depression years, we either wore it or drove it. It was really dog eat dog in those days, and nobody seemed to have an extra dime. Amenia tried hard to get ahead. We did everything to get the farmers to come in and shop and to do their business there.

"Amenia wasn't like a lot of small country towns that you've seen where they have a 'No U-Turn' sign at each end of the main street to make people drive around the block, so that merchants off the main street would get a crack at them. No, sir. Amenia wasn't like that. We had only one main street, and the signs at each end said, 'U-Turns are Permitted.' I guess it was some wag from CASSELTON down the road who had painted under one of those signs, 'for what?'

"But I was glad that I grew up in a small town. We kids had to make our own recreation. Three times a week we'd go over to the railroad tracks when we heard the freight train coming, and we'd count boxcars going through on our Great Northern branch line. If we were lucky enough to have a penny we might lay it on the track to see what kind of shape it would get squashed into by the steel wheels of the train. We thought we were pretty brave because it was rumored among us kids that it was illegal to squash a penny, and that the Secret Service would be out if they heard about it. I don't remember anybody ever sacrificing a nickel for a thrill like that.

"Going to a little high school, like Amenia, had its advantages. You got to participate in sports, to play in the band, to act in plays, and to run for class office. Why, it even made it possible for me to be class salutatorian when I graduated—the other senior was valedictorian.

"Our high school was so small in Amenia that one year we had a four-man basketball team. Believe you me, a kid had to be in good shape to play man to man on a four-man basketball team! The only embarrassing part of playing with only four players was just at the start of the game when one of our guys had to shake hands with two of their guys. We didn't have a nice big gym like you have here in Crosby. Our gym was up over Carley's grocery store and was just a cracker box with only one row of chairs around the edge of the floor. It had a low ceiling and a great big potbellied stove protruded a few feet out onto one corner of the playing floor. When our team was defending that end of the floor, our four-man zone defense was very effective. That hot stove was as good as a stationary guard. Some nights, I still wake up in a cold sweat remembering those screams and the smell of toasted elbow as an opponent would get careless around that stove."

By this time, the politician, me, had loosened up his crowd and himself and had convinced everybody that he was just another small-town citizen from North Dakota seeking their vote; and, if they'd just sit still in those creaking, old plywood theater seats, he'd give them a real political message. And that crowd, whether it was ten people or fifty, always sat expectantly, knowing there was a reward at the end of the political speech when cookies, donuts, and coffee would be served.

And so, the political message got around, and the public had a chance to assess the politician who sought their votes.

1

My Life Before Politics

Early Days

I was born in Devils Lake, North Dakota, on September 30, 1919. My father was the first County Agricultural Extension Agent of Ramsey County. His ability soon won him an assignment as agent in Cass County in 1921. My first memories are of life in Fargo. We lived on College Street, then the last paved street on the northwest edge of the city.

During the summer, the Fargo-Detroit Ice Company's blue-and-white wagon, looking like a canvas-covered prairie schooner, would come down our street twice a week. A magnificent team of big Belgian horses pulled the wagon, and we could hear their steel shoes clip-clopping from away down the block. The kids would rush to the curb, knowing that when the iceman shaped a block of ice to fit a refrigerator box, his ice ax would send chips of ice littering the pavement behind the wagon. The minute he lifted the block of ice, gripped in tongs, from the spring scale suspended from the rear of the wagon and slung the gleaming block over the heavy black rubber pad on his shoulder, we kids would rush forward to gather the melting chips of ice to suck on or gleefully chuck down an unsuspecting victim's shirt collar or pants pocket.

On very hot days, the pavement tar became so soft that we could pinch a piece from the edge and use it for chewing gum. Asphalt mixed with gravel was not used yet and pavement tar had only an occasional stone to disrupt good chewing.

Because my parents were loyal graduates of North Dakota Agricultural College and because we lived only a couple of blocks from the campus, I was introduced to college activities at an early age. Football, then as now, provided a status or ranking of colleges, and it was important to field winning teams. NDAC's Claudie Miller was my first football hero.

Perhaps I became aware of Claudie's exploits when, on a Saturday afternoon, my father and several of his friends spread a heavy sheet of brown wrapping paper to resemble a football field on our dining room table. Then, huddled over the static-laden description of the out-of-town game coming from our super hetrodyne radio, they would move salt shakers and dominoes on the flat wrapping paper to visualize the progress of the game. I learned not only the jargon of the football game but also the appropriate time to utter a mild swear word or two. By the time I was six years old, I was a knowledgeable member of the "knothole gang" who received free passes to NDAC football games as long as we sat in the stands behind the west-end goal posts. It wasn't the best place to watch a football game, but we didn't have to look into the Saturday afternoon sun, and the price was right.

We moved to Amenia in December 1925 when Dad became manager of the Carrie T. Chaffee Estate, a major remnant of the Amenia Sharon Land Company. The snow was deep that winter. When we turned our four-cylinder Dodge sedan north out of Casselton for the first time, we had to resort to a single track through a field because Highway 18 was hopelessly blocked with snow. The trip was precarious—sometimes on the highway and sometimes alongside in a field to circumvent the huge drifts. The car had no heater, and the windows frosted over. Jolting along slowly seeking the track through the deep snow was an introduction to rural living that I never forgot.

Amenia was a good little town—laid out in old English style with one square block in the center devoted to a public park. Houses, business places, and the consolidated grade and high school faced the park. Because Amenia had been established in the 1870s as the headquarters of the huge Amenia-Sharon Land Company bonanza farm, it had some amenities as a company town that were not found in other small towns. It had its own water and sewage system, electric generator, telephone exchange, and six metal streetlamps along concrete sidewalks.

But a person can be too effusive about Amenia's amenities. The city water was extremely hard and always in short supply. If, at night, someone's toilet-tank-flapper valve failed to seat, the town was out of water the next morning. During the many times that the city pump would fail or a main line would freeze and break, townspeople would melt snow or conserve rainwater for their Saturday night bath—in two inches of water in the bath tub. Ernie McDonagh, the village drayman, had a small business of selling 50 gallon drums of Detroit Lakes spring water for drinking to those who could afford it. Amenia's sewage was pumped to a nearby slough, a forerunner of today's sewage lagoon systems. Fortunately, Ottertail Power Company took over the electric light franchise, and later Northwestern Bell Telephone Company absorbed the Amenia Telephone Exchange.

My mother was a pianist and was always on call to play the piano or organ for church services, weddings, and funerals and to accompany students when they played solos at music contests. We started a school band in 1932. Paul Smith, an area farmer and clarinet player, was the conductor. My uncle, Louis Leet, loaned his old C Melody saxophone to me so I could begin playing an instrument. The old saxophone had been in an attic for years and was reluctant to return to service. But I worked at it and was finally able to honk out melodies on it.

I was even invited to come to an evening community gathering in Chaffee to play a solo. When my part in the program came, I tongue-moistened my reed and climbed resolutely up the stairs to the stage. About halfway through my solo, my mother, who was accompanying me, was startled when my sax emitted a discordant squawk. A large round leather pad whose glue had dried, finally fell out of the saxophone and rolled like a dollar to the edge of the stage and dropped off. The crowd went from stunned embarrassment to unrestrained laughter in seconds. I marched to the edge of the stage and down the stairs to retrieve the pad. Licking the glue on the back of the pad, I quickly pressed it back in place. It held. I again mounted the stage and replayed my solo. I've often said that I was so scarred by that humiliating episode that appearances before audiences have been painful ever since.

Though we lived in Amenia, our house had a barn behind it. When I was ten, my father decided that my brother, Jim, age eight, and I were old enough to join 4-H Club activities. He bought two shorthorn steer calves for us to raise as 4-H Club projects. The steers were tied in stalls in the barn when they were fed. On the 4th of July, my father took the day off and announced he would help Jim and me teach our 800 pound calves to lead. He secured a 30-foot rope to the halter of the first calf. Dad was next to the calf, and my brother and I gripped the rope at a discreet distance behind him. The steer did not understand what was wanted of him. He tossed his head and sashayed sideways. Then he took a few tentative steps forward and then backed up.

Suddenly a mighty blast from a neighbor's 4th of July aerial bomb sounded. The steer lowered his head and plunged down the alley. My father was jerked off his feet but regained a grasp of the rope that my brother and I had dropped. The plunging steer dragged my father along the cinder-surfaced alley until he could scramble to his feet and snub the end of the rope around a nearby telephone pole. The ride behind the steer had fixed the elbows of his shirt and his temper. When he had regained his composure, he said, "Next year, boys, you are going to be sheepmen."

And next year we were sheepmen. He bought us four old broken-mouthed purebred Shropshire ewes and a ram from NDAC. Jim and I took to sheep raising and stayed with it, building up our flock until I went away to college. One year we had the reserve champion fat lamb at the state 4-H achievement contest at NDAC. The Amenia Community Club bought that champion lamb at the 4-H sale. A month later, my brother and I were guests of honor at a Community Club banquet that featured our lamb in the form of chops and roasts. When a lamb chop from my good wooly friend was placed in front of me, my appetite vanished. All I could see were those trusting eyes of the lamb we had so lovingly fed, watered and cared for all those months before, and here was his trust betrayed in the form of a lamb chop!

The Rush River was less than a half mile from town. A railroad company dam held water in the river, but it seldom flowed. We learned to swim in that murky water. It never occurred to us that the cattle feedlot across from our swimming beach might be polluting the water. But I learned to swim well. When our Amenia Boy Scout troop went to Camp Shawandasee near Detroit Lakes, I took training in Junior Red Cross Lifesaving and became certified.

A few weeks after I had won my Red Cross Lifesaving badge, I was called upon to use it. My father's company coupe skidded to a stop in a cloud of dust next to our house, and he shouted to me to get into the car. We raced west out of Amenia toward the Civilian Conservation Corps dam project on the Rush River. "One of the CCC boys has drowned," my father said as we jolted over the rutted road.

"Nobody out there wants to go into the water to find him, so you'll have to do it."

We pulled up behind a small cluster of stunned young men standing on the river bank. Two men were on a raft, slowly probing the depths with long poles. I stripped off my clothes, hung them on a fence post next to the water and dived in. The brown water was cloudy because of all the silt that the men on the raft had churned up with their poles. I was good at swimming underwater, but the sunken branches and tumbleweeds that had blown into the river made for a frightening, clawing search. A large crowd gathered, and finally the drowned boy was located and raised to the surface.

It was time for me to get out, but I was stark naked. Then to my utter humiliation, I realized that my boxer shorts hanging on the post had been made by my mother from pieces of flour sacks and that the word "Pillsbury" was plainly visible across the seat! I was able to get someone to throw my overalls into the river so I could put them on underwater and climb out. My boxer shorts still may be hanging on that post. The raft my friends and I had built using four-oil drums lost its allure after it served as a recovery vessel for that drowned CCC boy's body.

I was fortunate to get in on the last of the threshing machine era. When I was 14, my dad decided I was old enough to drive a bundle wagon during threshing. I drove a young team of horses that didn't know anything about threshing either. A young friend named Vernon Henderson was on that four-wagon crew. He had an old team of horses that belonged to Emil Johnson, one of the farmers for whom we threshed. We had a threshing run of about six weeks. We had to feed our teams at six o'clock each morning. When I woke up in the mornings, my fingers were curled in stiff claws as they had gripped the pitch fork the day before. I had to pry them straight and work them back and forth to get them limber enough to start the new day.

On one side of the threshing machine feeder, a tractor-mounted hay bucker would bring a load of grain bundles to be deposited in a pile. A "spike" pitcher would throw them into the threshing machine. One by one, as the tractor-bucker dragged in each batch of bundles, a little dirt would be dragged in, too, until a small mound developed.

When the field was finished, the threshing machine was moved to another farm. Vernon Henderson and I started racing our empty bundle racks across the finished field. My young horses enjoyed the run, while Vernon's old team quickly lost interest. But he discovered that by sliding his pitch fork along the rack bed so that the tines protruded just behind his slowest horse, he could get a new burst of speed everytime that horse lagged behind.

Suddenly Vernon's racing bundle rack hit the mound of dirt left where the threshing machine had been stationed. It flew into the air—the rack going in one direction and the running gear and horses going in another. Fortunately Vernon was not hurt when the rack hit the ground, but the racing team kept running down a road until they came to a farmyard where they turned in. When Vernon and I caught up to them, they had run a wagon wheel right up the slot of a one-row corn binder. The farmer who lived there was not at home. We extricated the wheel and slowly led Vernon's exhausted team away. It was some weeks before two young chastened bundle team drivers could muster enough courage to tell the farmer to check over his corn binder before silo-filling season began.

When I left home to enroll at NDAC, my brother, Jim, who was two years younger than I, had developed into a muscular young man. He liked football, though our Amenia High School didn't have a football team until the year after I left. He developed into one of the better football players in our eight-man football team conference. My youngest brother, John, was slender and not athletically inclined.

My brothers and I had accompanied our father to nearly every football game at NDAC from the time we moved to

Amenia. While it was true that much of our football was viewed from the low-rent knothole gang end of the field, we learned a lot about the game. I was determined to go out for football at NDAC. It looked so easy! The recruited freshman football prospects with scholarships were brought in for practice a couple of weeks before the fall quarter began. I was not among the prospects invited in early for a football scholarship. But I decided to attempt to make the team as a walk-on anyway.

I checked in at the athletic department equipment room and told Larry Tanberg, who was in charge, that I wanted a uniform. Larry explained that they didn't have much left, but he threw me a set of shoulder pads with one pad missing, a pair of pants with no pads at all, and a pair of shoes that were too big. "Its the best I can do," he said apologetically. I clomped out to the field where practice was under way. I was a curious sight, I'm sure, with only one shoulder pad and pants that hung to my ankles. On the edge of the field, I happened to stand next to Arnie Seim who was about 6 feet 4 inches tall and must have weighed 240 pounds. I listened to the noise of battle on the field—the smashing of leather on leather and the oaths that followed.

I looked up at Seim and realized that a person could really get hurt out there. With some dismay at what I realized was my lack of courage, I trudged back to the equipment room and turned in my duds. It was one of the smartest decisions in my life. But I didn't need to play football to get into football games. After all, I was playing second alto sax in Dr. C.S. Putnam's Gold Star Band, and we had free seats on the 30-yard line.

My dad was regarded as one of the very best professional farm managers. He looked after 26 farms, the entire town of Amenia, and the Amenia Seed and Grain Company for the Carrie T. Chaffee Estate. Probably my admiration for him and his work caused me to register at NDAC in agricultural economics. The college had been plunged into a traumatic situation the year I registered as a freshman. Governor William Langer, in a fit of anger, had fired the college president and a number of department heads because they had refused to follow his mandate that they and their instructors contribute 2 percent of their salaries to the Governor's political campaign fund. The college immediately lost its accreditation. Enrollment fell almost as low as campus morale.

My father was president of the NDAC Alumni Association when the professors were fired. He and other alumni leaders saw that the state's institutions of higher education had to be insulated from the raw political power that Governor Langer used. With the help of student leaders, the NDAC Alumni Association blanketed the state in a successful effort to pass an initiated Constitutional Amendment to create the Board of Higher Education. Listening to the Constitutional Amendment campaign plans that took place in our living room was my first close look at North Dakota politics. My father would have been surprised had he known that Jean Mason Guy, his oldest son's wife, would one day be chairman of that newly created Board of Higher Education.

Though my college major was agricultural economics, I was genuinely interested in livestock. As a matter of fact, I believed that when I finished college, I would join my father in large-scale lamb feeding. His success as a commercial lamb feeder in those dismal depression years made the profit from buying lambs in Montana and feeding them at Amenia look enticing.

Since I had received good training in livestock judging during my years in 4-H Club activities, I decided to try out for the NDAC Livestock Judging Team. I did make the NDAC judging team that went to the Southwest Livestock Exposition in Fort Worth, Texas. There were four of us on the team and two alternates. We knew that livestock in Texas would be more of the range type and less of the feedlot type we usually judged.

And, in addition to the usual rings of horses, sheep, hogs and cattle, we would have to judge a ring of four mules. None of us had ever laid a hand on a live mule! On our trip to Fort Worth our coach, Ford Daugherty, arranged for us to stop for an afternoon at Oklahoma A&M to get a hands-on feel of a ring of mules. We had to learn fast.

There were 21 colleges and universities with four-man teams competing in the Fort Worth Collegiate Livestock Judging Contest. Each contestant had limited time to view and to get a feel of four similar animals in a "ring." The animals were numbered, and the contestants had to record on a card their ranking of the four animals. Later in the day, each contestant had to go before a contest judge and explain, in just two minutes, why he ranked the animals in a specific ring as he did. We were used to giving reasons for placing sheep, hogs, dairy cattle, horses, and beef cattle, but giving reasons why we placed the four mules as we did was another matter.

The mule judge was a heavy man in cowboy boots who wore a big Stetson hat. His chair was tilted back against the wall of the hotel room, and he chewed on a matchstick. I stood before him and launched into my reasoning on why I had placed the four mules.

When I finished, he took the match from his mouth and in a Southern drawl as heavy as Texas crude oil asked, "Son, have you all ever seen a mule before?"

Inwardly I bristled. "Certainly," I answered.

"How many?" he shot back.

"Well—er, four," I stammered. The judge grinned and looked out the window. "I thought from your accent that might be the case." I was startled to hear that I or any one on our team had an accent. Didn't we speak as plainly as radio announcers? Apparently he and I had different accents. "Well, son," he said, "you done good." Imagine my amazement when later I discovered that out of the 84 contestants, I ranked seventh in mule judging.

My Life Before Politics

World War II was raging in Europe. Gradually, President Franklin Roosevelt eased the United States into preparedness for war. On college campuses, much sentiment was against United States involvement in the European war and NDAC was no exception. "Hell no, we won't go!" was a popular answer to the military draft. My father served as chairman of Cass County's Draft Board. He knew that his three sons eventually would wind up in the military. The Civil Aeronautics Administration began a nationwide program to train young civilian pilots, hoping that a good number of trainees would enlist in the military services.

The program appealed to me and my college roommate, Bill Smith, who had been a buddy of mine since first grade in Amenia. At NDAC we both joined Sigma Alpha Epsilon fraternity. The pilot training course used little 85 hp Aeronca and Piper Cub airplanes. Those flying kites had fabric skins, and the student sat tandem behind the instructor. We went out to the airport twice a week to take an hour flying lesson. After the first takeoff, when my stomach seemed to not want to keep up, flying came easily. We learned to fly figure eight turns, to recover from stalls, and to take off and land.

It was hard to make a serious mistake in those slow awkward aircraft but not impossible. As I sat in an afternoon class on campus, I was startled to hear several sirens racing north on 13th Street toward Hector Airport. Immediately the thought of an airplane crash flashed into my mind. And just as quickly, I remembered that Bill Smith had gone to the airport for his one hour of CAA flight instruction. I couldn't keep my mind on my classwork. Minutes later word came back that two planes had crashed.

A student pilot in a bi-wing Waco coming to land failed to see a Piper Cub in the blind spot under his lower wing. The bigger plane landed on top of the smaller one several hundred feet in the air, and both planes came down out of control. The Waco pilot died instantly, but Bill and his instructor survived the impact. The instructor, whose back was broken, later recovered, but Bill's head injuries were too much, and he died. The student body at NDAC was stunned because Bill was widely known and liked.

I was numb and hesitated going back to finish the flying course. But I did. Because of winter we had to continue the lessons with the planes on skis. My final cross-country test came on an extremely cold but sunny January day. I was to fly solo to Wahpeton and land next to the Wahpeton School of Science, go in and have the aeronautics instructor, Art Sampson, sign my log book, and return to Fargo. The flight south to Wahpeton was fast because of a stiff northwest wind.

I circled the School of Science to make sure of the designated landing field. It was high noon, and the glaring white of the snow below failed to outline the existence of hard snow drifts with sharp icy crests. I came in for my landing against the wind, expecting my skis to touch down on smooth snow. Instead I landed along the top of a sharp, hard snowdrift. Upon impact, the skis spread and the fabric belly of the Cub caught on the snowdrift and ripped away. I was shocked to look between my feet and see snow shooting by! How fortunate I was to land parallel to the snow bank crests rather than into them!

Art Sampson came out and checked the airplane. "It will fly," he said, "but it will vibrate and will be cold against a northerly wind." He was right; it was cold. All feeling left my cold feet as I slowly bucked the wind back. By the time I arrived at Hector Airport, my coordination was suffering. I stalled the Piper about 20 feet in the air and it came down on its skis with a crash, twisted sideways, and slid down the icy runway. I was so cold that I totally ignored the disapproving eyes of my waiting instructor and the irritated complaining of the man who owned the airplane as he surveyed the torn fabric. I got my private flying license, but other events came along to steer me away from joining the military flying service.

About the same time that flying lessons and being editor of the *Bison* yearbook in my senior year were cutting into my school work, I met an attractive freshman girl on a blind date that Mary McCannel, Bill Smith's steady, had arranged. Although I had known many nice girls, the chemistry never had been so powerful as when I met Jean Mason of Fargo. I was accused of "robbing the cradle" for going with a freshman girl. But Jean was perfect for me, and I felt good about her wearing my SAE fraternity pin.

Getting a master's degree in agricultural economics had evolved as a goal of mine. I registered at the University of Minnesota in the Fall of 1941. I stayed in a small room off the hallway in a private home near the St. Paul farm campus. As I began graduate work, I slowly realized that my extracurricular activities at NDAC had prevented me from bearing down as hard as I should have on my studies. At times that first semester, I thought I should quit. It didn't help to have Jean back at NDAC and fair prey to all the wolves whom I imagined were circling around her.

Then on December 7, 1941, the roof fell in. The Japanese attacked Pearl Harbor! As I huddled over my little radio, listening to President Roosevelt talk to the nation, my heart sank when he intimated the destruction of ships at Pearl Harbor. My brother, Jim, was on a battle ship at Pearl Harbor!

I decided to sign up for naval officer training to begin after my first year at the University of Minnesota. But even more important, I must try to lay claim to Jean Mason before someone else did. I thought an engagement ring would be appropriate, but where would I get the money? I was going to graduate school on half a shoestring. Suddenly the thought occurred to me that I could sell my beloved French Selmer alto saxophone that had earned four years of free tuition for me at NDAC. The saxophone sold quickly, and I just as quickly rolled the money over in a down payment on a diamond ring. I pursuaded Jean to accept the ring on New Year's eve 1941.

I've never played a saxophone since, and I've regarded my decision to turn it in on a diamond engagement ring my greatest good fortune.

In May 1942, my father died in Rochester, Minnesota, after months of illness. I returned to Amenia to help my mother and youngest brother, John, make plans for a life without Dad. The Navy deferred my entrance into midshipman training until fall.

When I arrived on the campus of Notre Dame University in October to begin the Naval V-7 program, I was in for the most intensive and difficult study program of my life. Being a graduate engineer would have helped. There were days when I despaired of ever getting a commission. But I did get my Ensign commission on January 28, 1943. Two days later, I walked to the altar of the Fist Congregational Church in Fargo, and Jean Mason become Jean Mason Guy.

After receiving antisubmarine training at Key West, I was assigned to a new destroyer about to be commissioned at Orange, Texas, the DD579 William D. Porter, as gunnery and antisubmarine officer. Jean had been able to catch up with me as I received one training assignment after another. We were always on the brink of destitution on my Ensign's salary, but we enjoyed the challenge of making ends meet.

The *USS William D. Porter*

The *William D. Porter* turned out to be an ill-starred vessel.

As we took on supplies at a dock in Norfolk in the Fall of 1943, our coming assignment assumed mysterious undertones. We were not told what our mission would be, but the kind of supplies and equipment coming aboard seemed to point us toward the North Atlantic. Fleece-lined foul-weather gear in bundles hardly indicated the tropics. And antisubmarine gear, which consisted of towed noise makers to attract acoustic-sensitive torpedoes, made supply ship convoy duty probable.

Our destroyer was ordered to the mouth of Chesapeake Bay, where we were to anchor and tie up side by side with two other destroyers to await the black of midnight when our sealed orders would be opened.

At midnight, in the soft glow of a charthouse lamp, our captain tore open the manilla envelope to receive his instructions. His jaw dropped as he read and re-read. We were to proceed immediately to a spot in the open Atlantic, well offshore, and, with our two sister destroyers, we were to escort the battleship, USS *Iowa*, to England.

That assignment might have been regarded as routine except for the passenger list on the huge sleek-nosed battleship. That roster was a veritable who's who of the big names in the U.S. war effort. President Franklin Roosevelt headed the list of leaders going to Tehran to meet with Winston Churchill and Joseph Stalin. The President's delegation included Supreme Naval Commander Admiral Earnest J. King, Admiral William D. Leahy, General George Marshall, Averill Harriman, and Harry Hopkins.

Almost as soon as the captain had tucked the short message into his shirt pocket, a series of misfortunes began to sully the record of the USS *William D. Porter*, DD579.

In the gloom of night, Captain C.W. Walters ordered his ship to back away from the two destroyers with which it had been nesting. A soft breeze was blowing against the port bow, just enough to move the ship sideways as we pulled slowly aft. The heavy flukes of our anchor, tucked in the hause pipe on our bow, dug into the paint of the adjoining ship and caught their captain's gig hanging from davits, jerking it into the sea along with 100 feet of lifeline along the rail. The darkness hid the consternation on our captain's face, but all our crew felt it was a foreboding beginning.

As we moved toward the open sea, a 50-gallon drum-sized depth charge suddenly loosed its moorings and rolled down twin rails and off our stern to disappear in our foaming wake. There was no explosion because no primer had been inserted in the stored depth charge. But an incident like that was a black mark on our ship.

We proceeded, under orders of radio silence, toward the rendezvous with the battleship, USS *Iowa*. When her stacks appeared just over the horizon, we strained to see her massive but graceful lines take shape in the early light of dawn. We took our escort position about three thousand yards just forward of the *Iowa's* port bow. The other two destroyers were positioned directly ahead and off her starboard bow. With flashing signal light messages, we headed east. The grey and black irregular camouflage paint on all four vessels made accurately estimating their heading difficult. To make it even more difficult for any lurking enemy submarine to launch a successful torpedo attack, we changed course slightly and in unison every five to seven minutes. The standard naval zig-zag procedure.

Toward evening of the first night out, the wind had increased to hurricane force. When darkness fell, the waves were towering and breaking over bow and railing with such force that no one was allowed on the main deck. No longer were the ships visible, but glowing yellow dots on our surface radar screen accurately monitored their position. Keeping position was difficult in the darkness as the ship lurched and plunged in the mountainous waves. Suddenly the soft glow of our hooded bridge lights went out and flickered back on. We later learned that a wave had broken over the side, cascading sea water down a large ventilation tube, shorting out the forward electrical board, the nerve center of the ship. Fortunately, the otherwise redundant aft electrical board immediately picked up the electrical load and, though crippled, we proceeded normally.

When dawn broke, the peak of the storm had passed, and we assessed the damage. The ship's roster was checked, and grief set in when it became evident that one of our seamen had been swept overboard during the night without anyone's knowledge. We could not turn back, and even if we could, we knew it would be useless.

Then the chief engineer reported that one of our ship's four massive and powerful boilers had burned out. Any high-speed maneuvers, for which destroyers are famous, would not be possible without all four boilers' powering both screws.

The captain's face was grim as we pressed on. Misfortunes such as these had seldom happened one at a time, let alone day after day.

Then one night we left our escort position to intercept a contact we had picked up on our radar many miles ahead of our task force. The night was overcast with no moonlight. We approached our contact with all the crew at their general quarters battle stations. Was it an enemy or friendly contact? After a rapid exchange of infrared light signals, our contact identified itself as a friendly high-speed merchantman traveling alone. We broke away, securing from battle stations by bringing our guns and torpedo tubes back to center position, ammunition back in lockers, helmets to racks and off-duty crewmen back to their bunks. But what we didn't know was that we left our battle stations with a serious mistake waiting to happen.

The next afternoon we cut through the water in our usual assigned position on the *Iowa's* port bow. Promptly as scheduled, the clanging urgency of the general quarters bell jolted everyone to action for a drill, which we had gone through day after day. Men raced to their battle stations, donned helmets, pulled on earphones, jerked canvas off guns, and pressed buttons bringing full power to train gun barrels and torpedo tubes.

Below the pilot house in the Combat Information Center, the executive officer, Commander William Poindexter, was conducting drills, directing gun batteries by telephone, and ordering them to track their target manually because battle damage was being simulated, which put power and automation out of order. Gun crews and torpedo crewmen immediately left their computer and radar controls and moved their weapons as best they could by manpower alone. The executive officer ordered the torpedo crew to track the battleship off our beam and to prepare to simulate firing all ten torpedoes manually.

Bill Guy Remembers

When the torpedo men had a lead on their target, the order came to "Fire one!" Then, "Fire two!" When the order came to "Fire seven!", the dull hollow "whaamp" sound of an exploding impulse charge signalled the shooting of a torpedo out of its tube. The torpedo, or fish as it was called, seemed to float in midair in its sleek silvery beauty as it cleared the rail and settled flatly to the water where it sank in a huge puddle of foam. Its propellor, already whirring, churned the water, sending it on its course. The telltale crack of the impulse charge sound transfixed the captain, who was standing on the wing of the bridge. His face drained of color as he watched the fish begin its journey below the sparkling surface of the sea, a journey marked easily from above by the white wake of that programmed propellor.

We were committed to radio silence. How to warn the *Iowa*? "Send out, 'Torpedo on your starboard bow,'" the captain, his face now a purple red, ordered a nearby signalman. Pennants came jerking out of their locker and went flapping on their halyard to the top of our main mast. As the pennants reached their signal position, the captain realized to his horror that he was signalling "starboard bow" when the torpedo was approaching the *Iowa* on the port bow. The captain's eyes were glazed when he made the snap decision to break radio silence and warn the battleship on our short wave TBS. Grabbing the radio phone off its hook, he shouted, "Arsenal, Arsenal, this is Blue Duck. Torpedo approaching close on your port bow!" He repeated it twice more and sank back against the pilothouse bulkhead.

From my battle station above the pilothouse, directing the ship's antiaircraft 40-mm gun batteries, I saw it all. The huge battleship seemed not to respond to the captain's warning, but I am sure there was galvanized action in the *Iowa's* pilothouse as the helmsman threw the big wheel to a hard right rudder position and engine room bells signalled full speed on the port engine. The torpedo tube had been trained manually at what was considered point blank range. We watched the white trail as the missile seemed to be on an intercept course with the battleship, which had begun to show signs of turning away. The captain watched weakly, perspiration beading his forehead.

Suddenly, at what seemed the moment of impact, a plume of spray rose behind the battleship as the pressure-sensitive torpedo exploded close astern in her churning wake. There was no moment of elation on our destroyer—we knew the *William D. Porter* had done it again. Signal lights on the Iowa flashed. Admirial King demanded an explanation. Our captain, in a fit of desperation, signalled "accidental discharge because of salt water in a torpedo-impulse primer circuit." Admiral King did not buy that hasty explanation and ordered us to leave the four-ship task force and return to Bermuda where we would be held in quarantine, pending a naval inquiry into the incident.

A team of high-ranking naval officers went over our ship with a fine-tooth comb, refusing to let anyone go ashore for ten days. The embarrassing incidents of raking another destroyer's side with our anchor, losing a depth charge overboard, having the forward electrical board shorted out, burning out a boiler, and having a seaman missing at sea all came out in the inquiry, but why one torpedo mysteriously fired when the impulse charges were not primed could not be explained.

Finally, a young seaman on a 40-mm gun mount overlooking the torpedo tubes told the questioners that he had seen the chief torpedoman pull a spent primer shell from tube number seven after it had fired its missile. The chief torpedoman, on securing from general quarters in the dark of the night before, had neglected to remove one impulse charge primer after we identified the high-speed merchantman. That broke the case, but it broke many individuals, too. The captain, an Annapolis graduate, was ordered ashore, never to command a naval vessel again. The executive officer was given a letter of admonition for his file. The torpedo officer was transferred, and the chief torpedoman was given a sentence in Portsmouth Naval Prison. He had been decorated for heroism when a destroyer he was on was sunk off Italy only months before being assigned to the *Porter*. Now he would wear his decoration in prison.

The quarantine was lifted, and a new captain came aboard. Before they left, the Naval Inquiry Officers gathered all the Porter's officers together for a pep talk. "Put this event behind you," they said. "This is the responsibility of this ship's leadership, and you who remain have the qualities to make her top of the line." We took their advice and did just that.

The *Porter* was assigned to the Pacific Theater, but its troubles, unfortunately, were not over. For those on the morning 4 to 8 o'clock watch, June 10, 1945 came into view as a gloomy grey day with a low and thick overcast. The *Porter*, along with one other destroyer and four small LCS (landing craft support), had been assigned picket duty, positioned about 50 miles north of Okinawa. Her mission was to constantly sweep the skies with air search radar to spot "bogeys," as Japanese aircraft were called, as they flew to attack from the mainland of Japan.

The two destroyers also had radio contact with a flight of four gull-winged Corsair fighter planes, manned by Marine pilots, which circled in formation in a long loop overhead just below the low cloud cover. The fighter planes were there to intercept any incoming Japanese aircraft the destroyer's radar detected. Every two hours, fresh aircraft would relieve the patrolling Corsairs, as the two destroyers and four LCSs slowly made their seven-mile roundtrip on station below.

Destroyers, as a class of naval vessel, had been a prime target of Japanese kamikazi or suicide planes. Already around Okinawa, Japanese pilots, who sought martrydom by plowing their planes into U.S. ships, had sunk or put out of action 96 destroyers, or like-size vessels such as destroyer escorts and mine sweepers. The *William D. Porter's* 5-inch, 38 main battery guns had been doing so much shore bombardment in the Phillipines, Kerama Rhetto, and Okinawa that their worn barrel sleeves no longer guaranteed accuracy. With such a disability, radar picket duty was inevitable.

I had just finished the 4 to 8 o'clock watch on the bridge and had gone to the fantail to get a haircut from the young sailor who doubled as the ship's barber. As we stood talking, our bodies constantly and unconsciously compensating for the easy roll and pitch of the ship under foot, we heard the distant crack of a 5-inch, 38 gun on our sister destroyer. Looking up, we saw the black puff of the exploding projectile near a single plane that at first glance seemed to have been closely trailing the four Marine fighter planes passing overhead.

In a second, we realized that the single aircraft was Japanese, and we were its target. It began its steep dive from dead ahead. Our ship's general quarters bells began their insistent clanging to call the crew to battle stations. But there was no time left. I watched the dive bomber with its single bomb beneath its belly grow larger by the split second. It would hit us, I instinctively knew, so where was the safest place to be? The young sailor-barber made his decision. He dashed for the side and went over the rail into the ocean.

"He'll hit on the port, so go to the starboard," my survival reaction told me. I took a step to the right, but at that moment the plane, in a roar of its diving engine, struck our main mast, whipping him sideways as he crashed into the port deck just aft of amidships. There was no explosion. But in one sweeping motion as it hit the deck, the wreckage was dragged over the side as the ship knifed through the waves. The wreckage must have dragged under the ship and possibly the port propellor might have detonated the bomb for there was a violent muffled explosion under the stern. So sharp and strong was the explosion that it sent me flying into the air with the feeling that the flat side of a giant scoop shovel had struck on the bottoms of my feet. When I landed on the deck, I noticed the deck plates were bent.

The ship lost way abruptly. The deck hatches to the engine rooms flew open, and firemen and engineers came boiling up out of the steam in a struggling stream of humanity, covered with black bunker oil, laced here and there with bright red blood. The main deck was immediately slippery with oil, and as men raced to their battle stations aft, they slipped and slid, adding curses to the pandemonium of sailors dragging one another up out of the flooding, steam-filled engine rooms.

In minutes, the able crewmen were at battle stations. A fire in the upper powder magazine of the number five 5-inch gun turret had been quickly contained and put out before the crew was aware of it. If it had exploded the stored amunition, the ship would not have stayed afloat two minutes.

Captain C.M Keyes calmly ordered damage control measures in place. Following procedures drilled into the crew over the past months, all compartment water-tight doors and hatches were slammed shut and sealed. It didn't occur to us at the moment, but as the compartments were sealed, the clothing we wore were our only remaining personal possessions.

The ship was down by the stern as LCS 122 came alongside to take off the wounded. This was precisely what this little ship had been assigned to the picket station to do, and it did it well. The other three LCSs continued to trail our sister destroyer, looking like three puppies on a leash.

It was obvious immediately that the ship was sinking by the stern. Far off in Okinawa, a sea-going tug with huge pumps was dispatched to help us, but the distance and its slow speed made her help a long shot. Our portable Briggs and Stratton pumps were all working feverishly to keep up with the water pouring in through split seams below. Some badly ruptured compartments had been sealed off. The heavy black fuel oil from burst fuel storage tanks mixed with sea water, creating a sludge that the small portable pumps could not handle. One by one the pumps, with engines hot and smoking, gave out.

Everything on top side that could be jettisoned was pushed over the side. The heavy doors of the 5-inch gun turrets came off and were slid into the sea. Boxes of ammunition, 20-mm guns, spare 40-mm gun barrels, all ten torpedoes, and all depth charges were shoved overboard. Sailors used muscles and strength they didn't know they had as they wrestled heavy objects to the ship's side. The decks were slanted and slippery, footing was difficult. There was no water to slake thirst and no first aid for the cuts, bruises, smashed fingers. The stinging salt water and oil went almost unnoticed.

Two hours after the *Porter* had been struck, the captain realized that his ship would sink despite all our efforts. The sea-going tug could not reach us in time. Reluctantly, I am sure, he ordered the LCSs alongside and then gave the order to abandon ship. Men with oil-soaked clothing scrambled over the side and dropped to the decks of the LCSs. Finally the captain came over the side to join his crew, and the LCSs moved away. About five minutes later, the bow of the *William D. Porter* rose in the air as the stern disappeared, then slowly and majestically the bow sank out of sight. The DD579 was another casualty of war consigned to a final resting place 26 hundred fathoms below the ocean surface.

That afternoon, our heavily laden LCSs arrived at Okinawa and were loaded off on a large troop carrier, which processed naval survivors. The officer who met us as we climbed aboard, to my startled surprise, was Commander R.L. Body, who had been my advanced economics instructor at the University of Minnesota. Our paths would cross often in the years ahead when we both returned to the University. The survivor ship logged us in and provided us with laundry and one change of clothes. A day later, we were transferred to a troop carrier, which had been designated a survivor ship for naval personnel and a prison ship for Japanese prisoners of war. Because our wounded had been taken to a hospital ship, we had no way of ever knowing the extent of their wounds or fatalities. We did hear that the sailor I had been talking to just before the kamikazi hit us was picked out of the water by our sister destroyer.

Two days later, the "survivor" transport with our crew and 350 Japanese prisoners of war headed east to Hawaii.

The war was fast coming to a close. Germany had surrendered, and Jean and I were on our way to my temporary assignment in Washington, D.C., when the Japanese surrendered in response to the two devastating atomic bombs that had been dropped on their mainland. My brother, John, five years younger than I, had just arrived in the Pacific war zone as an engineer on a large landing craft when the war ended. All three of us brothers had chosen the Navy.

But the end of the war confirmed what we were afraid of. My brother, Jim, had died of malnutrition in a Japanese prison camp in the jungles of Burma. Jim had survived the sinking of the battleship *California* at Pearl Harbor, but the Japanese on Java had captured him after he survived the sinking of the heavy cruiser *Houston* and a seven mile swim to land. I was able to talk with a handful of his prison camp surviving shipmates when they were returned to Bethesda Naval Hospital in Washington, D.C.

Jim's body was later returned to the United States and was interred in the family plot at Riverside Cemetery in Fargo.

I was released from the Navy in October, 1945. Jean and I headed back to Minneapolis where I continued my graduate work in 1946. I received my M.S. degree that spring, just a month after our first child, William L. Guy, III, was born in the University Hospital.

My brother, John, was separated from the Navy and entered the State University of Iowa. After graduating, he and his wife, Ruth, began what was a very successful career, farming in southern Minnesota.

Launching Our Lives

When I finished my graduate studies in agricultural economics at the University of Minnesota in the Spring of 1946, I was eager to enter the job market and work toward a career in feeding livestock. I failed to land a job with the Central Livestock Marketing Association in St. Paul, but an offer from Balthauser and Moyer, a livestock commission firm at West Fargo intrigued me. B and M not only bought and sold sheep and lambs, but they fed out a great number of them at their West Fargo feedlot, nestled in a crook of the Sheyenne River. Ever since my years raising sheep in 4-H, I had been interested in commercial lamb feeding. Here was a golden opportunity to get hands-on training in buying and selling lambs and feeding them for market on a large scale. I took the job.

When October arrived, the selling season was over, and I began my work in the feedlots. A half dozen men labored to unload lambs, spread bedding, stack bailed hay, shovel grain into a big Bear Cat hammer mill, and do a dozen other activities that came with the job. My co-workers thought it strange that with my master's degree, I would stoop to such hard, smelly work every day—rain, blizzard, or shine. Some of the men were alcoholics who couldn't quite get over the night before.

The lambs—during that winter there were 17,000 of them—had to be watched closely and fed and watered daily. A small Caterpillar tractor dragged big self-feeders into the huge hay shed to be filled with chopped alfalfa, corn, wheat, barley and oats, all of which were smashed to bits in the whirling hammers of the mill and shot out of a pipe into the self-feeders. When full, the feeder would be dragged back to one of the many feedlots, and another empty feeder would take its place at the mill. It was back-breaking, dusty work. The lambs were eating constantly, and it was necessary to grind for several days ahead to carry over a weekend, holiday or a breakdown. The 100 or more self-feeders had to be continually attended because the fine-chopped feed easily bridged and would not drop down for continuous feeding. Someone would have to go along the feeders with a rod or pitch fork to start the fine feed flowing down. On holidays and Sundays, I often was the only one around to do the job.

Christmas Eve came, and the crew seemed to evaporate, leaving me to finish securing for the night. As I drove back toward the bright lights of Fargo, it suddenly dawned on me that this was Christmas Eve, and Jean and I had no Christmas tree for our small apartment. I drove to several lots where I had seen evergreen trees for sale. But it was after 7 p.m., and they were closed. Then I found a lot where a light still burned in the little trailer that served as an office. The man inside looked at my dirty smelly coveralls and shook his head, "We've been sold out since noon."

"But what about that pile behind this trailer?" I asked in alarm.

"Those are broken rejected trees," he said. "If you can find something there, you are welcome to it."

I picked through the pile. There wasn't anything saleable there. In desperation, I stood a little four-foot tree up. All of its branches on one side were crushed and drooping. But there was something about the tree I liked. Even with so much damage its good side was full and symmetrical. I pushed it into the backseat of my car and headed for home.

Jean had been waiting dinner, and her special efforts had been dried out in the oven and wilted, just waiting for me to come home. Her spirits were at a low ebb.

When I hauled the little tree into the living room, she saw its mangled branches, and she burst into tears.

My spirits sank, too, because I realized that I had failed a test in our first home on our first Christmas Eve.

"But Jean," I protested quietly, "this little tree was lying in the snow after all the buyers were gone, and it had no chance to be a part of Christmas. If we trim off its damaged branches and decorate it well, we can stand it in the corner and nobody will notice its handicap. And this little tree will return all the love we can give it."

Jean dried her tears, and after the delicious Christmas Eve dinner that my late arrival had somewhat spoiled, we trimmed our first Christmas tree. It looked beautiful and appreciative in the corner. But I had learned a lesson I never forgot—always buy the Christmas tree early.

Back to Amenia

I stayed with Balthauser and Moyer one year before becoming Assistant County Agricultural Extension Agent for Cass County under Hal Stephanson. Hal was a great person to work with, but I hankered to get out on my own. Our next-door neighbors in Fargo were Cormie and Millie Bean. Cormie had just received his master's degree in chemistry from NDAC. We often got together to fantasize about starting a farm chemical business that would formulate and sell fertilizers, insecticides, and herbicides. Soon after taking the county agent job, I decided to join forces with Cormie Bean and make our dream come true.

With no experience and very little money, we formed the Guy-Bean Farm Supply Company and bought a large lot with trackage and highway access near the West Fargo Union Stockyards. I quit my county agent job and went to work planning our farm supply business. We decided at the same time that we would begin to farm our family's land at Amenia the following spring. With no machinery and no farm credit rating, this would have been impossible had not my widowed mother been willing to lend the minimum funds necessary to start both the business and farming.

Our farm supply lot adjacent to a Northern Pacific Railroad spur was low and swampy and needed about three feet of fill to bring it up to grade level of the stockyards' road. Cormie and I undertook to construct an 80-ton, quonset-style fertilizer warehouse on a shallow basement with a deck for off-loading from railroad cars and on-loading trucks.

We learned about the construction business fast—the hard way. An early winter set in, and the ground froze before a contractor could start hauling in fill dirt in huge frozen chunks from an abandoned railroad spur nearby. The fill would not settle and compact. Our small round-roofed warehouse with Bean and Guy doing all the construction went into the winter with no shingles because the composition shingles we bought were too brittle to handle in the winter cold. We ordered two obsolete boxcar bodies for $40 a piece from the railroad company. They arrived in January on our siding, resting on two flatcars.

We urgently contacted the railroad section foreman for advice on how to get the two boxcars off the flatcars and onto the ground. He shook his head and advised us we would need 40 men and heavy steel rails to slide the boxcars to the ground. We didn't have access to 40 men or steel rails. We decided to use long 6 x 6 posts for rails to bridge from the flatcar to square cribs built up adjacent. Just when we got ready to put our plan into action, Cormie was rushed to the hospital with a burst appendix. I was left alone to lower the boxcar bodies and get it done soon before demurrage set in.

I obtained a truckload of short house-moving timbers from a retired house-moving friend to build my two-square cribs alongside the flatcar. With a small hydraulic jack, I raised the boxcar body enough to slide a 6 x 6 rail under each end. I poured water on the rail surface and let it freeze to make it slick. I pushed on the offside with the small hydraulic jack and inched the boxcar along the rails and off the flatcar onto the cribs. By jacking the car body up to remove one crib timber at a time, I lowered it to the rails on the ground.

I had bought an International truck to start farming. With the truck, I was able, bit by bit, to nudge and pull the boxcar bodies to the location on our lot where they would rest as storage for herbicides and insecticides. A few days later, the section foreman came by and asked how I had gotten a crew of 40 men together. "I didn't need them," I explained. "I took them off myself." The section foreman left, obviously irritated that I was unwilling to tell him how many men had helped me.

Cormie and I struggled to keep enough cash flow to stay in business. When we unloaded the 100-pound sacks of fertilizer from a 40-ton car load, we would rest our aching, sweating bodies and ask ourselves how many guys with master's degrees had worked at loading the car. The only fertilizer users in 1948 were sugarbeet growers. We had a massive educational challenge to get farmers interested in using fertilizer on other crops and pasture.

Bill Austin, a large and successful farmer at Casselton, was one of our first customers. He wanted a phosphate fertilizer that also had a high nitrogen content. We had no such analysis, but we suggested that he might order phosphate and nitrogen separately and mix them himself. We delivered the two bagged fertilizers to his farm in early spring. During a rainy spell, Austin's hired help emptied the bags, mixed nitrogen pellets with the phosphate, and piled it all on the concrete floor of an old horse barn. It was out of the rain to be sure, but the nitrogen slowly absorbed the moist air flowing down the barn alley, and the pile of fertilizer began to set up like a poor grade of cement.

When the rain stopped and field work commenced, Bill Austin found his fertilizer pile was a mass of big chunks that didn't crumble easily. In great distress, he sought our advice. We had heard that Warren Walkinshaw, an Argusville crop sprayer, also spread fertilizer by air, and we suggested that might work. And so with grim determination, Austin had his fertilizer chunks loaded into the plane's hopper. Then almost as though he were on a bombing run, Walkinshaw flew the field, allowing grapefruit-sized chunks of fertilizer to rain down only to smash in white plumes when they hit the ground. This was farming at its best.

A month later, Bill Austin was back at our store seeking to contract the aerial spraying of a new weed killer called 2,4-D. As luck would have it, we had just laid in a small supply of the liquid chemicals and an itinerant aerial crop sprayer from Oklahoma was available to put it on. We did not know that we had the most virulent form of 2,4-D, nor did we know that the diesel fuel carrier that the aerial sprayer would use would make the 2,4-D even more virulent. But we went ahead and sprayed 500 acres of Austin's flax. Since flax was selling for about $7.50 per bushel, he was anxious to get the weeds out of his field to enhance his yield.

The day after we sprayed, Austin came to our office with tears in his eyes. "You've killed my flax," he almost sobbed. We drove out to look and sure enough, his six-inch flax plants were all kinked over and looked to be in the last throes of death. "I'm going to plow it up and reseed," he wailed. It was late in the season, and I suggested he leave some strips in the plowing so the true damage could be proven more accurately later. Then the skies opened up with a three-day rain which prevented plowing. Slowly the flax began to recover. He didn't plow and actually had a good flax yield. But because it was less than his neighbor's yield, he sued Sherwin Williams Chemical Company. He lost the suit. We were not fair game for a law suit because we had neither money nor product liability insurance.

A month later, Bill Austin was again at our office door. "I've got web worms in my sugarbeets," he said. "I need Paris Green dusted on them by air. You fellows are the only ones with Paris Green around here. If I could get it anywhere else, I wouldn't be here." With that compliment in hand, we agreed to hire spray pilot Duayne Strand to dust our Paris Green on the Austin sugarbeets. We waited to begin dusting until the end of the day after the wind had gone down. Strand had flown the last load as the sun was sinking to the horizon—a red ball in the west.

Bill Austin drove his new stream-lined Buick out to the end of the pasture that served as a landing field. Strand brought his big bi-wing Steerman in for a landing against the blinding sun. He did not see Austin's Buick. As his plane raced along the ground, it gradually slowed until it hit a big bump—running right up the back of Austin's car and down over the hood. Surprisingly, the plane was not damaged. But Bill Austin just stood there speechless, looking at his crushed car and then looking at crushed Guy and Bean. "What else can you guys do to me?" he asked helplessly.

Guy-Bean Farm Supply opened a warehouse facility in the old Northern Pacific Railroad freight depot in Casselton in 1950. But the Korean War made up our minds to close down our business for good in 1952. The war demand for sulfuric acid reduced the availability of treble super phosphate. In retrospect, the war did us a favor; it forced us out of business at a time when we could get out—on a break-even basis. Cormie Bean went on to become an executive with Dow Chemical in Michigan, and I went to full-time farming at Amenia.

Back to Farming

Jean and I had every opportunity to begin careers in the city, but we liked the independence of thought and action that farming would give us.

It was a calculated risk to expect Jean, a city-bred woman, to take to living on the Amenia farm that would have to be rebuilt from scratch from field fertility to pasture fences to the farm buildings themselves. The 820-acre farm belonged to my parents, but they had never lived on it. The tenant farmhouse, in which we were to live, was old and run-down. It had no indoor plumbing, and the electric system consisted of a light socket hanging from the ceiling in each room. Cass County Rural Electric Cooperative had not built lines to surrounding farms yet; but years before, Ottertail Power Company had strung its line to the four farmsteads clustered at the foursection corners, two miles west of Amenia. The electric service was minimal and barely sufficient to energize appliances. The farmhouse had been heated by a potbellied parlor coal stove and a big black wood-burning kitchen stove.

We went to work. Each bit of the house renovation uncovered something else that needed redoing. We put in hardwood floors, then replaced all the windows. And while the walls and floors were torn apart, we rewired and installed central oil-burning heat and plumbing for a kitchen and two bathrooms. Walls were replastered and papered or painted. A new front entrance replaced the porch, and a large utility room was added to the rear of the house. A water pressure system was installed, and a septic tank served a disposal field under nearby trees. The outer walls had insulation blown into them, and the house was resided and shingled.

Our son, Jim, was born in March 1948. A few months later, Jean arrived at the farm with our new baby and two-year-old Billy to make a home in a house that was still in the throes of renovation and barely livable. As I look back at those days, I marvel at the strength and determination that young people have.

Jean came to love that farm. When Deborah was born in May 1950, we had settled in. The house was livable. A dilapidated old barn and a large sagging sheep shed were torn down. A chicken coop and granary were moved away from the house. A large shop was built, and a metal quonset machine shed was added.

When our daughter, Holly, was born in 1955, Jean had become a committed farm wife. She lent a hand in livestock emergencies, especially when our 350 ewes were lambing and our 30 sows were farrowing. With four children and outside duties as a Sunday school teacher, 4-H club leader, and county president of the Farm Bureau Women's Organization, she had her hands full.

Our youngest daughter, Nancy, was born in September 1958. That gave us a full house with three daughters and two sons—all of them different personalities—but all healthy and good kids.

Top: The Guy family in 1926. From left to right, my father, William Guy Sr., me, Johnny, my mother, Mable and Jimmy.

Bottom: Jim (r) and I with our champion lambs in 1934.

Top: The Guy family in 1940. From left to right, my mother and father, John, Jim and me.

Center: Me as a naval officer in 1944, and my ship, the William D. Porter, sinking as a result of a Japanese Kamikaze attack, June 10, 1945.

Bottom: Jean and I at our wedding January 30, 1943.

Top: The Guy farm two miles west of Amenia, 1961.

Center: Taking a break in the field in 1955 with (l-r) Jean, Jim, Deb, and Bill III.

Bottom: Passing sheep lore on to Bill III (l) and Jim (r), 1960.

2

My Early Experiences in Politics

Getting Into Politics Is Easier Than Getting Out

I've often been asked how I got into organized politics, and I have to confess that I just kind of wandered into it, step by step.

When Jean and I moved into the Amenia community, it didn't take long to learn that our neighbors, bless their hearts, seeing this young couple moving into their midst, already had decided that we were a couple of patsies to assume some of the community responsibilities. About three weeks after we'd moved in, several of our neighbors came over to suggest that I run for the school board because the entire three-member school board had resigned in disgust after the school kids had taken down the 40-foot flag pole and run it like a battering ram through two sets of doors in the front entrance of the school. They had had their fill of student discipline and school board responsibilities.

So, reluctantly, I said, "Okay, I'll run for the school board." Because nobody wanted the job, I was easily elected. There was a kind of giddy feeling in winning an election even though it was only a school board election, and I was elected without opposition. The thrill of winning an election kind of gets in your blood.

The people around Amenia remembered me as a member of a family whose politics definitely had been Republican. It was not unusual then that a neighbor came by one cold spring morning in 1950 and said, "Let's go over to Buffalo this afternoon to the District Republican Nominating Convention." Having nothing special planned for the day, I agreed. I had never attended a political convention and was aroused by visions of hundreds of enthusiastic, bannerwaving citizens meeting and forging their ticket of chosen candidates like a skillful blacksmith would heat and shape a piece of fine steel.

That afternoon we arrived at the Buffalo gym to find three cars parked on the gravel street outside. "Do you suppose we have the wrong day?" I asked. "Could be," was the answer. "But let's go inside and see."

Inside the gym, we were greeted by four men who had pulled their folding chairs up in a circle and were sprawled casually in heavy coats, overshoes, and caps, their thumbs tucked into their waistbands or under their overall shoulder straps. The room was so cold that a hint of vapor showed in the air whenever one of them spoke. Not only was the gymnasium unheated, but the electric lights had not even been turned on. Tattered remnants of colored crepe paper streamers hung from sagging wires that had been stretched along the walls. Folding chairs were scattered in disarray exactly where they had been left when the orchestra packed up its instruments at the close of the school dance a few nights before.

"Where was the crowd?" I wondered. "Where were the delegates for this district political convention? Was this all there was to a convention?"

"Well, I guess we're not gonna get any more," said Louis Easton, the district chairman. "We better get started." He hauled out some tattered books and slapped them down on a dusty chair beside him. I was depressed. "How do

My Early Experiences in Politics

you hold a political convention with only six people?" I wondered.

"Let's see now," Louis said. "Harry Wadeson is a holdover for the Senate, and I suppose Alex Watt and Russell Idso are going to run again for the House." Two of the men present nodded their heads and "'lowed as how they'd run again for the House." I was appalled. Two incumbent House members, the district chairman, and the elderly father of one of the House members were all who made up the District Nominating Convention—except for my friend and me! Was this democracy in action? Louis Easton looked at his chart of precinct committeemen and then glanced over at me and very seriously said, "We haven't had a precinct committeeman in Amenia township for several years. Here, take these petition forms and get six of your neighbors to sign, and you'll have enough signatures to be on the ballot for Republican precinct committeeman."

Even in my disappointment at no one's showing up for the convention, I was somehow pleased to be called to duty in the Republican party that had dominated North Dakota for many years. I took the forms and gently folded them so they would fit into my shirt pocket.

As we left that cold gymnasium and walked toward our car, the elderly father of one of the House members shook his head sadly. "I think cars are what's done it," he said. "'Forty years ago when people had to come by horse and buggy or even by train, we'd get three or four hundred people out for a District Nominating Convention. Now when you can drive by car to Buffalo from any part of this district in an hour, people don't give a damn!"

I took the petitions along to the Amenia Post Office the next morning and got eight signatures from the first eight people I asked as they stood around talking and waiting for their mail to be sorted. But that night, my conscience began to bother me. Here I was signing on as a Republican precinct committeeman because I'd been asked to. But really, deep down in my own heart, I was more nearly aligned with the philosophy of the Democratic party.

"What should I do, Jean?" I asked my wife. "I feel like a hypocrite! There's no Democratic party in North Dakota as near as I can tell and certainly, there's no Democratic party in our eleventh district. I am interested in politics, but there's no future in North Dakota in politics unless you're a part of the Republican party."

"Well," Jean said, as she put her freshly dried evening dishes away, "there could be a Democratic party in North Dakota if people wouldn't give up before they start. Why don't you go to the county auditor and get some petition forms and get signatures for Democratic precinct committeeman? It isn't too late, you know."

So I did go into Fargo, I did get those petition forms from the county auditor, I did get the required number of signatures to run for Democratic precinct committeeman, and I did file those petition forms with the county auditor in time to be on the ballot. But what a jolt was in store for me.

When our precinct election board counted the ballots following the general election that fall, Bill Guy had won both the Democratic and Republican party precinct committeeman posts. I had enough write-in votes in the Republican column to win and no one else competed against me in the Democratic column, so I won in both columns!

I suddenly was faced with a choice that comes to few people. Would I be a Democratic precinct official or a Republican precinct official? With some real misgivings about ever finding enough Democrats in my legislative district to form an organization that would meet in anything larger than a telephone booth, I took the responsibility of Democratic precinct committeeman for Amenia township in a party that had elected only two governors in the state since North Dakota was created in 1889!

But I was in politics; and, from that moment on, I never regretted my choice of joining the underdog Democratic

My Early Experiences in Politics

party. That underdog position simply made me more determined than ever to start some ripples in organized politics.

A Majority of One!

In my early years as a lonely Democrat in Amenia, I naturally followed with great interest developments in the national party. The name of a newcomer to the list of possible candidates of presidential timber arrived on the scene at the National Democratic Convention in 1956 at Detroit, Senator John F. Kennedy.

At first blush, Kennedy seemed too shallow to be pursuing the nomination as the Democratic candidate for President of the United States. But the seed was sown, and John Kennedy began quietly and effectively to assemble a staff for the onslaught to win the nomination for President in 1960.

I was attracted to John Kennedy because, under his easygoing, boyish good looks, I saw a fighter at heart. I read the national news magazine stories about Kennedy's Senate subcommittee that was investigating the racketeers who had infiltrated some major national labor unions. The labor movement was too important and affected the lives of too many good people to allow a few self-serving, dishonest, racketeering, would-be labor leaders to grasp positions of authority within some unions and through their activities give organized labor and the reputations of working men and women a bad name.

Spokesmen for some large unions criticized young John Kennedy, and yet, I believed that most rank-and-file labor people were thankful that the Congress was looking into the machinations at the top of their unions.

John Kennedy was the featured speaker at a Midwest Democratic conference which I attended in Des Moines about 1958. Kennedy was seated at the head table next to the Iowa State Democratic chairman. Kennedy's speech concerned labor racketeering. The son-in-law of the Democratic state chairman had been under investigation in the Senate probe of racketeering in St. Louis labor unions. Senator Kennedy stood at the lectern and delivered a solid, critical speech about labor racketeering and to everyone's discomfort, actually mentioned the state chairman's son-in-law by name. In retrospect, I realized it took a lot more courage to criticize the son-in-law than to ignore the son-in-law or adapt the speech to something other than labor racketeering.

I was impressed with that young senator, and I was equally impressed with the radiant, dark-haired beauty who attended the banquet that night—his wife, Jacqueline. I introduced myself to Mrs. Kennedy following the speech and told her how much I appreciated having a national leader speak out on a sensitive subject which most politicians would have lacked the courage to face. I also told her that an earlier visit by Senator Kennedy to North Dakota had created many new friends for him in our state.

When I got back to our farm home near Amenia, I wrote a letter to Senator Kennedy, congratulating him on his excellent presentation at the Democratic Midwest Conference in Des Moines. I also stated that should he seek the Democratic nomination for President, he could count on my assistance.

I had completely forgotten this letter nearly two years later when an incident on a cold, blizzarding day in January 1960 revealed a glimpse of the thorough Kennedy organization.

I was farrowing hogs several hundred yards across the river from our farm home. Quite often I would walk over and back because it was too much of a hassle to start a truck or a car in the cold for that short trip. Going over to the hog house with the strong northerly wind at my back was not uncomfortable even though the visability from flying snow was almost nil and the drifts were getting high. I took care of the sows and their little pigs and prepared to return to our house across the river.

Bucking that gusting and moaning north wind with its driving snow was enough to jerk a person's breath away even though I was warmly padded in a heavy hooded parka, insulated work coveralls and heavy boots. As I drew abreast of the door of the vacant house where seasonal workers on our farm stayed in the summer, I decided to step into the cold kitchen to get out of the wind for a moment while I caught my breath. I opened the creaking kitchen door that hadn't been used for several months and walked in on the cold, slippery linoleum. My breath came in white vapor that froze to the fur of my parka, but at least I was out of the wind for a few moments.

Suddenly the phone on the wall began to ring. I was taken by surprise because I thought the phone was disconnected when our seasonal workers moved out after the fall work was done. I picked up the receiver to see who might be calling this vacant house and realized that our home phone across the river was connected on the same party line, and the call was probably directed to our home. I said, "Hello." In the distance a voice answered, "Is this Bill Guy?" "Yes," I replied "What can I do for you?"

The distant voice very clearly said, "This is Bob Wallace. You don't know me, but I'm calling from Chicago as a representative of the Senator John Kennedy for President organization. You sent a letter to Senator Kennedy a couple of years ago, indicating that you would be willing to help out if the Senator decided to run for the Presidency."

"That's right," I said. "And I still regard the Senator as an excellent candidate." "Fine," Mr. Wallace said. "Now, would you agree to try to get on the North Dakota delegation to the National Democratic Convention so that you can work within that delegation for the Senator?"

I thought for only a few seconds; I knew I couldn't go to the National Convention and use up valuable time and limited finances because I had decided to run for the State

Senate again that year after having been defeated in two previous attempts.

"I don't plan to go to the National Convention," I said, "but I will do all I can to influence those who are chosen on the North Dakota delegation to support John Kennedy."

Bob Wallace spent a few moments trying to convince me that I should seek a position on the delegation, but I assured him that I had considered that possibility many times leading up to our conversation and I definitely had decided that I could not attempt to be a delegate in 1960. I needed all the time I could find to campaign for the State Senate.

Finally, I was able to hang up after assuring Wallace that he could count on me to do what I could in North Dakota for John Kennedy.

As I hung up the receiver, I made a mental note to call the telephone company and ask them to disconnect the phone or at least take if off our billing until new occupants moved in later in the spring.

I plunged back into the storm, forcing my way into the blizzard, wondering how coincidental it was that I should have stepped into that vacant farmhouse at the moment that particular call came through. As I struggled through the snow toward our farm home, I had no way of knowing that a sudden turn of events would cause me to give up what looked like a sure race for the State Senate, and instead, would plunge me into a campaign for Governor as the endorsed candidate of the Democratic-Nonpartisan League party. I made good on my determination not to go to the National Democratic Convention but to spend my time and money campaigning in North Dakota.

Our North Dakota delegation to the National Democratic Convention followed our State Convention's traditional rules that all of our delegates' votes should go to that Democratic candidate for President who the majority of our delegation supported. That was known as the "unit rule," now outlawed in a National Democratic Convention.

North Dakota's delegation arrived in Los Angeles under the leadership of State Chairman Abner Larson. Another powerhouse in our delegation was Dave Kelly, the National Committeeman. Daphna Nygaard, National Committeewoman, was also present and effective. Our delegation had only 11 votes, but we had sent 22 delegates, each with a half vote. John Kennedy was a strong contender, but many thought his Catholicism, eastern liberal politics, and Boston accent did not square well with heavily Protestant North Dakota whose Democratic outlook was western and conservative.

Adlai Stevenson and Lyndon Johnson were also favorites among some of our people, but the majority of our delegation supported Senator Hubert Humphrey of neighboring Minnesota. As a matter of fact, Hubert Humphrey had our delegation sewed up under the unit rule.

Probably nothing would have changed the delegation's commitment to Senator Humphrey except the Senator's withdrawal. And that is exactly what happened. Senator Humphrey not only withdrew suddenly but told his committed delegates that they were free to support whomever they wished. Humphrey's delegations were thrown into an uproar. Immediately our North Dakota delegation sought a majority position for one candidate so that our entire 22 half votes, or in reality, 11 votes, would go to one candidate.

Our delegates argued with one another and cajoled. But there was no way that any candidate could get a majority until finally, John Kennedy came within a half vote of achieving that success. That evening before the convention convened for the first balloting for the Democratic candidate for President, our delegation could not break the deadlock and trigger the unit rule to support one candidate.

I had sent telegrams to Delegation Chairman Abner Larson and National Committeeman Dave Kelly in which I stated that as our party's candidate for Governor, I supported the nomination of John Kennedy even though to do so might be adverse to my own interests as a gubernatorial candidate in North Dakota.

Less than an hour before the convention's first ballot fireworks were to begin, one of our North Dakota delegates, Clarence Larson from Agate, changed his half vote to Kennedy. That gave Kennedy a half vote majority in the delegation and triggered the unit rule, which lined up all 11 of our North Dakota delegation votes for the Senator. Delegates backing other candidates were crushed, but they were forced to capitulate to the slim majority.

The convention hall was tense; the balloting would be extremely close! Because the well-organized effort for John Kennedy included many states who were committed to him on only the first ballot, some of those states were legally released from their commitments and could move to another candidate should the balloting go to a second round.

Robert Kennedy and his brother-in-law, Sargent Shriver, had been working diligently with North Dakota and other Midwest states to line up support for John Kennedy. Wyoming had only a handful of votes, but it was a crucial state because the delegates told Robert Kennedy they would cast their few votes for John Kennedy as the last state in the balloting if their few votes would push him over the top. If their votes did not push Kennedy over the top, they would vote for another candidate.

As the roll was called, the atmosphere in the convention hall was highly charged. Some of the states, including Minnesota, passed on the first go-around because they wanted the flexibility of moving in with the candidate who appeared headed for victory. When Robert Kennedy and Sargent Shriver heard North Dakota's 11 votes called out for John Kennedy, a look of excited anticipation passed over their faces because if all went well, there were sufficient votes left for Wyoming to cast its small number of votes to nail down a Kennedy victory on the first ballot.

As the scoreboard totals kept mounting, the delegates nervously watched and held their breaths. Finally, the totals under John Kennedy's name reached the critical point when Wyoming, almost drowned out by the roar of the crowd, cast its few votes to put John Kennedy over the top.

In any tight election, you can point to a number of factors that made the difference between victory and defeat. But certainly the decision by Clarence Larson, a burly Scandinavian farmer from Agate, North Dakota, who seemed the most unlikely person to cast a vote for an eastern liberal Catholic senator, had to be one of the decisive moves in that convention. Without Clarence Larson's last-minute decision, John Kennedy might never have become President!

Robert Kennedy visited North Dakota several years later and told me that when the Kennedy organization heard North Dakota give its full vote to their Senator, they knew they could depend on Wyoming to throw its few votes to Kennedy and push him on to victory on the first ballot even though some large states were procrastinating to force the nomination into several ballots. John Kennedy visited the North Dakota delegation soon after that first ballot victory to thank them profusely for their support.

The story of Clarence Larson, who was the unlikely hero to the Kennedy forces, illustrates about as well as anything can the importance of one person's vote in our democratic system of government. No politician worth his salt can minimize the importance of every single voter and vote that is cast. I've won and lost enough close ones so that I can never forget it.

Off and Running

By the time John Kennedy burst on the national scene, the North Dakota Democratic party was becoming something more than a curiosity. The reason for this was the developing relationship between the party and the Nonpartisan League.

For many years, the Nonpartisan League was regarded as a faction of North Dakota's Republican party, and the League always filed its candidates in the Republican column. Because of this, the real election took place in the June primary to see whether the League or the regular GOP candidates would win. So weak was the Democratic party that it was almost a foregone conclusion that the winner of the NPL vs. Republican fight in the spring primary would win in the fall's general election.

In the early 1950s, young people in the Democratic party began to see that the Nonpartisan League was held in the Republican column simply because the old state officeholder leadership in the NPL wanted it there, and the conservative leadership in the Republican party could see that the Nonpartisan League served a useful purpose of splitting the progressive thinking voters in North Dakota between the Nonpartisan League and the Democratic party. This made both liberal parties less apt to win the top offices than if all the progressives were united under one banner. It was not surprising that some Democratic party "young turks," as they were known, began infiltrating the Nonpartisan League with the idea of moving the League into the Democratic party.

In the 1960 convention of the Nonpartisan League, the movement to shift the League to the Democratic party reached its climax. The second floor ballroom of the old Patterson Hotel in Bismarck witnessed its last great political drama and heard the strident acrimony that set off political reverberations still felt and talked about where old politicians gather. The ballroom of the Patterson Hotel was convention hall again as it had been year after year for Nonpartisan League politics. The floor of that aged convention hall sagged and creaked as people walked across it. Many a delegate wished that the rooms below were stacked full of tightly baled hay to give some support should the floor finally give way.

My Early Experiences in Politics

By League convention time, Congressman Quentin Burdick and I were considered the front running candidates for the Democratic nomination for the U.S. Senate and for Governor. Burdick was identified with the NPL and had been their candidate in past years. Neither one of us wanted to be involved in what we knew would be an historic donnybrook at that Nonpartisan League convention.

We left the milling crowds in convention hall and in the hotel lobby to lock ourselves in a small basement room with a portable television set, some scrub pails, and broken hotel chairs for company. Television coverage was new to North Dakota politics, and the local TV stations were experimenting with publicizing and reporting political conventions. With our little 12-inch television set, Quentin Burdick and I were able to watch the excitement in convention hall upstairs.

It was not long before the battle began. People well known in North Dakota politics gestured and shouted. Halvor Rolfsrud was being challenged for reelection as chairman of the Nonpartisan League. Halvor was one who did not see any advantage in moving the NPL to the Democratic column. He fought the attempt to unseat him. Herschel Lashkowitz, the colorful mayor of Fargo, spoke in his usual flamboyant and vehement style. Mayor Lashkowitz seemed to fuel his own emotions, as each fiery phrase reached a higher pitch than the last one. Quentin and I could not help but smile when the local TV station, without any ulterior motive I am sure, placed an overlay advertisement for Elephant-brand commercial fertilizer on the screen during one of Lashkowitz's speeches. I am sure many of Herschel's political enemies saw that overlay and gleefully pointed out that this was a very appropriate overlay ad to run during the mayor's speech.

The furious debate and vociferous charges and counter charges reached a roaring pitch when Emmons County rancher Clarence Haggard leaped to the stage to try to hold the fort by keeping the young insurgents from taking the microphone. He brandished a neck yoke with a steel ring at each end, which to the uninitiated is used to hitch a team of horses to the tongue of a farm wagon. He swung the clanking neck yoke around his head as he shouted. All who were struggling to get to the microphone stayed a discreet distance from the arc of his whirling weapon.

Suddenly a move was made. The connecting cord to the microphone was yanked out of its socket, and fists began to fly. Such a staid person as Bill Martin, president of the Cass County Farmers Union, took a haymaker swing at Mayor Lashkowitz. The fist failed to reach its mark, but the rush of air visibly wounded the mayor.

Pushing, shoving, swearing, and outthrust chins were the order of the day as determined people jammed the aisles. Some delegates leaped up from their chairs to shout and gesture only to have other delegates slip into the chairs beneath them to grab contested seats that had been denied them at the beginning of the convention. What the television cameras were recording in that turbulent scene was the passing of the Nonpartisan League from the Old Guard to a new breed of young insurgents.

Political reporters from other states sensed that this was not just another raucous political convention. Mercer Cross was one of those reporters. He was a tall, thin, nervous-type newsman who had just landed in Bismarck as a reporter for the Minneapolis *Tribune*. He couldn't believe his eyes. Politics had never been this way back in Minnesota. When he thought he had seen enough tumult for a story, he rushed toward the basement of the Patterson Hotel to unlimber his typewriter. Somehow, in the confusion of his rapid descent down the lobby stairs in which he had to battle people crowding up the stairs to see the excitement, Mercer cut his finger. Blood flowed. Mercer's face turned pale. The tension he was under was bad enough, but to add real blood, his own, was too much. His lips quivered. He sought to stanch the bleeding finger with his handkerchief, and he tried desperately to type with the wad of white cloth wrapped around the finger. The keys got a little bloody, and the wadded handkerchief made typing very difficult indeed.

Before long, the typewriter keys, the handkerchief, the finger, and for that matter, the story itself were all bloody. But why shouldn't they be? Mercer Cross was writing about the last bloody convention in North Dakota's wild, turbulent history. And Quentin Burdick and I watched the story unfold as we glanced from TV to his typewriter.

The Nonpartisan League did vote to join the Democratic party by endorsing the same candidates, and a genuine historic merger took place the next day at the Democratic convention in the Bismarck Civic Auditorium when NPL delegates came marching down the aisles en masse and took their seats beside the Democratic party delegates.

Those were two unforgettable conventions. They had all the excitement, intrigue, smoke-filled rooms, buttonholing, huddles, badges, hilarity, heartburn, headaches, despair, and laughter that any delegate could hope for. And suddenly it was over. The gavel banged out its message for the last time. A new political movement was born even though many were afraid to see the umbilical cord snipped.

I had been nominated as the first Democratic-NPL candidate for Governor, but not until a stiff challenge from Lavern Schoeder had been turned back. Jean and I stood at the edge of an aisle, shaking hands with delegates as they jostled each other good naturedly and pushed their way for the last time toward the exits and home. We felt good. There was a heady feeling, a euphoria, in being nominated—until the sobering realization sank in that I held the new party's banner.

On the stage of the convention auditorium, a few newspaper reporters still sat at their long tables hammering out their last-minute stories. Above the jumbled chairs, the county signs were standing askew in the sections so recently occupied by cheering, enthusiastic delegates. The floor was littered with everything from popcorn to balloting tallies—crumpled up and scattered.

The scene conveyed a feeling of anticlimax in light of the exciting events that had just transpired.

My First Encounter with Television

At the conclusion of that exciting 1960 convention, I had my first encounter with the medium that was playing an increasingly important role in our political life—television.

The candidates who had just been nominated huddled with the state chairman in front of the stage like a football team receiving instructions from the quarterback. Suddenly a TV station program director rushed up and asked, "Do you candidates at the top of the ticket want 30 minutes of live television time starting on the stage in eight minutes?" The TV station had planned the telecast for longer than the convention had lasted, and they needed some action to fill the remaining minutes.

Free television time! I'll say we wanted it! In seconds, we were on stage, pulling our chairs in place behind the long table that members of the press had just vacated. The table was covered with a 10-foot long sheet of white wrapping paper used as a tablecloth.

"What should I say?" whispered U.S. Senate nominee Quentin Burdick. "Why don't you jot down some thoughts in the few minutes we have before we go on?" I suggested. Burdick frantically began to write his thoughts. My own thoughts shifted furiously to what I would say in front of that television camera. Getting one's mind to function clearly is difficult when you only have a two- or three-minute deadline.

In what seemed like a matter of seconds, I heard the announcer saying, "And now ladies and gentlemen, I present the Democratic-Nonpartisan League nominee for the United States Senate, Quentin Burdick."

My Early Experiences in Politics

At the end of the table, Quentin leaped to his feet, grabbing his notes, which happened to be written on the ten feet of white paper tablecloth. As he struggled toward the rostrum with his trailing load, I had the presence of mind to reach out with my foot, stop that trailing paper cloth, and tear off the last eight feet of his notes. The sudden jolt to the Senator's rush toward the rostrum almost jerked the paper from his hand, but in a panicky moment, he was able to recover his oversized notes and arrive at the microphone, exuding that smiling self-confidence that a candidate for the U.S. Senate should have on camera.

Striving to Become a Household Word

As candidates struggling to become household words, we were to discover that television is a wonderful medium to reach the public. But it has the potential to create behind-the-scenes crises as well as incredibly humorous situations.

One afternoon, soon after the convention, I was driving a tractor on our farm while cultivating sugarbeets. I looked up from the row and saw my wife driving into the field at a speed that indicated something had happened that was very important for me to know about. In a few minutes, I reached the end of the field, and Jean rushed over to shout above the pop-pop-pop of my John Deer B. tractor, "KXJB-TV has called and said they will give the Democrats thirty minutes if you can get into the West Fargo studio by a quarter to six." My watch said 4:45—and the station was 30 minutes away!

But free television time was something that politicians, especially poverty-stricken Democratic-Nonpartisan Leaguers, could not turn down. I shut off my tractor, jumped into the car, and Jean sped me back to the farm. I was out of the car, bounding up the back porch stairs, tearing my dusty clothes off as I went. I practically slid into the shower and out in one movement as I washed the day's accumulation of sweat and dirt from my hair and body. Five minutes later, I was racing out of the house, buttoning my shirt, dragging my jacket and tie along with me. KXJB studio was 28 miles away, and I would have to bend the speed limit a little to get there on time.

When Jean and I arrived at the studio on the edge of West Fargo, we were met by several other Democratic officers in our organization, whom KXJB-TV had alerted to join the panel program. As we hurried in, I talked excitedly to County Chairman Myron Bright about what subjects we should cover. Four of us were to be on the program. We made plans hastily as we were led into the large hayloft-like studio where the filming was to take place. This was in the early days of North Dakota television, and it so happened that two television stations used the same facilities. At one end of the lofty studio was a glass-enclosed balcony from which the television engineers could look down on the filming below.

The program director hastily sat us down behind a long desk, pointed at the camera, and said, "When the small red light alongside of the lens comes on, that means you are being filmed." I asked if we could watch ourselves on a studio monitor screen. He said, "No, we can't do that because the program being shown by the other station in this building is on the only monitor we have."

I glanced at the show on the monitor clearly visible to us and only a few feet away. It was an exciting cowboy show. The sound coming from the monitor was loud enough so that it could be heard above our voices.

"I hope you'll turn down the sound on that monitor," I suggested. The program director turned and shouted up at the glassed-in balcony, "Hey, turn down the sound on the monitor!"

Nothing happened, and it was apparent that either the monitor could not be turned down or the instructions were not reaching the right person. Suddenly, the cameraman swung his gimlet-eyed lens at us, and a tiny, red light snapped on. We were being televised and were on our own!

My Early Experiences in Politics

It was amazing what people could do on television when forced to. Our foursome carried on a discussion of the issues and candidates on our ticket; and before we knew it, our time was up. But all during this time, the monitor was a distraction to us because in the western film, bandits rode alongside a jolting stagecoach pulled frantically down a mountain trail by a team of four horses. Shots were fired over a period of several minutes until the holdup men were able to stop the stagecoach. Loud orders emanated from the bandits to the stagecoach driver, and keeping our minds on our political subjects was difficult when such exciting action was taking place on the large television screen facing us only a few feet to one side of our table.

When our program was over and when we had congratulated ourselves for having obtained 30 minutes of free television expense and for using it about as effectively as four people could on the spur of the moment, we left for home.

"Let's go and see mother and dad in Fargo," Jean suggested. It was a good idea, and frankly, it was close enough to supper so that it might even result in a free meal. As we walked up the steps at Dad and Mother Mason's Fargo home, Jean's father opened the door to greet us.

"Say, I saw that half-hour television show that you were just on. I thought it was pretty good. But," he asked, "what on earth was all that galloping and shooting in the background?"

I doubt that any political candidate anywhere has ever had to put up with galloping and shooting as background noise although I think some candidates' presentation probably could be livened up a bit if they would try it.

My next brush with television came a few weeks later when I visited Grand Forks to campaign for Governor. The local district chairman greeted me and suggested that maybe I would want to make a one-minute live presentation over the local television station.

"It's a great opportunity," he said, "because they've decided to try selling a one-minute spot to politicians for $17."

I checked my billfold to see if I could cover a $17 television charge and found that I could just make it.

The KNOX-TV studio was in a large, round-roofed, quonset-type building. One end of the building was devoted to filming. That end was separated into two large studio rooms by a folding door that extended 20 feet from the floor to the ceiling. On one side of the studio space, a glassed-in booth was situated so that the announcer could view the rooms on either side of the folding door.

The program director led me to a battered desk placed in one of the two studio rooms and explained how the filming would be done. "You will be introduced by the announcer in the glassed-in booth," he said. "And when you see that small red light come on next to the TV camera lens, then your presentation will begin. When the light snaps off, you will know that your time is up. The announcer in the glassed-in booth will then give the disclaimer indicating that it was a political advertisement."

The instructions sounded simple enough until I realized that there was a five-minute live advertisement for the stock car races at the Grand Forks fairgrounds just before my one-minute presentation. In the other studio, behind the folding doors, was an old, crumpled jalopy that was started up to give the stock car racing advertisement some real, live noise and color. The folding doors between our two studios did not quite close, and the exhaust pipe of the old, battered stock car was just a foot or so from the opening. As someone in the car would tromp down hard on the gas pedal to give that exciting roar of a racing car, plumes of blue smoke would come billowing out of its exhaust pipe.

It seemed an eternity that the blue smoke kept rolling into my side of the studio. As a matter of fact, it became so thick I could barely make out the camera that was to film my one-minute speech. My eyes were watering. Suddenly,

My Early Experiences in Politics

I heard the faraway voice of the announcer in the glassed-in booth saying, "And now ladies and gentlemen, the Democratic-Nonpartisan League candidate for Governor, William L. Guy."

The stock car's engine had been stopped, and through the blue gloom of smoke that hung in the air, I dimly saw the TV camera's red light come on. With tears in my eyes, I took a deep breath to start talking. I began to cough. Each time I would begin to say something, a cough would overtake me. Suddenly the red light blinked off, and I heard the announcer intoning in the safety of his glassed-in booth, "Ladies and gentlemen, you have just heard from the Democratic-Nonpartisan League candidate for governor, William L. Guy. This is a political advertisement." My 60 seconds were up.

I stumbled out of the smoke-filled studio and realized that these were the most expensive coughs I had ever coughed.

I was very discouraged by that humiliating experience before the TV camera at KNOX that night. But the next day, to my amazement, people who had never heard of Bill Guy were talking and laughing about him. I received more name recognition from my one-minute fiasco than I could have received had things gone well.

A Humbling Experience

Television is fine, but North Dakotans expect personal contact with their politicians. That was as true in 1960 as it is today.

The first organized event that Jean and I attended during our opening 1960 campaign swing around North Dakota was a coffee party that Mrs. Alice Wagner, a Democratic stalwart for many years, had arranged in Valley City. She had invited many of her elderly women friends from around the neighborhood to her home. It was clearly not a gathering of politically interested people. But it was an indication of what we would run into in the hundreds of neighborhood coffee parties that became a part of the campaign in the months ahead.

I was apprehensive and inexperienced at both campaigning and coffee parties. Mrs. Wagner led me around the room to shake hands with her elderly lady friends. We came to one very petite lady in her 80s who was balancing a tea cup on her lap. Mrs. Wagner, the enthusiastic, optimistic person that she was, introduced me as "the next Governor of North Dakota."

"Why," said the little old lady, "I am so pleased to meet you, Mr. Dahl, but I thought you were an older man."

I stifled my shock when I realized that this little old lady thought she was talking to my Republican opponent, C. P. Dahl, who was 25 years older than I was. The incident was amusing and probably fortunate for me that it happened early in the campaign, because it underlined the fact that to most North Dakotans at that moment, I was an unknown candidate who had a long way to go.

A Case of Mistaken Identity

In 1960, Jean and I struck off across the state early, beginning the campaign well before the primary election because we wanted to do all we could to help to elect Quentin Burdick to the U.S. Senate. Senator William Langer had passed away in office, and to fill that vacancy, a special election was held in conjunction with the June primary election. Quentin Burdick was endorsed by the Democratic-Nonpartisan League for that Senate seat, and Governor John Davis was endorsed by the Republican party as their candidate. Jean and I headed west in our 1959 blue-and-white, six-cylinder Chevrolet station wagon with a large, gold-and-black sign secured upright on the roof proclaiming one word, "Burdick."

Our campaign swing took us into the southwestern part of the state, and one late afternoon about 5 o'clock, we parked near an intersection on Bowman's main street. As we peered at our road map to find out how far it was to Regent for an evening event, we were startled by a young boy about 11 years old standing just outside the car window on my side. He held a package of gumdrops in one hand.

"Say," he said, "how'd you like to have a gumdrop?"

The thought of eating a gumdrop at that moment did not exactly appeal to me, but I didn't see any reason why I should insult the young man by refusing.

"Thank you," I said, accepting the gumdrop from his grimy hand. There followed a pause of a few seconds and suddenly the expression on the young man's face changed.

"Hey!" he said. "You ain't Burdick!" and he reached through the open window and grabbed the gumdrop right out of my hand. With a disgusted look, he turned on his heel and marched off. When I thought of the gumdrop that came from his grimy hand, I wasn't sure whether I was lucky or unlucky that I had been put down by this young supporter of Senator Burdick.

Lost on the Land...

A statewide campaign is a grueling affair at best. Jean and I often would work 18 hours a day, living out of suitcases and sleeping in strange places each night. To make our limited campaign funds stretch as far as possible, we gladly accepted almost any friendly offer for a roof over our heads at night.

Such an offer came from Ray and Esther Vendsel. Ray was running for Congress. He and his wife lived on a ranch in Renville County up near the Canadian border.

"When you are finished with your rally at Berthold," Ray said, "come on out to the ranch and get a good night's sleep. It's easy to find. You go straight north of Carpio for six miles on Highway 28, then turn right and follow that road for four miles in an easterly direction. Then turn north one-half mile and then east one-half mile. When you reach this point, you're about a mile away from the ranch, and you will see a light in the distance. It will be the only light visible anywhere. Just follow the trail toward that light, and you'll soon be at our ranch house."

So about midnight under a moonless, black sky, we bounced over the Renville County roads in our Chevy station wagon until we thought we were about a mile from the Vendsel ranch house. Sure enough, when we came over a little rise, we could see a light in the distance. But the road suddenly seemed to "peter out" into a field road or even a cattle trail, but it was headed toward the light, and we followed it.

After traveling about a mile and a half over what I thought was an incredibly poor road to any ranch, we finally arrived at the light, which was on a slowly moving tractor that was pulling a field cultivator! We were embarrassed to stop the surprised farmer in the dead of night at the edge of the field to ask him where the Vendsel ranch house was. He sent us backtracking and a few minutes later, we were relieved to find out that, sure enough, there were two lights on the horizon in that sparsely settled area—one on the slowly moving tractor and off to the right in the distance the yard light of the Vendsel ranch.

And in the Air

The Democratic-Nonpartisan League did not have the money to organize carefully in every county and city of the state. And it didn't have transportation and lodging funds for its candidates. It didn't have financing for billboards, television, radio, and newspaper advertising. Much of the campaign had to be carried out through the good help of hundreds of volunteer friends and supporters in all parts of the state. Once, I was scheduled for a political banquet at 6:30 in Devils Lake and a late evening reception in Fargo the same night. Ordinarily such a conflict of appearances would be impossible to resolve. But in this instance, an

My Early Experiences in Politics

attorney friend, Glen Swanson, who was later to become a district judge, offered a solution.

"I have a Cessna Tripacer out at the Devils Lake Airport," he said. "We can fly to Fargo as soon as you have spoken at the banquet here in Devils Lake, and you can make both events."

That seemed like a good way to handle the dilemma, and I boarded Swanson's little single-engine airplane at the Devils Lake Airport about eight o'clock that evening. The ceiling was low and murky and brought darkness early. A light mist was falling. I had some grave misgivings in my heart as we took off into the wet night behind the throbbing engine in that little airplane.

After flying for what seemed like 15 minutes with the visibility very restricted, the ceiling exceedingly low, and the rain pelting the windshield, we noticed a dim flashing light off to the right. "That must be New Rockford, isn't it?" shouted Swanson over the noise of the engine.

The dim cabin light hid my look of dismay, and I shouted back, "Are you asking me? Who's navigating this airplane anyhow?"

"Don't worry," he said, leaning over to speak into my ear. "We have electrical instruments aboard which home us in by radio to our destination."

I swallowed uneasily and nodded my head. We churned on through the murky darkness, and suddenly I was aware of a faint glow coming through the overcast in the distance.

"There," shouted Swanson triumphantly. "There's Fargo just as I thought. the wind has drifted us a little bit south, but there it is right ahead!"

"That isn't Fargo, Glen!" I shouted. "I may not know how to navigate, but I have enough sense of direction to know that isn't Fargo!"

"You can't argue with modern navigational equipment!" was Swanson's confident reply.

We flew toward the dim light ahead and in a few minutes, we were right over the top of it. Looking down,

I was jolted to realize that it was not Fargo at all, but the runways below were those of the Grand Forks Air Force Base. Glen was quietly dismayed at his navigational error, but I was quietly relieved to know where we were.

From the Grand Forks Air Base, we were able to fly low through the rain and fog to Grand Forks and then south above Highway 81 to Fargo. When we landed at Hector Airport in Fargo, I knew how people felt when they knelt down to kiss the solid ground. I looked back at that little dripping airplane and wondered what would have happened had we not accidentally come across the Grand Forks Air Base or if that little piston-driven engine had failed in the darkness. At that moment, I made up my mind that conditions would have to be very desperate before I would again venture out in a single-engine airplane to fly through fog and rain at night.

An Early Woman's Liberationist

The Equal Rights Amendment was not a part of the 1960 campaign, but I had a slight preview of it when I was campaigning in Williams County with big, bluff, and colorful "Chief" Clarence Poling, who was running for the legislature. We were going door to door in a small town, had finally covered all of the houses, and were handshaking our way down the single street of business places. We came to a small grocery store. Chief Poling was well known in the county because he was a veteran legislator and county commissioner. He knew nearly everybody in the county, and nearly everyone knew and loved him.

We advanced toward the battered counter in the little, overstocked grocery store and steered toward the busy woman who was straightening some goods on a shelf.

"Hi, Emma," was the Chief's cheerful greeting. "We are around here to ask for your vote in the coming election."

The woman wheeled around, folded her arms, looked Chief Poling in the eye, and said, "Chief, I absolutely refuse to vote for you unless you promise to equalize the rights between women and men!"

"Why, Emma," the Chief said in his most conciliatory tones, "I would be glad to promise to do that, but first, you women will have to give back all the rights you have now so that I can redistribute some of them to the men if we're going to get equality."

The woman seemed satisfied with the Chief's line of malarkey; but in retrospect, I know that his line of reasoning never would go over big among equal rights advocates today.

Being A Democrat Could Be Hazardous to Your Health

Since only two other Democrats had ever been elected Governor of North Dakota since statehood in 1889, it was easy to understand why a Democrat-Nonpartisan Leaguer in 1960 was not given much of a chance. As a matter of fact, being identified with the Democratic-Nonpartisan league was considered in many small North Dakota communities to be quite daring and different.

Jean and I made a campaign stop in Steele one afternoon to visit the Cunninghams, who printed the local newspaper. Across the street, the children had just come out of school for their afternoon recess. A small boy about 10 years of age and full of curiosity saw the big Burdick sign wired upright on our station wagon roof and came over to see what was up.

When he learned that I was the Democratic-NPL candidate for Governor, his face lit up, and he reached out to shake my hand. Then looking carefully up and down the sidewalk to make sure no one was watching, he raised the tab on his shirt collar to disclose a Guy campaign button pinned underneath.

I was pleased, of course, and asked, "Why don't you wear that Guy button out on your shirt pocket where everyone can see it?"

"What!" he exclaimed. "And get killed!"

I was learning to take my left-handed compliments in small doses.

Not All Are Chosen

During my first campaign for Governor, I received a surprise invitation to speak to the annual convention of the North Dakota Stockmans Association. I had to do it, and I don't mind admitting I was scared. Sure enough, when I entered the lobby of the Knights of Columbus Hall in Dickinson, the coat hooks were all hung with Stetson cowboy hats. This was cattle country, and I was a sheepman. Even worse, I was a sheepman from Cass County. And even worse yet, if it could be worse, I was a Democrat in Republican country.

When it was my turn to speak, I took a hitch in my courage and strode up to the front of the hall. There I stood looking down at all those stern-faced cattlemen. They sat there looking down at me it seemed. I cleared my throat bravely. "I know that sheep is a dirty word out here, and I admit that I am a sheepman. I also know that you cattlemen are a proud and independent lot and don't think much of us sheepmen. But I want you to stop and think for a moment."

"Nearly two thousand years ago when there was a star over Bethlehem and the Angels of the Lord came down to find someone with credibility to spread the glad tidings of great joy, they didn't look up you cattlemen; they looked up us sheepmen!"

I had those cattlemen in my shepherd's crook from there on in.

Top: Campaigning in Fargo in June of 1960 with John Kennedy (l) and Quentin Burdick (r).

Center: A young Democrat-NPL legislator, 1959.

Bottom: Standard fare on the campaign trail, 1960.

3

A Democratic-NPL Governor is Elected

Now Comes the Hard Part

By 11 o'clock on the evening of November 6, 1960, it had become obvious that I had won the election—the third Democratic governor elected in North Dakota since statehood in 1889. We watched the returns on television in our farmhouse near Amenia. A half dozen friends from the community had come over to make an election-returns-watching party out of it. By 11 o'clock, the phone was ringing constantly from friends and supporters around the state, not to mention the reporters from various newspapers as far away as Minneapolis and even Washington, D.C.

In the first few moments when I realized I had won, the feeling of elation was mighty heady stuff; but as the phone calls stretched on into the night, it became apparent that there would be little sleep the next day or two. At 4 o'clock in the morning, my wife and I turned in only to have the telephone continue to ring. We put a pillow over it to no avail. We finally stuffed it in a dresser drawer and packed it solidly with clothes and pillows to muffle any sound. We would have pulled the jack out of the wall had there been a jack to pull out, but we were on a rural party line and to pull any cord out of the wall would have disrupted the phone service to four other farms. The muffling of the phone in the dresser drawer really was not effective, but it did soothe our consciences a bit when we pretended we did not hear it.

The next morning, Bell Telephone was "Johnny-on-the-Spot" and voluntarily strung a separate line the two miles from Amenia to our farm, much to the relief of the other farms on our party line.

Winning the election for governor meant that the work began immediately, even though the salary didn't start until two months later. I was besieged by people who were interested in backing or opposing legislation that they thought might come before the upcoming session. The Legislative Research Committee sent me legislative interim reports. Every organization from co-ops to the chambers of commerce to the labor unions placed me on their mailing lists so that I would receive the information they were circulating to their members.

It was soon obvious that my tiny office in our farmhouse was just not adequate to do the job, and I moved to Bismarck to live in loneliness in a Grand Pacific Hotel room.

The Peterson brothers, John and Vernon, owned the Grand Pacific Hotel. They had been friends of mine since college days. John Peterson had been the best man at our wedding, and we had kept in touch with him and his wife, Helen. The Peterson brothers told me that I could have my hotel room free of charge while I prepared to take over the reins as governor. I thanked them for their kind offer, but I told them that I had won the nomination and the election without any commitments either expressed or implied to anybody or any organization and certainly not in exchange for financial help. And contributions from corporations such as the Grand Pacific Hotel were illegal. I didn't want to mar my record by accepting their kindness, so I paid the hotel bill out of my own pocket.

A Democratic-NPL Governor is Elected

My friend Charles Conrad took the lead in lining up several public meetings on subjects such as education, mental health, welfare, and employment.

As these meetings took place, and as I listened to people testify, I was also thinking of the people I wanted to attract into state government to serve as department heads during my term in office.

Filling the chinks of any spare time I had was the job of assembling my first message to the legislature. This turned out be a much larger challenge than I had anticipated. Had it not been for the volunteer work of my good friend, Lou Dunn, the clerk of the North Dakota Supreme Court, I don't know how I could have had all of the drafts typed up and edited in time. She even worked at typing a revision on New Year's Eve.

Governor John Davis had accepted an invitation to take a voyage with other governors on a naval ship to South America. He was not on hand to be of assistance to me in most of the transition period, and the legislature had made no provision for staff or funds for the governor-elect. I found that conducting the duties of a governor-elect without the benefit of the governor's staff and without state financial assistance cost me about $1500, which at that time was a substantial sum. One of the first legislative suggestions I made was that the legislature appropriate transition money to help a governor-elect in the two months between the election and the inauguration. I think the legislature, then predominantly Republican, agreed to this suggestion in a hurry, thinking that the next governor obviously would be a Republican and could use that kind of assistance. Curiously, the next governor was not to be elected until 12 years later, and the governor was Arthur Link, another Democrat-NPL party member. Governor Link had little use for transitional funds because he received all of the assistance and staff support possible from me as the outgoing Democratic-NPL Governor.

Another Mistaken Identity

Governor Davis suggested in mid-December that I, as governor-elect, accompany several other North Dakotans to a Missouri Basin Interagency Committee meeting in Sioux City, Iowa. I welcomed the chance to gain firsthand experience with that 10-state organization, which also included federal agency representatives who worked with water resource development in the Missouri Basin. At that time, North Dakota was striving mightily to get Congress to authorize and fund the Garrison Diversion Irrigation Project as an integral part of the total Pick-Sloan Missouri River Basin Water Resource Development Program.

We flew from Bismarck to Sioux City, in a Bureau of Reclamation twin-engine C-45 Beechcraft. As our plane rolled to a stop in front of the terminal building, I saw a long, black Cadillac limousine and another big car parked in apparent readiness for our arrival. The president of the Sioux City Chamber of Commerce knew that several governors would be coming to that meeting, and he had come out in the limousine to greet the governors as they arrived and to give them the red carpet treatment.

The first man to step out of our airplane was prominent farmer-conservationist Henry Steinberger, looking very distinguished with his flowing, white hair.

"Governor Guy!" greeted the Sioux City Chamber president. "So glad to have you in our city."

"I am sorry," Henry said. "My name is Steinberger," and they shook hands.

Then, tall, dignified, bald-headed Oscar Berg stepped down from the airplane to the asphalt ramp. Our host had recovered, and he extended his hand apologetically to Oscar.

"Governor Guy, we are so glad to have you in Sioux City," he said.

A Democratic-NPL Governor is Elected

Oscar smiled a little and said, "I am not the Governor. My name is Berg. I'm Executive Director of the North Dakota Water users Association."

Then, Bob Dorothy of the Bureau of Reclamation, a very handsome man with an outdoors sun tan, stepped from the airplane, and the flustered Chamber president reached out his hand and smiled wryly.

"Governor Guy, I should have known you!"

Dorothy said, "I'm sorry, I am not the Governor. I am with the Bureau of Reclamation. My name is Dorothy."

By this time, the pilot, with his crewcut, and I, with my crewcut, had alighted from the airplane. Panic was written across the face of the Sioux City Chamber of Commerce president. He eyed us quickly and then made his decision. Reaching out his hand in extreme embarrassment to the pilot, he said, "Governor Guy, I don't know how I could have mistaken you."

The pilot thought the scene was very funny by this time and couldn't conceal his mirth.

"This is Governor Guy," he said, pointing to me. The Chamber president's jaw dropped, his face flushed, and he swallowed a few times and wordlessly shook hands as we crawled into the back seat of his limousine. We had both learned something—the young crewcut farmer who was governor-elect of North Dakota would have to go some to look like a governor.

Political Shenanigans, North Dakota Style

Taking office as the third Democratic governor since 1889 was not without incident. A rumor had circulated that the opposition would seek a court injunction to prevent my taking office. They would claim I was ineligible to be governor because I had served in the legislature during the previous session when the salary and expense allowances for the governor had been raised. Some observers even felt that a North Dakota constitutional provision governing the eligibility of legislators for other elective offices might prevent my taking office.

Judge Peter Sathre, the chief justice of the North Dakota Supreme Court, was an irascible old man whose political career traced back to the formation of the Nonpartisan League in the early years of the century. About 9 o'clock on the morning of inauguration day, Judge Sathre came down to the governor's office, which had just been turned over to me to prepare for the afternoon ceremonies.

"Governor," the judge said with eyes twinkling. "I think there are people who are up to no good, and something needs to be done about it."

I had heard the rumors, too; and I asked him, "What should we do about it?"

"It would not surprise me," the old judge said, "to see some lawyer come parading down the center aisle of the House of Representatives about 60 seconds before you are given the oath of office at your inauguration this afternoon and present papers which would enjoin me from giving you the oath. I suggest," he continued on, "that we meet here in your office in a few minutes, and I will give you the oath of office before the required witnesses so that when you march into that legislative chamber for the inauguration ceremony this afternoon, any oath of office given there will be purely for ceremonial purposes."

I could see that the old judge's willingness to meet political fire with political fire had not diminished over his many years in public life.

So, Judge Sathre, in his flowing, black robe and his flowing, white hair, returned to the governor's office and before witnesses, quietly had me raise my right hand. With my left hand on the Bible, I took the traditional oath of office.

Five hours later in the public inauguration ceremony, I stood for a second time and took the oath of office. The Chief Justice had a smile at the edges of his mouth, and his eyes twinkled as he had me repeat the oath he had already given me in my office. The inauguration ceremony

A Democratic-NPL Governor is Elected

was not interrupted, but a few hours later I was informed that a group of political opponents, located in Jamestown, had filed a motion with the District Court to have me declared disqualified to serve as governor because I had been a legislator when certain emoluments for the governor had been increased, rendering me constitutionally ineligible to serve. The District Court sent the case immediately to the Supreme Court where it was heard.

Many people were apprehensive about the lawsuit because they could remember all too well how a previous governor 25 years before had been disqualified after his election because he had once purchased a Minnesota resident fishing license. That was successfully used as evidence that he did not satisfy the five-year residential requirement to be governor of North Dakota. I did not have the apprehension that many felt, and I went to the inauguration ceremonies for John F. Kennedy in Washington, D.C., without much fear that a decision of our North Dakota Supreme Court would suddenly turn my carriage into a pumpkin.

On January 19, 1961, I received a phone call in my hotel room in Washington, D.C., from my aide, Lloyd Omdahl, back in Bismarck.

"Bill," he shouted excitedly over the telephone. "The Supreme Court has upheld you! They found it constitutional for a Democrat to be the governor of North Dakota."

I was relieved, but it was only the beginning of sporadic political harassment to which I would have to become accustomed in the months and years ahead.

It was, indeed, unusual for North Dakota to have a Democratic governor. Some people of our state had trouble getting used to that fact, and people outside North Dakota would be even more confused by not having a Republican as the chief of state in North Dakota.

And I Didn't Drive A Chrysler Either

Soon after taking office, my wife and I were invited to the Bismarck Chamber of Commerce annual banquet held at the St. Mary High School gymnasium. The speaker for the evening was Heartsil Wilson, a Chrysler Corporation vice president.

Those assigned to sit at the head table had gathered in a small room off the banquet hall to receive their seating arrangements. The president of the Chamber of Commerce brought Mr. Wilson over to meet my wife and me.

"I'm so pleased to meet you," beamed Mr. Wilson, knowing in his mind that in North Dakota he was safely in Republican territory. "You know, it's always good to meet a Republican. Why, back in Michigan, my Chrysler colleagues and I were Dick Nixon's strongest supporters!"

Our Chamber of Commerce friend thought things were getting out of hand and was flustered and embarrassed.

"But, Mr. Wilson," he stammered. "Governor Guy is a Democrat!"

Now it was Mr. Wilson's turn to be embarrassed. His jaw dropped, and his shoulders sagged.

"That's all right, Mr. Wilson," I said brightly. "Would it help you to know that I get 22 miles to the gallon with my Chevrolet?"

Heartsil Wilson's stricken face broke into laughter, and he slapped his knee.

"I deserved that," he said.

The following day, Wilson called me from Winnipeg, Manitoba, where he had a speaking engagement.

"Governor," he said, "I'll never forget that 'put-down' that you slipped me last night in Bismarck. I really walked into it and deserved it."

We've been friends ever since.

One Good Turn Didn't Result in Another

I considered myself quite fortunate in January 1961 to "inherit" two exceptionally competent governor's office

A Democratic-NPL Governor is Elected

employees whom my predecessor, John Davis, had hired. Bonnie Chase became my personal secretary and assimilated mountains of work like a baler baled hay. Becky Zoller was my experienced receptionist-typist. I knew I could depend on them to do the right things.

On about my second day in office, I found a round pink candy mint on one corner of my desk. How thoughtful of my new staff, I thought. They surely know how to get this governor off to a good start in the morning. I continued to find a mint every morning when I came to the office. Apparently my receptionist was the one who placed a mint in the same spot on my desk everyday—or was it my personal secretary?

Suddenly the mints stopped coming. I thought it strange that I no longer found mints on my desk in the morning after they had been placed there, one a day, without fail for more than a month. I became concerned that I had done or said something to cause my fall from the staff's favor. I quietly questioned Bonnie who referred me to Becky, my receptionist. "Why those mints have been given to me to give to you each morning by John Gunness," she explained.

I was surprised. I knew John Gunness as the executive director of the North Dakota Petroleum Council, which represented the oil industry in our state. He was their lead lobbyist with the legislature, which was in session.

A few days later, I happened to meet John, coming down the great hall from the Senate Chambers.

"John", I exclaimed, "I want to thank you for those mints you've been giving me. I didn't know until the other day that they were coming from you. How come they've stopped coming?"

John's face reddened. He shifted his feet nervously and with a smile, he said, "Well, damn it, Governor, you vetoed my bill!"

Now it was my turn to laugh. "John", I said, "I didn't even know you were interested in any particular bill. What kind of a lobbyist are you anyway? Thinking you can bribe the governor with mints and then not tell him what you are trying to bribe him for?" I guess my describing the mints as bribery was putting it too strong. But my meeting with John solved the great mint mystery—and cemented a friendship that lasted several years until John lost his battle with cancer.

My (second) swearing in by Chief Justice Sathre, January 4, 1961.

Top left: My inaugural address to a stunned Republican legislature, January 4, 1961.

Top right: A new governor in action, 1961.

Center: Visiting Chick Swenson on his farm south of Bismarck, 1962.

Bottom: Addressing the North Dakota National Guard at Ft. Riley, Kansas, during the Berlin crisis of 1962.

4

Being Governor
(and the Governor's Family)

The Governor's Family

Except for the family of the president of the United States, no other family of a public office holder must endure such continual, intense scrutiny as does the family of a governor. Families of judges, congressmen, mayors, and legislators can lead normal lives and seldom draw the attention of the public or news media. But a governor's family sacrifices much in the way of privacy and the right to be individuals. Everyone in the family and all its activities often are positioned to make the Governor's term in office successful.

I doubt that anyone can be successful as Governor unless that person's spouse totally supports the Governor's political philosophy and work demands. But even more important, that spouse also must assume added responsibility of raising the children in the family with less help from his or her office-holding mate, while the whole family activity is conducted in a fishbowl.

I was extremely fortunate. My wife, Jean, was an exceptionally good mother to our children, and also was adept in public relations. Her views of political matters were close to mine, and our discussions of people and issues helped to clear the debris before decisions were made. Jean was an ideal First Lady. She was skilled in social graces and had an inner warmth that attracted people to her.

When we took up housekeeping in the governor's residence, we had five very active children. The governor's residence had just been completed. Governor John Davis and his family had occupied it only nine months, which was barely time to decorate and furnish it. Immediately our detractors voiced concern that five young children would certainly tear the beautiful new governor's residence apart.

The children were all different and would react differently to 12 years in the governor's residence. Our oldest, Billy, was 14 when we moved from the farm and small town of Amenia to Bismarck. Billy was a quiet, serious-minded, goal-oriented young man. He was able to shrug off the glare of the public spotlight. He knew when he was a freshman in high school that he wanted to be a certified public accountant and a lawyer. He didn't deviate from his plan except to spend four years in the Navy during the Vietnam War. He became a CPA and an attorney in a Moorhead, Minnesota, law firm. He married his high school sweetheart, Marilyn Walter, who now heads the Department of Education at Concordia College in Moorhead. They have two children, Stephanie and Mark.

Jimmy was 12 when he left his beloved trap lines along the Rush River to move to Bismarck. He didn't care for the city or for crowds. Being in the public eye was difficult for him. He never wanted to be seen riding in the Governor's official car. He was happiest when he brought home old lawn mower engines from Porter Brothers junkyard and repaired them to running condition. Jimmy had always wanted to farm. He and his wife, Jane Bergman, and their children, Cari and T.J., operate the Guy farm at Amenia.

Of all our children, Deborah, at 10, was the most gregarious. The fish bowl living didn't bother her a bit when she arrived in Bismarck. She plunged right into school

Being Governor (and the Governor's Family)

activities and soon was spending her summers as a lifeguard at the Bismarck swimming pool. A toboggan accident, which broke her back, nearly left her paralyzed. She put her law enforcement degree from Minot State College to work in the personnel division of the N.D. State Highway Department. She and her husband, Jim Igoe, who works at the electric power generating plant at Underwood, have two children, Cody and Caiti.

Perhaps Holly, who was 5 when we came to Bismarck, suffered most from being exposed to the public. She was a very shy youngster and resented the spotlight. Her college work at Willmar, Minnesota, got her away from North Dakota and made it possible for her to meet and marry Dale Mossberg, a young house builder. Holly has made a career of supervising disturbed girls in a county home for young women. She and her husband have one son, Jamie.

Our youngest daughter, Nancy, was barely 2 when I was elected Governor. Perhaps because she spent her earliest years in public life, she adapted easiest. Of all the children, she has been the most active in precinct and district politics. After a few years of stenographic and sales work Nancy returned to night school for a degree from Minot State College. She and her attorney husband, Greg Stites, have no children.

Perhaps children who are raised in a governor's family have certain advantages. But there are also many disadvantages. I certainly would not seek that fishbowl environment in which to raise a family. The support of the schools, church, and community friends helped fill in the deficiencies of time and attention that our children might have suffered. But above all else, our children had the benefit of an exceptional mother.

The Show Was in the Balcony

Sometimes family roles and official roles conflict. Being a normal parent or child and a member of the first family of the state isn't always easy, as we were reminded in 1964.

Our oldest son, Bill, had little use for team athletics, but for some reason he took to high school wrestling.

The Bismarck High School wrestling coach, Jerry Halmrast, was a man who demanded top physical conditioning and close attention to technical details from his student wrestlers. He would station a motion picture cameraman on the balcony, looking down at the wrestling action on the mat below so that the films could be used to provide careful analysis of the successes and failures of each match.

During one wrestling meet in the Bismarck auditorium, my wife and I took our position on the front row bench in the balcony opposite the balcony from which the wrestling action was being filmed. Our son had his hands full in his match, and even though he had the shouted encouragement from his father and the sympathetic motions of his mother, who was totally immersed in the action, the match went badly.

Unbeknownst to his mother, the cameraman had shifted the direction of his lens from the straining wrestlers on the the mat below to Jean Guy in the balcony across. As Billy's shoulders were finally pinned to the mat and the referee signaled it with a sharp slap on the floor, my wife was overcome with despair and rocked back on her backless bench with both feet flying up in the air in complete sympathy with her defeated son below.

It was not until the coach was showing the film of the matches the following Monday that Billy realized that his mother had provided more action in the balcony than he had on the mat. There must have been at least a sliver of pride in his mother's enthusiasm and loyalty as our red-faced son received the laughter of his fellow wrestlers as they watched his mother tip over backward in utter dismay on her balcony bench.

Being Governor (and the Governor's Family)

Where Did You Get That Number One License Plate?

The Guys tried to be a normal family, enjoying normal vacations; but sometimes, the pursuit of the normal had its funny aspects. Our family's first vacation after moving to the governor's residence took place in the summer of 1961. We loaded our 3-year-old Chevy station wagon down with all the gear that you need for a two week's stay at a Minnesota lake cottage in July. Somehow, five children and two adults were squeezed in between boxes, suitcases, and life jackets.

A flat tire and a dirty carburetor slowed us down so badly during the trip that it was midnight before we arrived at Walker, Minnesota. We still had to drive 10 miles through the dark and lonely woods before we would arrive at the cottage we had rented but never had seen.

"We'd better stop at that all-night filling station for gas," I told my sleepy wife. "We may not find the cottage on the first try."

The young station attendant drowsily maneuvered the gas-hose nozzle into the gas tank. He stood there under the white fluorescent station lights looking blankly at the rear of the car. Suddenly he leaned over to examine the license plate. "Say, how do you get that North Dakota number 'one' license?" he asked.

"Well, you have to be governor," I said, matter of factly.

He straightened up with a roar of laughter. "What?" he cried in disbelief. "In a Chevrolet?"

I could see that this Minnesotan was not going to let any North Dakotan pull his leg.

We did find our cottage that night, but it was beginning to get light in the east before quiet settled on our sleeping family.

The next morning, we took inventory of what came with the cottage, what we had brought along, and what we needed from town.

Bill Guy Remembers

The list seemed long when I checked it off with Jean. It included everything from pancake flour to fishing licenses.

I had been given a gold-plated fishing reel as a public relations gift from Minnesota's Governor Elmer Anderson. I needed to complete it with a rod. A very elderly gentleman behind the Walker hardware store counter asked to see my reel so he could fit a rod to it. Suddenly, he held the gold-plated reel almost to his glasses as he read out loud, "Governor Bill Guy from Governor Elmer Anderson." The old man's eyes shifted suspiciously to me and he hissed, "How did you get this? Did you steal it!" I could see I didn't look like governor material.

As I made my way from one Walker store to the next, my supply of cash dwindled. I crossed one item after another off my list. Finally, I had but one item left—a six-pack of beer. We were not beer drinkers, but we had been told that the best way to win the heart of one of our neighbors was with a cold beer on a hot day.

I went into the municipal liquor store and placed my order for the beer. To my dismay, my pocketbook yielded only 50 cents. "Do you cash checks?" I asked the clerk. "Talk to the manager," he said, jerking his thumb toward the office at the rear of the store. The manager turned out to be a woman.

I repeated my request to have my personal check cashed. She eyed me suspiciously. "What is your name?"

"Bill Guy," I said.

"Where do you live."

"Bismarck, North Dakota," I answered.

"Do you know anybody in Walker?" she asked.

"No, I don't," I replied apologetically.

"What kind of work do you do?" she asked.

"I'm the governor of North Dakota."

"I'm sorry, we don't cash personal checks," she snapped, turning on her heel and stomping off.

I ruefully left the store wondering what I had said wrong.

Being Governor (and the Governor's Family)

When I returned to the cottage, I told Jean of the humiliation I had endured trying to leave a few tourist dollars in Walker. "Well," she said, "tomorrow I'll go to town. Maybe they will cash my check." She did, and they did.

Number One License Plates Don't Look Right on a Chevy!

We were reminded again the next year that a Number One license plate was a bit pretentious for our aging Chevy.

Bill and Nan Murray had invited us on a Minnosota fishing trip. We didn't take long to accept.

We headed for Lake of the Woods. A week of cruising on the Canadian Border water on a luxury launch lay ahead of us. Our suitcases, fishing tackle, bedding, and provisions were piled high in the back of our 4-year-old 1959 Chevrolet station wagon.

We were not an impressive sight with a thin coat of Minnesota muddy road spray dried to the sides of the car. We pulled into the Canadian Customs Office check lane at their little station opposite International Falls, Minnesota. A tall Customs Officer came out to greet us with a clipboard and pencil in hand.

He marched to the front of the car and leaned back, peering at our dirty license plate. He frowned and scratched his head. Finally he started for the back of the car. As he passed my window, he said, "I'll have to get the license number off your rear license plate. All that is left on your front license is the number 'one!'" It was another case of our old Chevy station wagon's not living up to number one billing!

Let Me Check our Policy

It's one thing when people in other states don't take you seriously, but it's quite another when your own citizens are dubious about you.

Often, when I flew to Fargo on state business, I called ahead to have the Air National Guard bring one of the automobiles from their motor pool over for me to use while I was in the city.

In the Summer of 1967, I flew into Fargo's Hector Airport and decided, at the last minute, that I needed a National Guard vehicle. I went to a phone booth and placed a call to the headquarters of the North Dakota Air National Guard just a few blocks away.

A young guardsman answered the phone. I identified myself as Governor Guy and asked if he would have a car sent over for my use. He said, "Just a minute, Governor, I will have to check to see what our policy is around here." He left the phone for a few minutes while he did his "checking of policy."

This made me smile because as the Commander in Chief of the Air National Guard, I thought that perhaps it was my responsibility to set policy. However, this young airman recruit was struggling with one of his first encounters with the top brass. Yes, I did get the car and General Homer Goebel's face was red when I laughingly told him of my encounter with his young airman. I chided him by saying, "I'm glad its the policy around Air National Guard headquarters to humor your Commander in Chief when he requests transportation."

Let's Call the Governor

The people of North Dakota want to be close to their governor. That's one of the state's great charms.

Perhaps governors in other states did not accept telephone calls directed to the governor's residence, but we did in North Dakota. Many people seemed surprised when Jean or I answered the telephone. Jean tried to ward off all calls to me at night when I was asleep, except in an emergency.

Being Governor (and the Governor's Family)

Middle-of-the-night calls usually were made by people who had consumed enough alcohol to bolster their courage. This did not seem to be the case at three o'clock one morning when our bedside phone rang and a young voice with a Southern accent asked my wife, "Is the governor of North Dakota in?" When the caller convinced Jean that it was a dire emergency, she woke me up.

When I had assured the caller that I was indeed the very sleepy Governor of North Dakota, he said in a heavy Southern accent, "Governor, is it true that there is really a North Dakota?" He emphasized that he was not fooling or pulling my leg but simply wanted to know if there really was a North Dakota.

I asked him where he was calling from. He replied, with a tinge of Southern pride in his voice, "Ah am calling from Florida."

"What state is Florida in?" I asked as I replaced the phone, satisfied with my rebuttal.

My wife, who had been listening to the call, said, "I'm proud of you. You usually aren't that sharp until almost noon."

On another occasion, soon after my inauguration, I was awakened out of a sound sleep late one night by a voice who was apparently calling from a heavily patronized bar. I could hear the blaring jukebox and the overtone of loud voices and clinking glasses in the background.

"Governor," the voice shouted, "are you Catholic?"

Very sleepily, but courteously as a public servant should be, I said, "No, I am not. I happen to belong to the Presbyterian Church."

"Damn it!" exploded the voice at the other end of the wire. "You have just lost me 50 dollars!" And he slammed down the receiver.

Security

At times, I wondered whether our open government and accessible elected officials might present some dangers along with the unquestioned benefits.

The Guy family hardly had thought about security when we moved into the governor's residence. Attacks on government officials or their families in North Dakota were unheard of. That kind of sinister activity seemed to be the norm in other parts of the world, and it was common knowledge that the governors of some of the larger states worked under elaborate security precautions. But as the decade of the 1960s opened, the mood of the nation began to change. Hate mail and threats increased, and public officials and law enforcement people became targets of increasingly bold individuals and single-interest groups.

There were many reasons for this change. Minority groups, youth, and women had begun to challenge the status quo, and rhetoric and actions against the establishment had become more strident and hostile. Redneck response to civil rights demands was oftentimes brutal. The establishment brought on much of the heightened animosity when it attempted to suppress civil rights by looking for a communist under every bed and by protecting a system that gave those in office too much power.

It all exploded when John Kennedy was shot dead in hate-filled Dallas. Then other acts of violence cropped up here and there. Governor Mark Hatfield's home in Oregon was sprayed with bullets from a passing car. A Molitov cocktail smashed the Mandan, North Dakota, police chief's front window of his home. An ammonium nitrate bomb demolished a University of Wisconsin building. You didn't have to go back to the days of Huey Long's assassination or Chicago Mayor Anton Cermak's murder while on a speaker's platform to know that there were lots of kooks running around.

I discovered that the governor of North Dakota was the only governor in the nation with no security system whatsoever. For years, we proudly regarded that fact as evidence of the gentle nature of life in our agrarian state. But concern for the safety of the North Dakota governor mounted.

Being Governor (and the Governor's Family)

With no coaching from me, the Board of Administration had direct lines from the governor's office and governor's residence installed to the Bismarck police station. The red phone had only to be picked up, and the Bismarck police dispatcher immediately answered. This arrangement offered some comfort as it guaranteed that help was only two or three minutes away should it be needed.

Many states station a highway patrolman or an armed guard for around-the-clock security at the governor's residence. Seeing a policeman in uniform stationed in the reception room of a governor's office was common. Most governors had an armed chauffeur, and some governors, like those from Georgia, New York, and Michigan, legally were accompanied by several armed bodyguards at all times.

The North Dakota Highway Patrol offices were moved to a suite on the ground floor of the capitol building, directly under the governor's office, to provide a shorter response time for security needs. The patrol installed a knee-high button on the inside of the chair cavity of the governor's desk. A touch of that button brought a patrolman to the governor's office on the double. The first morning after the button was installed, a patrolman twice burst into my personal office in response to my accidentally brushing the button with my knee. The problem was solved by recessing the button sufficiently so it could not be triggered accidentally. The button gave me a measure of assurance that emergency help was only seconds away, but I never had to use it.

Only once did I use the red emergency phone. One morning, about 4:00 o'clock, the front doorbell rang at the governor's residence. I slipped into my bathrobe and trudged into the front hall to peer through the narrow glass window next to the door. I could not recognize the man standing in the dim porch light. I called through the door to ask him what he wanted. He said he had come to get his daughter. This response sounded like that of a kook to me, so I picked up the red phone to call the Bismarck police.

Within two minutes, two burley officers in blue came up the sidewalk behind the intruder.

I opened the door to confront a very frightened man. His daughter, from Harvey, North Dakota, had come home with my daughter from some regional school activity the evening before, he said, and he had come to take her back to Harvey. I didn't believe it because I knew of no such house guest. But a quick investigation did reveal an extra guest sleeping with my youngest daughter—a guest who had arrived at our house after my early retirement to bed. I was embarrassed and the frightened man from Harvey was embarrassed, but there was consolation in the speed with which the Bismarck police responded to the red phone.

On another occasion, I was called to the state entrance of the governor's residence by the insistent ringing of the door chimes. It was 8:30 on a Saturday morning, and we seldom had morning guests come to the state entrance rather than our personal entrance. I opened the huge door, and there stood a black man in a dark suit with a white shirt and black tie. He was perspiring heavily, and beads of sweat stood out under the brim of his dark hat. It was a cool fall morning, and the man's appearance caused my alarm bells to ring. "I want to talk to the Governor," the man said. Obviously he did not recognize me as the Governor and, thinking quickly, I said, "He left for his office in the capitol five minutes ago." "Where's that?" the man asked. I pointed to the street in front of the residence and gave him directions.

When the man turned, I closed the door quickly, slid the deadbolt, and grabbed one of the seven phones in the house. In a couple of seconds, the Highway Patrol at the capitol building were alerted about their approaching visitor.

The following Monday, I was told that a Highway Patrol officer had taken the man into custody, and a sanity hearing had been arranged. After tests were made, the man was diagnosed as needing psychiatric treatment, and he was sent to a Veterans Administration hospital in St. Cloud, Minnesota.

About six weeks later, an official from our Department of Health came to my receptionist. "I have a report on the man who wanted to see the Governor," he said. "It is a priviliged report, but because it involved the Governor, I think he'll be interested." I looked at the official report from the St. Cloud hospital. Years before, the visitor had been shot numerous times, and several bullets remained in his body, including one in his head. "This FBI report will explain the situation," the health official said, handing me more documents. The man had served time for murder, and the bullet in his head had come from a gun wielded by his father-in-law. He had a long criminal record, and he had been in and out of mental hospitals. I don't know if that out-of-state visitor was a threat or not, but he did show me how vulnerable a North Dakota governor was.

On another occasion, a man requested to see me at my home after working hours. I foolishly agreed to an appointment that evening. After thinking it over, I decided to check with the Highway Patrol. They soon learned that the man had been released recently from the State Hospital at Jamestown. A patrolman stationed himself in a closet just off the state entrance to the living room in the governor's residence. The man arrived on time, and when I ushered him in, he declined to take off his top coat.

He sat in an easy chair facing me with both hands in his coat pockets. His conversation was rambling and made little sense. Suddenly he said, "Do you expect to finish out your term, Governor?" My heart sank at the implication, and the officer listening in the closet was on the verge of bursting forth to end the visit. But the conversation dwindled down, and the man eventually left. In discussing the incident afterward, my Highway Patrol protector was disturbed at how little security the state provided the governor and his family.

We never allowed incidents such as these to reach the news media, fearing that they would only provoke ideas among the kooks who otherwise might not give us a second thought.

Late in my final term in office, I was determined to do as much as I could to improve security for the governor who would succeed me and for his or her family. After a careful study of what could be expected from bulletproof glass, I asked the Director of Institutions to quietly have it installed in all the governor's residence windows. Though it would be of little protection to my family in our few days left in office, I felt good about leaving a more secure home for my successor. The bulletproof glass was installed so quietly that there was no public notice.

Bird Lovers Hide Your Faces

We were reminded of the dangers of the times—and also how security could cause intense discomfort—in 1964. Less than a year after he had been wounded by the shots that killed President Kennedy, Governor John Connally of Texas came to Bismarck to speak at a political birthday party given for me.

The Governor stayed overnight in our governor's residence guest room. It was that time of year in late September when the migration of blackbirds and purple grackles each evening filled the dense growth of trees behind our home with a raucous, squalling, nervous mass of thousands of birds. The night was unseasonably warm, and because the Governor's residence was not yet air conditioned, all windows were open to catch some cool air.

The Governor's Texas office staff had asked that we provide some security for Governor Connally. And so a local policeman was assigned to patrol the yard during the night. Every half hour, the policeman would leave his patrol car parked in front of the house and circle around behind the house to check that all was well.

Being Governor (and the Governor's Family)

Each time he went behind the house, the thousands of birds in the nearby trees would rise into the darkness, screaming and squawking at the interruption of their rest. In 15 or 20 minutes, the birds would noisily return to their perches and slowly quiet down.

Once again, the policeman would make his trip around the house, sending thousands of birds squawking into the night.

When morning arrived and a tired-looking Governor Connally came to the breakfast table, I asked how he had slept. "To be honest, Bill, I didn't sleep very well. I have never heard so many birds outside my window in all my life. For some reason or other, all night long, about the moment they would settle down, something would happen, and they would go screaming out of the trees again."

I thought how ridiculous it was that the policeman had to make his half-hour trips around the house when the birds themselves would have given a loud warning had anyone approached our home from that side.

The Right to Assemble Peacefully

The 60s and early 70s were turbulent times in America, and some of that turbulence spilled into North Dakota.

Colonel Ralph Wood of the Highway Patrol informed me that he had received information that a peace demonstration would be held May 16, 1970, at the Nekoma, North Dakota, site of the antiballistic missile construction. The people in the small communities near Nekoma, hearing of this, were nervous about what to expect. College students from as far away as the University of Minnesota were rumored to be headed for the University of North Dakota to assemble for the trek to Nekoma. David Dellinger, one of the Chicago Eight, was reputed to be the leader.

Tragic violence in other antiwar demonstrations had left people dead and property destroyed. It was understandable why mayors, town marshalls, state's attorneys, and sheriffs should be concerned about the violence that might erupt at any point along the 100-mile route from the University of North Dakota to the ABM site.

On May 12, I wired President Richard Nixon, informing him of the planned demonstration to be held four days later. I stated that our law enforcement resources were limited and that the federal government, through appropriate civil or military authorities, should assume responsibility to protect life and property at the actual ABM construction and supply sites, commencing at 6 o'clock on the evening of May 15 until the end of the day of May 17. I said that North Dakota would assume responsibility for protecting its communities and institutions other than the federal ABM site itself.

Only hours after sending my telegram to the President, I received a telephone call from Assistant Attorney General Richard Kleindienst, who protested my refusal to send state law enforcement personnel to protect the ABM site. He spoke forcefully for about five minutes. When he finished, I told him I was always glad to listen to his point of view, but that I wanted it clearly understood that North Dakota would not assume the responsibility for the federal ABM site security. "Do you have commercial air travel to Bismarck?" he asked. I smiled at his Eastern concept of North Dakota and replied, "You can catch a Northwest Airlines flight out of Washington at 5:30 p.m. and be in Bismarck by 9:30 p.m." He said he would fly a riot control planning team to North Dakota that afternoon. The team, headed by Johnnie Walker, arrived that night and met with me at the governor's residence. Two other Department of Justice men accompanied Assistant Attorney General Walker. Highway Patrol Chief Colonel Ralph Wood and Adjutant General LaClair Melhouse attended the evening meeting on May 12.

"The Justice Department has several task forces to send out to plan how to cope with civil disturbances," Walker said. "We are trained to meet situations such as the ABM demonstration."

The following day, the Department of Justice task force moved up into the northeastern part of the state to review the situation.

On May 13, I received a request from George Starcher, president of the University of North Dakota, to come to Grand Forks to talk with the students to allay fears that the North Dakota National Guard would be opposing a peaceful ABM demonstration with loaded weapons.

I flew to Grand Forks and met first with a dozen professors who seemed to be uptight about the possibility of another Kent State tragedy in which Ohio National guardsmen had fired on and killed several students. I pointed out to them that it had never been the North Dakota National Guard's practice in riot control to supply loaded weapons to all troops. We did, however, have a few selected veteran guardsmen assigned to sniper control duty who would carry loaded weapons. I pointed out that the ammunition was available, and, in an extreme situation, could be distributed to guardsmen; but I could see no possibility of any development that would warrant that action.

I also pointed out that sniper protection was not necessarily an anti-demonstrator plan but could protect demonstrators from vigilante action that might occur against them along the many miles of road to the ABM construction site.

Following my conversation with the professors, I attended an informal assembly of several hundred students at a dormitory complex and spoke to them for about an hour. I answered many of the same questions that the professors had raised.

The atmosphere was tense and explosive. While I was talking to the students, a note was placed on the lectern, "Attorney General John Mitchell wishes to talk to you." I thought it was a practical joke and continued talking with the students. But after we had concluded the meeting, I went to the dormitory director's office and asked if the note was authentic. He said it was, and I returned Attorney General Mitchell's call.

Mitchell was adamant that I use the North Dakota National Guard to secure the ABM site. I told him I would not since I believed this to be a federal responsibility, and our National Guard troops' first responsibility was to protect life and property in the communities and political subdivisions over which the state had direct responsibility under the law.

He protested that we had 3600 National Guardsmen and that he might consider asking the President to federalize them to take over the ABM site security. I told him as strongly as I could that if the President were to federalize the North Dakota National Guard, I would immediately ask him to replace the North Dakota National Guard with Fifth Army troops since our ability to react to an emergency as a state would be drastically reduced.

Mitchell again emphasized the number of National Guard troops available to me in North Dakota. I countered by telling him that he had 600 federal air police at the Grand Forks Air Base, plus helicopters and other means of transferring federal troops that could be brought in from Ft. Sheridan if he really thought such strong-arm tactics were necessary. "Do you plan to be at the demonstration site?" the attorney general asked. "Only if they need one more warm body to swell the crowd," I answered. "You see, I, too, protest the waste of tax money that the ABM represents." John Mitchell ended the conversation with a curse.

I strongly believed in people's right to assemble peaceably, and I saw no reason why the North Dakota National Guard and the Governor of North Dakota should have to oppose a demonstration that President Nixon and his attorney general seemed to be afraid to oppose.

Being Governor (and the Governor's Family)

I had spoken against the original legislation, which authorized federal funds for the Antiballistic Missile System, and congressional committee statements and press releases thoroughly documented my opposition. Attorney General Mitchell knew this, and I believed for political reasons he did not wish to involve the President and federal troops in a situation where a Kent State type of confrontation could be embarrassing to the Nixon Administration.

As it turned out, on May 16, rain saturated the already muddy ground, which not only dampened demonstration spirits but also made it difficult to drive to and walk to the actual ABM construction site.

To prevent any incidents when demonstrators' blocked highways because of the muddy conditions, I ordered the National Guard to provide two tow cars driven by guardsmen in civilian clothes to assist, without charge, those vehicles that became mired in ditches or fields or country roads along the demonstration assembly route. I didn't want irate farmers reacting to damaged fields and driveways.

The North Dakota National Guard was put on weekend drill status, and some units were shifted to locations closer to the northeastern part of the state. The order, however, was that at no time was the National Guard to interfere with the peaceful demonstration nor were they even to be present or visible along the assembly routes and at the ABM site.

In a call to my house on Friday evening, May 15, demonstration leaders asked for permission to plant small trees on the highway right-of-way near the ABM site as a symbol of creating life rather than destroying it. I gave them permission to plant the trees.

The demonstration took place peacefully. The contractor, Morrison-Knutson, had gathered its big machines and shut them down at my request. No federal troops were present, and I was not told if any federal preparations had been made.

There were recurring reports that the federal government had hired the Pinkerton Agency to infiltrate the demonstators to be available for security purposes if it was required. It was even suggested that there might have been as many Pinkerton agents swelling the modest crowd as there were actual demonstators.

The inflammatory speeches, which Dellinger and John Froines, another of the Chicago Eight gave at the Friday evening meetings on the University of North Dakota campus failed to ignite the emotions of the majority of university students.

The ABM demonstration was noteworthy for the restraint of both the demonstrators and the law enforcement agencies.

A rock concert during the afternoon in the Turtle River State Park siphoned off many of the youth who otherwise might have continued the demonstration. After the crowd returned from Nekoma, the Turtle River State Park had some problems late that evening and the following morning because of the vandalism and irresponsible behavior of some who attended the rock concert.

John Mitchell's experience with me over the ABM demonstration security stayed with him as a bitter memory. That became known when my wife sat beside him at a formal State Department dinner on February 24, 1971, in Washington, D.C. In her conversation with Mr. Mitchell, it became clear that his concern was not for the security of the ABM site, or for the safety of the demonstrators, or for the cost to the federal government. His only concern was for the political ramifications that might have stemmed from a civil disturbance confronting federal security at the ABM site and how it could have affected the political image of President Nixon adversely.

The North Dakota National Guard weekend drill cost the taxpayers of North Dakota $58,000, which was later appropriated from the State Contingency Fund with no protest from anyone.

In retrospect, I commended Adjutant General Melhouse, his officers, and his troops for their restrained and calm approach to their duties during the historic ABM demonstration at Nekoma, North Dakota. I also commended the demonstrators, who were well behaved. Both the troops and the demonstrators displayed North Dakota character, as I thought they would. Perhaps that's why I was less concerned than was John Mitchell.

The Flipside of Ethics

I've always thought the fact that North Dakotans were different was all to their credit.

In 1965, the Winchester Arms Company conducted a promotional campaign to recognize 100 years since the west was won. I suspect that the promotional campaign had something to do with dampening the cries demanding gun control in the United States.

The company presented each governor with an anniversary model gold-plated Winchester rifle, an exact duplicate of the lever-action gun that had served the frontiersmen on the plains so well. I accepted the beautiful, authentic, gold-plated replica and immediately gave it to the North Dakota State Historical Society.

Later, I was telling Governor Warren Hearnes of Missouri about giving the rifle away. "Bill," he asked, "what on earth made you give that gun away?"

"Well," I answered, "the people of my state would not look kindly on a public servant who took gifts from special interest groups. I am sure they would turn me out of office in the next election if I did."

Governor Hearnes laughed and said, "In my state, if the people knew their Governor was so dumb as to turn down a gift like that, they would turn him out of office."

Top: Jean and I watching election returns in 1968.

Bottom: My indispensible wife, advisor, supporter, and confidant Jean in 1972.

Top: *The first family of North Dakota at Christmas in 1963. From left to right, Bill III, Jean, Holly, Nancy, Debby, Jim and me.*

Bottom: *On vacation at Otter Tail Lake, Minnesota, in 1962. From left to right, in the back, Debby, Jean, Bill III, and me. In the front, Jimmy, Holly, and Nancy.*

5

There's a Lot to Being a Governor That Doesn't Have Much to Do With Governing

The Crowning Embarrassment

When I got into office, I quickly discovered that the governor had a lot of ceremonial duties to perform. Crowning a beauty queen had seemed like such dreamy duty. My first such experience was at the 1961 Minot Fair. A huge stage had been built on the race track infield in front of the grandstand. Miss Minot of 1961, accompanied by two very young attendants and six princesses, was to be crowned on that stage at the conclusion of the evening grandstand show.

One after the other, seven new convertibles glided up to the front of the stage. The queen and her princesses left their cars and one by one mounted the stage, each on the arm of a sharply uniformed military escort. They took their places on the stage under the bright spotlights.

I fidgeted in the shadows in the wings, nervously examining the rhinestones in the fragile crown I was to place on the lovely queen's head. The trumpets blared. It was my cue. I strode purposefully into the white glare of the spotlights. I smiled reassuringly at the nervous young queen. My heart pounded as I placed the crown on her honey-blond tresses.

Knowing that the crowd expected me to kiss the queen, I stooped over to carry out the delightful mission. The young queen recoiled with a start that sent her crown rolling. I retrieved the crown, and with trembling hands and blushing embarrassment, replaced it on her head.

The bugles blared again—my cue to lead the queen to her waiting convertible at the front of the stage. She took her place, seated tall and beautiful, on the top of the back seat with her flowing gown completely covering the back cushion. The two little 8-year-old attendants hopped into the front seat like squirrels.

There was no place for me to ride. I stepped back nonplused. One by one, the other convertibles came forward to pick up their princesses. As each car rolled away, the military escort stepped back smartly into the line that was formed with me at the end.

Suddenly, in a panic, I realized that I would soon be answering to military commands. As the last convertible pulled away, the senior military escort barked out the command, "Attention!"

I stiffened automatically.

"Right face!" At that very moment, the floodlights went out, and we were plunged into blessed darkness. "Forward march!" the officer shouted. The line of military escorts moved sharply to the right, but I spun sharply to the left.

With the command, "Forward march!" ringing in my ears, I was making tracks as fast as I could to safety and anonymity in the milling crowd that was leaving the grandstand. I had much to learn about crowning queens. It never would be as easy as I had thought.

Dakota Territorial Centennial

Those who knew Marion Piper would say she was the ideal chairman for North Dakota's observance of the Dakota

There's a Lot to Being a Governor . . .

Territory Centennial in 1961. For most of the year, Marion wore the long skirts and a broad brimmed black hat with a large red rose that were in vogue 100 years before.

Her enthusiasm was infectious and overpowering. Her face would be wreathed in smiles as she breathlessly and animatedly explained her next project. It was difficult to keep from being swept up in the rush of enthusiasm that she brought to every conversation.

Early in February, she made her grand entrance into my office full of smiling excitement to say she wanted my approval and cooperation in staging an old-fashioned 4th of July on the capitol grounds. I nodded without even knowing to what I was agreeing. But I do faintly remember saying facetiously that I would go along with the speeches and the bands and all of the planning that would go into the old fashioned 4th of July on the capitol grounds if she could assure me that I could shoot some skyrockets off the roof of the capitol the night before to open the event. She smiled broadly and swept out of the room.

I had forgotten about that encounter with Marion when, about 9 o'clock the evening of July 3, the telephone rang, and Marion's sweet voice said, "We will be ready for you to fire the skyrockets from the roof of the capitol at 11 o'clock tonight." I gulped in stunned silence and said weakly that I would try to be present.

I am not one who enjoys heights. As a matter of fact, when I climb up to change light bulbs in the living room ceiling chandelier, I get the giddy feeling that perhaps I will have to hire somebody to help me down.

But I gritted my teeth and, with three of our children, headed for for the capitol building. Marion whisked us on the elevator to the seventeenth floor and through a seldom-used door onto a roof that extended out just below the topmost level of the capitol. There, in the gloom of the night, I climbed hand over hand up a perpendicular steel ladder to the topmost roof behind the billowing skirts of Marion Piper in her 1861 costume.

When I had adjusted my eyes to the darkness of the night above the capitol, I became aware that other figures were moving about. The pattern of the lights of the city far below showed where the waist-high wall around the edge of the roof met the night sky.

Marion introduced me to a dark figure she identified as the sergeant from the Marine recruiting station. The sergeant showed me two 3-foot lengths of heavy steel pipe, set upright on the roof and held in place by sandbags. "We will drop the skyrocket into one of these two pipes," he said, "and you touch a match to the wick and jump back."

A fireman in full firefighting gear and carrying a hand extinguisher came into view in the shadows. I felt reassured.

Waiting for the rockets to be placed, I glanced behind me. Suddenly, I saw silhouetted against the roof edge the figure of my daughter, Debby, her hair blowing in the night breeze as she gazed down 19 floors to the ground below. I rushed over and grabbed her, my knees feeling weak as I wondered how I had allowed myself to get into such a frightening predicament.

But the moment came. I struck a large wooden match and reached over to light the fuse on the skyrocket. I had scarcely drawn back when it soared up out of the pipe in a loud hiss that diminished to a thundering boom that seemed to scatter multicolored stars in graceful paths across the heavens.

After firing a dozen or so big rockets, which must have been historic since they were fired from the highest point in that part of the state, I made my way down the steel ladder. When we arrived on the ground floor, I looked at Marion. She was bubbling over with excitement. "That idea was surely great, Governor," she said.

I swallowed my gradually receding fright, again counted our children, and vowed to be very careful before agreeing to anything that Marion suggested for the rest of the year.

There's a Lot to Being a Governor . . .

Before Catalytic Converters

One of the hazards of being Governor is the programmed personal appearance where you are part of the show.

Minot was celebrating an anniversary, and beards, old costumes, and antique cars were the fad. Jean and I were invited to ride in an anniversary parade in one of the many ancient cars. We agreed because it looked like fun. We rode on the cracked leather seats of an old car that resembled a carriage without horses.

The floorboards beneath our seat were worn and contained holes and breaks through which we could view the moving drive shaft below. The ancient engine seemed to burn as much oil as it did gasoline and, if it had an exhaust pipe, it leaked badly.

A steady haze of hot, acrid smoke came up through the floorboards and hung under the canvas canopy top as we ground slowly along. Finally, my wife and I realized that this poisonous exhaust was beginning to affect us, and we hung further out from our perch to get snatches of fresh air.

It was a strange sight indeed to see the horseless carriage chugging slowly along in the parade leaving a blue haze through which the Governor on one side of the car and his wife on the other leaned out and away, seeking a breath of air to survive until the end of the route.

We did survive, but after that we always looked at old cars with a wary eye when we were asked to participate in parades.

Elephants Are for Republicans

Natural transportation isn't necessarily better. "Would you ride the elephant out in front of the grandstand tonight?" asked an old college friend, Roy Pedersen, who was in charge of the evening program at the old Red River Valley Fair in Fargo.

"Are you kidding?" I laughed. "A governor is supposed to be full of dignity, you know."

"Gee, I knew you would," Roy enthused. "Just be back of the tents behind the stage on the race track infield in front of the grandstand at 8:30 tonight."

I arrived on time back of the stage to find a huge elephant languidly searching tufts of grass with his trunk. His hide was grey, creased, and toughlooking. He was covered all over with a sparse crop of very bristly hair. He eyed me, and I eyed him.

The elephant trainer came over with his short spiked stick. He unshackled the leg iron on the huge beast and ordered it to sit down. Surprisingly, it did settle its rump on the sod and awaited the next order.

"Just crawl up his back and sit on that little square rug," the trainer said. I crawled up and hung on for dear life while the little rug seemed to move in all directions as the elephant regained his feet.

Slowly and docilely, the mammoth creature moved down the track in front of the grandstand. The crowd roared. They sensed uneasiness behind my fixed smile. Each ponderous step sent the rug surface I was seated on in a series of gyrations that resembled a rudderless sailing ship in a stormy sea.

We reached the stage, and the elephant was ordered to kneel. I slid forward, each hair bristle feeling like a probing needle. With relief, I walked to the microphone. "Ladies and gentlemen," I said, "tonight I had my first Republican elephant ride. If you don't mind, I think I'll just stick to riding Republicans after this!"

Water — What was that Stuff at Devils Lake?

In 1966, I was invited to participate in the dedication of the new water system in Devils Lake. The new system brought pure, fresh, delicious water from wells located in an aquifer 19 miles southeast of the city. Devils Lake had

There's a Lot to Being a Governor . . .

long had the reputation of having brackish-tasting city water with its salt content so high that many travelers avoided staying there. The city water seemed as salty as that in the lake for which the town was named.

I was doubly pleased to be invited to the dedication ceremony because I was born in Devils Lake in 1919, and some of my roots were still there.

When my turn came to say a few words, I spoke of how much Devils Lake had done for me. I said, "It was here that I learned to speak at the unheard of age of three months. It came about when my mother placed the first teaspoonful of Devils Lake city water in my mouth, and I was heard to say in loud, clear tones, 'Good grief, what's that!'

"And some bird fanciers credit the vile taste of the lake water in Devils Lake for teaching the whooping cranes how to whoop and the whistling swans how to whistle."

Anyone for Coffee?

Maybe it's some of our water that makes us such avid coffee drinkers.

The Sargent Central Band at Forman was named the Governor's Band for 1962. Late in the fall, we went down to present that outstanding musical and crack marching organization with a state flag. Following the program in their new high school auditorium, some of my local friends sat down with Jean and me for a cup of late evening coffee.

Representative Ole Breum was there with his wide grin and sparkling eyes. Ole was an inveterate coffee drinker. As I saw him down his fourth cup of coffee at 11 o'clock at night, I asked, "Ole, doesn't drinking coffee like that cut down on your sleep?"

"No," Ole said, smiling, "I don't find it that way at all. I find that sleeping cuts down on my coffee drinking."

Of course, I had known for years that our citizens—especially those such as Ole Breum of Scandinavian heritage—were serious coffee drinkers. But I learned in 1954 in my hometown of Amenia that they are not necessarily discriminating coffee drinkers.

The occasion of my discovery was a volunteer firemen's fund-raising carnival in the high school gymnasium. I was chairman of the lunch committee. Our post was the kitchen in the gym's basement. We sold coffee, cheese sandwiches, and doughnuts out of the kitchen serving-counter window. Although our prices were reasonable, they were set to make money.

All started well that night. We had three large 3-gallon white porcelain pots of coffee, steaming on the two ancient electric stoves. We were proud of our coffee. It was rich, fullbodied, and settled by the addition of raw eggs.

The first pot of coffee was sold out cup by cup, and we immediately started a fresh pot brewing. To our horror, we realized that our old under-powered stoves were just not heating water fast enough to keep up with our dwindling supply of hot coffee.

In desperation, we sought out the school janitor, Bill Favorite. "What can we do?" we pleaded. He thought for a moment, and then his face brightened.

"You can drain hot water from the furnace boiler in the school next door."

We decided to give it a try. We found the steaming water from the pet cock on the furnace boiler was not only hot but a rich brown from the rust of the boiler tubes. We barely had time to pour fresh coffee grounds into each pot full of hot, rusty water before the urgent demand of carnival-goers called for more 10-cent paper cups full of the brown steaming brew.

We sold 1600 cups of our questionable coffee. We had no complaints, and many came back for more. I'm convinced that people drink coffee out of habit and have no taste for what is good or bad as long as it is labeled coffee. But then, the town's well water was so hard and salty that almost anything you put into it, including coffee, improved its taste.

There's a Lot to Being a Governor . . .

A Sailboat Trip From Pick City to Newtown

In 1961, John Peterson, co-owner of the Grand Pacific Hotel in Bismarck, invited me to accompany him on a six-day sailboat cruise on Lake Sakakawea. To publicize the wonderful sailing potential of this great body of water, we invited two reporters, Dick Dobson of the Minot *Daily News* and Cal Olson of the Fargo *Forum*, to make part of the trip with us.

Our first leg was a day-long sail on Peterson's 21-foot Pearson sailing sloop from the Sakakawea State Park marina near Pick City to the Mosset Bay area on the Fort Berthold Indian Reservation, where the Little Missouri entered Lake Sakakawea.

We arrived at our destination at dusk. Jean had sent along four thick, juicy steaks for our first evening meal. To our dismay, as we cruised the shoreline, we could find no place with an accumulation of driftwood for a campfire. The rising water apparently had floated all driftwood out from the shore.

Fortunately, we stopped at the dock leading to Cliff Mosset's tiny fishing camp resort. Cliff was part Indian and was married to a Native American woman. When Cliff learned that we couldn't locate driftwood for a fire, he invited us into his small one-room fishing shack near the water. The shack had a small two burner gas stove, a table, four chairs, and meager supplies for visiting fishermen. The supplies consisted of a small assortment of fishing hooks, plugs and leaders, a box or two of candy bars, and a couple of cases of Coca Cola.

By this time, it was 10 o'clock at night, and our stomachs were growling from hunger. We accepted Cliff's gracious offer enthusiastically. Soon, the smell of steak frying in a large, cast-iron pan filled the air in the tiny shack. The smell of good food put us in a jocular mood.

I had never fried steak before, but now I was getting advice from every side. Finally, in desperation, I turned to

Cliff Mosset and said, "Everyone has given me advice but you. It's your pan and your stove. What do you have to say?"

Cliff stepped forward and said, "Just put the steak in the pan, and let it fry until the blood has risen to the surface. When this process is complete, turn the steak over and let the blood again work its way to the surface. If you want the steak rare, you can take it off at this point. If you want the steak medium, let about half of the blood return into the steak as it fries. If you want the steak well done, let it fry until all the blood has disappeared from the surface."

"Well," I exclaimed, "it's good to have such a simple explanation of how to cook steak. I imagine this is part of your Indian lore."

"Indian lore, hell!" Cliff Mosset retorted. "I am a graduate of the Army Cook and Baker's School."

Help From the Audience

Getting to know North Dakota's Native American citizens was one of my great pleasures as a candidate and as a governor.

The name Burdick had long been a favorite among North Dakota Indians. Congressman Usher L. Burdick was an authority on Indian lore and spoke a bit of the Sioux language. It was only natural that Quentin Burdick should inherit his father's love for the Indians. Quentin even learned a passable knowledge of the Sioux tongue.

In May of 1960, Quentin Burdick visited all the Indian reservations as he sought to win a seat in the United States Senate. Jean and I were with him on many occasions. When we were campaigning at Selfridge in Sioux County, our small audience was at least one-third Indian.

I sat on the stage of the small meeting hall, listening to Burdick exhort his listeners. Suddenly a very elderly Indian in the second row let out three sharp coyote yips—woop! woop! woop! Quentin, with outstretched hand, said some-

There's a Lot to Being a Governor . . .

thing in Sioux, and the old Indian subsided with arms crossed.

A few moments later, the old Indian again erupted with three sharp coyote yips. Again, Quentin said something in Sioux and gestured with outstretched hand. And again the old Indian retreated into his thoughts.

Finally, the speeches were over and we headed back toward Mandan. "You were sure great tonight, Quentin," I said. "You certainly handled that old Indian well when you asked him in Sioux to shut up."

"Asked him to shut up!" Quentin exploded. "I told him to do it again in ten minutes! He added a little excitement to a dull program."

Indian Lore

While running for governor in 1960, new and baffling experiences confronted me on every hand.

One day I attended an Indian pow wow in the old battered community building at Fort Totten. I was told that the Indians were predominantly Democrats, and that this was a place to make some new friends.

The Native-American people, I was to learn, are wonderfully warm but quiet and undemonstrative people, and they do not react to the back-slapping type of politician.

A brief Indian dance opened the program in a big, poorly lit room with a worn floor and a ceiling and walls with chipped and falling plaster. A few of the Indian men got up and made welcoming speeches, but the women sat impassively along the sidelines.

I was having trouble relating to these people because this was my first experience with them. I knew that I had to get to know them better and that I had to take the initiative because they were too shy or reticent to do so.

Seeing a very old gentleman quietly puffing his pipe along the sidelines, I sat down beside him and struck up a conversation. "I suppose a man of your great age must have considerable skill in predicting what kind of a winter we are going to have," I said hopefully. I expected that an old Native American like this man surely would know all the Indian lore about examining the bark on the north side of the tree, gauging the depth of the fur on the bellies of squirrels, and noting the date that the geese moved south to determine how severe the coming winter would be.

The old man was very quiet, and for a moment, I thought he wouldn't answer. Then he took his pipe from his mouth, looked at me, and said, "I really don't know what kind of winter we are going to have, but I was reading Ben Husett's Almanac yesterday, and Ben says it is going to be a mild winter."

I was thoroughly deflated because Ben Husett was available to the white man, too, and his predictions were based on weather charts and past records and had nothing to do with the bark of a tree or the depth of the hair on the belly of a squirrel.

Sitting Bull's Bones

Sitting Bull, the Sioux medicine man and wily adversary of the early white settlers, was buried at the edge of Fort Yates in Sioux County, North Dakota. Legend embellished the feats of the famous redman. As cowboy and Indian tales became standard fare in the movies and on TV, the name of Sitting Bull took on new prominence.

Hoping to cash in on the tourist attraction that Sitting Bull's grave might have, a band of white South Dakota marauders stole north across the border with larceny in their hearts. In the dead of the night, they carried out their macabre mission.

Digging hastily in the small cemetery where the remains of Sitting Bull were said to be buried, they completed their grave thievery before sunup. Slinking south to their tourist site near Mobridge, South Dakota, they claimed to have reburied their North Dakota loot in a fresh grave. Making

There's a Lot to Being a Governor . . .

sure that no one would check their questionable but dastardly deed, they poured a huge thick concrete slab over their new tourist attraction.

The Native Americans of Fort Yates were outraged to think that anyone would desecrate their tiny cemetery. "Those thieves did not get the bones of Sitting Bull," tribal chieftain Aljoe Agard told me several years later. "Some day I'll prove they didn't get Sitting Bull's bones. We know that a certain kind of tomahawk was buried with him. Some day we will dig down and find such a tomahawk with some bones to prove that they did not get the right set of bones."

"As a matter of fact," Aljoe said with a faraway look in his eye and a faint smile, "I am sure we will find such a tomahawk!"

Scalp Hunters Would Not Be Interested

Many things about the young generation in 1969 grated on the nerves of their elders. The long hair disturbed many parents. But so many people were following the young generation and letting their hair grow long, so I felt I should abandon my trademark crew cut and do likewise to remain a comfortable conformist.

While visiting the Fort Berthold Indian Reservation at New Town and standing in line at a luncheon, I conversed with an old friend, Nathan Little Soldier, the tribal chairman.

Nathan, his eyes twinkling, glanced at my hair and said, "I see you have let your hair grow out."

I said, "Nathan, I don't mind Republicans and other types noticing that my hair has grown out, but it makes me nervous to have my Indian friends notice."

"Oh," Nathan laughed, "you don't have to worry. With all that gray hair, your scalp would make a very poor trophy."

Top: Bismarck Mayor Evan Lipps receiving a peace pipe from Standing Rock Tribal Chairman Aljo Agard as I look on, September 1963.

Bottom: One of the fringe benefits of office. A surprise birthday party for me at the Wahpeton State School of Science, 1970.

6

The Presidents I Knew

The Inauguration of John F. Kennedy

My election as Governor of North Dakota thrust Jean and me into national politics, as we quickly learned when we were invited to attend John F. Kennedy's inauguration. Attending an inauguration of the President of the United States is an inspiring experience. But preparing to go to the nation's capitol, struggling through airport terminal chaos, flagging down taxis, standing in line to be seated at restaurants, tiring visits to national shrines, inflated prices for everything from a dish of yogurt to a hotel room— all make for an exhausting and often frustrating four days. I say four days because during that event, Washington, D.C., hotels will not rent a room for fewer than four days even if you only wanted to stay two days.

Perhaps the high-stress aspects of an inauguration visit are less on people from the congested cities because they are used to having to live that way, but to visitors from the hinterland states, their first pilgrimage to view the presidential inauguration is an experience that few would care to repeat.

Our first presidential inauguration was in January 1961 when John Kennedy took the oath of office. We flew from Bismarck in the old twin engine National Guard transport, the "Minnie H," named after a famous Devils Lake steamboat. The old C-47 had a seating compartment that could accommodate about 12 passengers. Two pilots and an enlisted man made up the National Guard crew. Tables had been installed between airline-type seats facing each other, so dining or card playing was comfortable. The National Guard provided white table cloths and very tasty box lunches for our in-flight meals.

The old airplane was not pressurized, so it had to fly at altitudes below 10,000 feet to stay within the range where additional oxygen was not needed. The propellers on the two big engines thrust the ship along at about 150 miles per hour, but head winds or tail winds altered the ground speed drastically. Because the airplane was restricted to low altitudes, it did not fly above turbulent air, and it was commonplace to fly for hours through the white-out of clouds. At times, ice would build up on the wings and propellers. De-icing would send chunks of ice banging into the fuselage, making the passengers uneasy. At times like that, the dark green parachute packs, swaying on the rack in the rear compartment, came to mind. Usually the "Minnie H" would have to set down for fueling at Madison or Chicago. Those were welcomed opportunities to feel solid ground underfoot and maybe take another motion sickness pill before reboarding.

John Garaas and his wife, Barbara, and Major Vic McWilliams and his wife, Tobi, accompanied Jean and me to the Kennedy inaugural. We stayed at the old Jefferson Hotel, a delightful place that catered to theater people as well as to politicians. The six of us were assigned a suite of three adjoining rooms.

When Jean and I first arrived in Washington, we attended a briefing for Governors and First Ladies to receive schedules and instructions. Much of the information duplicated that which had been sent to us previously, but there were many last-minute changes. The logistics of the inaugural, with so many officials and dignitaries from here and abroad converging on the capital, were horrendous.

"Please listen," the security spokesman pleaded. "All governors will be provided an escort, consisting of a driver, a military aide, and a plainclothes security man. They will be with you at all times when you move from event to event."

"But I don't need a bodyguard," I protested. "I brought along a military aide from the North Dakota National Guard. Thanks for the car and driver, but I do not need a security man."

"I'm sorry, Governor," the stern-faced security chief said. "These are my orders. You may not need protection, but there are governors here who are definite security risks. Rather than make them look conspicuous surrounded by bodyguards, it has been decided that all governors will be assigned the same number of bodyguards."

"All right, fellows," I said, with a grin to my assigned bodyguards, "I have but one order to give you and one order only. Don't lead me in front of or behind any of those governors considered security risks. That way we have a better chance of staying out of the line of fire!"

Only hours after arriving in our hotel, I was handed a note from the desk clerk saying that "Mr. Pearson had called and asked you to return his call." I did not know who Mr. Pearson was. Could it be that the John Deere dealer from Hunter, North Dakota, Henning Pearson, was at the inaugural? Or was it more likely to be wealthy farmer Walter Pearson, from Arthur, who was here? I called the number. A very proper female voice came on the line. "Mr. Pearson and his wife would be pleased to have you and your wife join them and other guests at their Georgetown home for dinner day after tomorrow in the evening." I was mystified. "What Pearson is calling?" I asked. "Mr. Drew Pearson," was the frosty reply as if there were no other Pearsons. I must have hesitated in total surprise but gathered my senses to say that I would consult my wife and call back.

We did accept the invitation and enjoyed one of the most memorable evenings of our lives. Drew Pearson, the famous columnist, and his wife were practiced in the art of entertaining. We knew none of the other guests, but they didn't seem to be acquainted before the party either. 12 guests had differing interests, ranging from a small machinery manufacturer from Kansas to a diplomat from Greece. The conversation was fascinating. Drew Pearson entered into it only to ask an occasional question, to steer the talking to subjects he was interested in, I guess.

The formal dinner setting was a sparkling montage of a dimly lit chandelier, centerpieces, and a formidable array of silverware and shining dishes on a gorgeous soft white tablecloth. Drew Pearson's wine goblet shone in the reflected candlelight when he raised it to toast me, saying, "To the Governor and First Lady of North Dakota who have finally brought two-party rule to that state." I was taken completely by surprise and hesitantly raised my wine goblet, too. "You don't raise your goblet when you are toasted," hissed the brassy, overbearing woman seated on my left. I was demolished and realized that I was swimming in a society beyond my depth. But checking later, I discovered that it was just as proper to raise my wine goblet when toasted as to not raise it. That glorious dinner was the opening of a friendship with Drew Pearson and his wife that lasted until his death years later.

During the morning of the day before the inaugural, snow began to fall. Huge, heavy, wet flakes came down in layers. By late afternoon, traffic all over Washington was barely moving—and the snow showed no signs of letting up. The airports were closed, and we were told that more than 80 incoming flights had to be diverted. Fortunately for us, we had a car and driver assigned to us because the thousands of cabs that roam the city's streets seemed to vanish. The snow had accumulated to a foot on the level, and traffic barely crawled, with wheels spinning in the slippery mess. We left a gala event at the Mayflower Hotel at 4 p.m., and our car took two hours to negotiate the ten blocks or so to the Jefferson. Those cars with chains were able to get started once stopped. But everywhere, passengers in cars without chains were out pushing to get the cars moving. The slightest incline became a formidable hill and required a mixture of pushing and cursing to start. Shoes and stockings were soaked, and trousers were wet to the knees.

At midnight before the big day, the snow ceased falling, and cleanup crews were out in force. Small Army tanks were pressed into service to drag the hundreds of abandoned cars off Pennsylvania Avenue so it could be plowed out for the inaugural parade only hours away.

Inaugural morning broke sunny but cold. The ceremonies and parade would proceed as planned. Jean slipped into her wool dress and sweater with practiced ease. She was to be seated below the balcony from which the President was to speak. But I approached my rented formal morning coat with its long tails, grey vest, and striped trousers with apprehension. The outfit had been worn on too many occasions and was one size too big for me, but the Inaugural Committee had prescribed it and a tall silk hat as the uniform of the day. When I was fully decked out, I looked like a clean-shaven Abe Lincoln.

We had not anticipated the terrible traffic jam the snow-blocked streets caused. Our military driver and aide were becoming increasingly frustrated as we slowly followed heavy traffic toward Capitol Hill. Major George Gorman turned to me and said, "Hold that stovepipe hat of yours up so the police can see it, and I'll get out and see what I can do." From that point on, George in his Air Force uniform and coat would get out of the car to seek a policeman. In every instance, the policeman would glance over at our car, and, seeing my tall silk hat looming large in the backseat, he would hold back traffic to wave us through. I began to feel like a VIP as my black silk hat won us preferential treatment.

The tall silk hat also won me entrance to the heavily guarded capitol building through which I had to pass to get to the stand built out over the steps, which housed the hydraulic-controlled lectern from which the President would speak. Ambassadors, congressmen, and governors, all in tall silk hats, jammed the tight seating area behind the lectern and looked down at the large crowd assembled below in the chilly morning air. I found my assigned seat with Governor John Eagan of Alaska on my left and Governor Bill Quinn of Hawaii on my right. Quinn's coat was open at the throat, and a smile lighted his tanned face. But Governor Eagan's coat collar was buttoned tight around his scarf and his teeth chattered beneath a pained scowl. "Gosh," I thought, "these Hawaiians haven't learned how to act when it's cold." I learned weeks later that the frigid ceremony caused Governor Quinn to come down with pneumonia.

The new President's swearing in was impressive. And the crowd savored every word of his speech, seeking those elusive clues as to what kind of a national leader he would be.

The most memorable phrase in the new President's speech was: "Ask not what your country can do for you, but what you can do for your country."

There would never be another presidential inaugural quite like that one. Subsequent inaugurals of President Lyndon Johnson and President Richard Nixon just did not measure up in comparison.

That night, our driver took us to the the National Guard Armory, for the Inaugural Ball, featuring Louis Armstrong and his orchestra. It was a formal affair with tuxedos, tails and formals. Snow plows had opened lanes for the congested traffic. When we arrived, the crowd of people was being processed in an orderly manner.

Louis Armstrong, mopping his brow with a white handkerchief, was at his best. His trumpet and gravel voice kept thousands standing to watch and listen while thousands more struggled to dance on the rough surface of the crowded dance floor.

We recognized many people who were prominent in national affairs, and many people whom we had met in political life came by with a smile and an outstretched hand. Once, when the music stopped, we were standing next to James Symington and his wife. Jim was the son of Stuart Symington, the United States Senator from Missouri. Later in 1967, President Lyndon Johnson appointed Jim Symington as protocol officer. But that night, he was about to make his entrance into the federal bureaucracy. While applauding the last melody from the orchestra, I asked Jim what his plans were. He smiled as he said, "President Kennedy has offered to appoint me deputy director of the Food for Peace Program."

"Good heavens," I replied. "Are you qualified to head the Food for Peace Program?"

"I think so," Symington grinned. "You see I like food, and I'm a peaceful man!" Thus, presidents appoint their deputy administrators.

As the evening came to a close, the crowd turned its thoughts to getting home. Instead of forming orderly lines at the many cloakrooms, tuxedoed men mobbed the doorways, pressing in so tightly that once a person had traded a ticket for coats, backing out was difficult. The pressure pushed tables back from the doorways, and men were forced into the cloakroom, adding to the chaos. Fist fights and shoving broke out and much cursing accompanied the efforts of too many to fight their way to the cloakroom doors. Somehow Jean and I got our coats, hats and rubbers, and made for the main exit to meet our chauffeured car.

Outside the armory, everything was pandemonium. Snow was still falling, and streets and sidewalks were heavy with slush. We waited and waited in the chill air, but our car was not in the long line that slowly wound past the entrance to pick up passengers. The waiting stretched on and on. Bejeweled ladies in mink wraps, who ordinarily would not allow themselves to be seen in anything but a limousine, scrambled to board the buses—anything to get away from the armory. Adlai Stevenson, with an open coat and no hat, slogged through the slush in his patent leather shoes, looking forlorn as he tried to find his chauffeured car.

Thoroughly chilled, but better off than most, our fortunes brightened when we heard a voice call our names. It was Governor Peter Coleman of Samoa in his slowly moving limousine. He had recognized us and could see we were in trouble. We didn't need to be asked twice. We piled into that nice warm back seat, thankful that our coach had not yet turned into a sleigh. The military car and driver who had been assigned to us never did show up. We learned later that he had made a wrong turn on the freeway and had driven nearly to Baltimore before he was able to turn around.

Camelot

In 1962, my wife and I were guests at our first state dinner in the White House. The guests of honor were the Grand Duchess of Luxembourg and her son.

One rectangular table was set up as the head table, and all other guests were seated at round tables, each accommodating 10 guests. My wife, Jean, had the privilege of being seated at the head table just two seats removed from President John Kennedy and with very interesting table partners; Douglas Dillon, Secretary of the Treasury, and author John Steinbeck were seated on either side of her.

The Kennedys, by their presence, added a glow of elegance and buoyancy to the occasion. The gold tableware seemed to shine more brightly, and the white tablecloths seemed to sparkle.

My wife stood at her place as the guests were finding the seats assigned to them. John Steinbeck walked up. "Isn't this lovely, my dear," he said. "This is the most thrilling evening of my life."

How strange it seemed to me that this man, whose books, such as, *The Grapes of Wrath*, seemed to probe the harsh and the cynical, could be so swayed by the elegance of the occasion that he would make such a statement.

A State Dinner in the Johnson White House

Standing in front of a mirror to adjust a black tie in a Washington, D.C. hotel room in preparation for a formal White House dinner did not happen to me very often. Wearing a tuxedo gave me a starched, harnessed-up feeling. I wondered if people who go to many formal events ever get used to it.

Jean looked like a million dollars in her blue sequined formal. She wore it last at the Lyndon Johnson inaugural two years before.

Jean in her fur and I under my Stetson hat set out for the great adventure. The lobby of the Statler Hilton was crowded for seven forty-five in the evening. The White House invitation said 8 p.m. We would be right on time.

I wondered if getting a cab would be troublesome. The red-coated doorman, with whistle between his teeth, waved a passing cab up to the hotel entrance. It was a black cab. That was a fitting vehicle color for going to a White House formal dinner.

"To the southwest entrance of the White House," I told the cabbie. He didn't flinch. Do you suppose he made that run often?

As we neared the southwest entrance to the White House grounds, we pulled in behind a line of limousines. They hesitated one by one at the White House gate, submitted to police inspection, then turned sharply right and rolled on through.

A big, new, dark blue Cadillac limousine was in front of us. I wondered who was in it.

Our turn at the gate came. Four uniformed police, wearing bright orange reflective vests, were busily checking cars and passengers. They carried long flashlights with red hoods over the beams.

A policeman took the card that came with our White House invitation. He handed it back. "Ever been on these grounds," he asked our driver, who replied, "No, sir." "Okay," the policeman said, "follow that limousine up close. When you've discharged your passengers, you leave by the southeast gate." "Yes, sir," our cabbie answered.

We followed the line of slowly moving limousines as they wound around the sweeping drive that eventually led to the rear receiving entrance of the White House. All cabinet members, Supreme Court justices, and congressional leaders had their own limousines with chauffeurs. Limousines, which already had discharged their passengers, had swung around and were parked along the curb of the wide driveway. Policemen were everywhere. The line of cars stopped one by one in the glow of light coming from under the arched awning extending about 40 feet out from the White House to the driveway.

Our cab stopped. Not many arrived by cab. Most would rent limousines to travel in style. But who would you impress? A handful of policemen on the White House lawn? They were too busy to care whether you arrived in a sleek limousine or a lowly cab. Policemen moved quickly to open both rear doors of the cab.

We stepped into the friendly light of the entrance. A red carpet beginning at the curb covered the concrete sidewalk leading to the open door. We were about to enter a world of sparkle and elegance—the White House.

A smiling young military officer stepped forward and directed us into the oval reception room. Formally attired attendants were stationed at the two coat check rooms. One was on each side of the room. No coat check tipping there.

Governor Nelson Rockefeller and his wife were checking their coats across the room. She was wearing a lovely maternity-style formal. They greeted us with smiles. We had come to know them well. They were as nice as they were wealthy. He was the senior governor of the nation, going into his ninth year in office. Governor Otto Kerner of Ilinois and I were next senior, beginning our seventh year in office.

We were directed up a heavily carpeted stairs to the main floor. At the top of the stairs, a young naval officer with gold braid drooping from the shoulders of his uniform met us. He scanned the many small white envelopes spread out on a table. An envelope for each guest had his or her name on it and contained a card on which a table number was written. Husbands and wives dined at different tables.

I tucked the envelopes into my pocket. A white-gloved young Army officer stepped forward to escort us to the spacious marble-floored foyer—really the front entrance— which opened out onto the front driveway and lawn. That elegant, towering, foyer, with its white entrance columns, separated the east and west wings of the White House.

Jean took the arm of her military escort. I followed. We moved across the foyer to the long, wide red-carpeted hall which led to the East Room where the formal reception would be held.

At the spacious doorway to the east room a smartly uniformed young Air Force officer took the cards from Jean's military escort.

"Governor and Mrs. Guy of North Dakota," he intoned into a portable microphone. Jean's military escort stepped back, bowed, and took his leave. Once again, I moved up to be her escort. The East Room was joyous bedlam. More than 100 people were already there, resplendent in black tuxedoes and formal gowns of every description.

Another young military officer in charge of the reception line met us at the door with list in hand. After checking his list, he informed us that we would follow the Nelson Rockefellers in the reception line.

I put on my glasses to better see the interesting personalities already gathered. There was Douglas Fairbanks, Jr., still as swashbuckling and handsome as ever. George Meany was talking with Supreme Court Justice Byron "Whizzer" White. We renewed acquaintances with Secretary of Labor Willard Wirtz and his wife. Former Governor of Florida Farris Bryant, now an aide to the President, had always been so kind to us. We met Supreme Court Judge William O. Douglas and his new, pixie-like, 23-year-old wife. "I know your state well," the judge said. "I used to herd sheep out there." The judge was born near Fergus Falls where his father was a minister in a country church.

Suddenly and dramatically, a ruffle of drums sounded down the hall. The Marine Corps Band struck up "Hail to the Chief." Four uniformed military men entered to the cadence of the music. Two carried rifles. Two others carried the Stars and Stripes and the President's flag. When the flags were secure in their stands, the four men wheeled smartly around and retired in step to the music.

The President and his wife, arm in arm, entered the room smiling and nodding their acknowledgement of their guests' applause. They were followed by the honored guests. Vice President and Mrs. Hubert Humphrey, Chief Justice and Mrs. Earl Warren, and House Speaker and Mrs. John McCormack.

A reception line formed. President Johnson was first in line. His gracious and petite wife, Lady Bird, was last in line. The honored guests were stationed between them. Strict protocol governed the order in which people were presented to the President and the other members of the receiving line. A gentleman was always presented to the President first. A lady was always presented after her husband or escort. The cabinet members and their wives were first in line. Next came the members of the Supreme Court and their wives. All the Cabinet members and all of the Supreme Court judges were present. Ambassadors would come next by protocol, but apparently none had been invited. Governors followed.

The reception line moved slowly. Behind us in the line were the congressional leaders, followed by key congressmen, followed by guests not involved in government. That last group contained many exceptionally interesting people. There were actresses Joan Crawford and Audrey Meadows. Ray Shierer, NBC White House correspondent, stood tall above the multitude. Trumpet player Al Hirt's beard set him apart from the rest.

A military officer stood facing the President. He announced the names of each couple as they moved up to shake the Chief Executive's hand.

"Governor, you're sitting at my table," beamed the tall Texan. Inwardly I said to myself, "You've got me confused with someone else, Mr. President, because my card says I'm to sit at table twelve."

Chief Justice Warren was a big vigorous smiling bear of a man in his 70s. Vice President Humphrey always appeared happy and was the picture of supreme confidence and optimism. House Speaker McCormack was a wonderful old man who obviously was fighting the ravages of advancing age. Their wives were the nice type of women you would expect to meet in your home town—no airs or pomp, just sweet smiles.

Once through the receiving line, we continued through the doorway into one of the three living rooms that opened on three sides so that you could cross from one side of the White House to the other.

We saw the white cloths on round tables in the state dining room. They were richly elegant with their settings of gold-rimmed china and gold-plated table wear. Candles and centerpieces added a touch of magnificence. Each table was numbered, and a place card above each plate designated the seating arrangement. Each round table seated ten.

I looked for my Table No. 12. It was the President's table! He would sit with his back to the ornate fireplace centered along the east wall.

The huge chandeliers sparkled softly. Uniformed waiters waited quietly at attention along the wall. Introductions at each table were being made among guests who might be meeting for the first time.

Mrs. Hubert Humphrey, with her quiet sense of humor, would sit at the President's right. Mrs. Earl Warren would sit at his left. Republican minority leader Everett Dirksen and Democratic majority Mike leader Mansfield were seated next to these women. Mrs. Gower Champion, the dancer of 20 years before, and Mrs. Nelson Rockefeller were seated next to the senators.

I was seated at Mrs. Rockefeller's right. Popular singing star Nancy Wilson was seated on my right. Judge Smith of Texas completed the guest list at the President's table.

Applause greeted the President and Mrs. Johnson as they entered the room. It died down, and a solemn table grace was given. Guests were seated, and a chatter of voices that would continue through dinner began.

The ornate menu described the courses: fish, breast of pheasant, wild rice, and Minnesota blue cheese. Three wine goblets were filled with different wines as we moved from fish to pheasant to dessert.

A lectern was placed on the table. The President stood and raised his champagne goblet. "I propose a toast to liberty," he said, "and to the leadership in our three branches of government who protect that liberty." Silently, the standing guests raised their goblets in response. The guests were seated and the President spoke. His words were solemn and sincere. He spoke of three dear friends and their wives from three branches of our government: The Judiciary and Chief Justice, Earl Warren, who was once the Republican governor of California; the Executive branch and Vice President Hubert Humphrey, once the mayor of Minneapolis; and the Legislative branch and House Speaker John McCormack. The President finished his short talk and was seated. The table lectern was removed.

One by one, the three honored guests responded with a toast to the President and a brief statement of admiration for the nation's Chief Executive. Three times the guests rose and toasted their President.

Lyndon Johnson listened and gazed thoughtfully at his hands folded in his lap. The toasts were finished. The applause died down, and the after-dinner talk rose to a babble.

Nancy Wilson talked of the singing tour in Germany that she would begin in three days. Mrs. Rockefeller talked of the values of life. Even though she was married to such a wealthy man, her values were basic and sound. Senator Mansfield was reserved, considerate, and quiet. He was the kind of man who would make a good fishing partner. Senator Dirksen was of the outgoing and the back-slapping variety. There was never a dull moment within earshot of him.

The Strolling Strings, all young, red-jacketed airman musicians, moved among the tables, serenading with their violins. Voices rose to be heard. Violins played louder to be heard.

And then dinner was over. The President rose and made his way slowly through the standing, smiling guests. He chatted here and pumped a hand there. He found Mrs. Johnson, and they held court among the milling guests in the great red-carpeted hall. Back in the East Room at the opposite end of the hall, the chairs were beginning to fill. Two hours ago it was the reception room. Now it had row upon row of satin-bottomed chairs, all facing a temporary stage occupying about one-third of the room. We were to see an abbreviated 30-minute version of "Hello Dolly," featuring its original singing star, Carol Channing.

The President and Mrs. Johnson, with their honored guests, were seated in the front row. The lights in the chandeliers dimmed, and stage lights came on. A small orchestra struck up the snappy music that characterizes "Hello Dolly." Carol Channing was beautiful in her 1890 gown of red, decorated with huge hearts outlined with sparkling red sequins. An enormous but fragile fan-like hat topped her tangerine-tinted wig. Her voice was quite deep and husky. She smiled the smile that was her trademark. The President applauded enthusiastically, clapping his hands above his head. Miss Channing was obviously thrilled and blew Mrs. Johnson a kiss. The performance was exciting and thrilling for both the audience and the performers.

After the show, the President moved along in front of the stage, reaching up to shake hands with the beaming cast.

Suddenly, a flourish of music from the orchestra announced the arrival of a four-tiered, red-frosted cake. "To celebrate your fourth anniversary of "Hello Dolly," the President said. "Oh, Mr. President, you knew we were coming, and you baked a cake," Miss Channing cooed. The guests surrounded the stage star to shake her hand. She was as lovely at close range as she was behind the footlights on stage.

The crowd slowly surged toward the marble-floored foyer. On one side, a red-uniformed military orchestra struck up the dance music. The guests waited for the President and his wife to begin the dancing. They were a graceful dance couple. Dancing began in earnest. Mr. Gower Champion and his wife, Marge, the famous dance team of the 1940s, danced sedately. Miss Channing created a stir with her dance partners. The President had a sweeping style, which moved him rapidly around the dance floor. The Vice President was an excellent dancer. His footwork was interesting to watch. His dancing with Miss Channing was almost professional.

The President was tired. It was easy to see why. He and Mrs. Johnson slipped away to their third-floor private living quarters about eleven thirty. Many tired guests had been waiting for that signal. Leaving a White House social affair before the President retired would have been rude.

We walked out into the cool night air. It seemed as though we had been part of a wonderful dream. Columnists would write about that affair as being one of the outstanding social events in White House history. What a privilege to be guests at such an awesome and elegant affair.

President Johnson Could Talk and Eat at the Same Time

Eating with Lyndon Johnson was not always such an elegant experience, as I learned in 1967. The Vietnam War was dragging on. It was an unpopular war, fought for a cause that many people could not relate to the United States' interest. Most popular was the argument that if South Vietnam fell to Communist North Vietnam, the rest of the Southeast Asian countries would fall like dominoes to Communism, and the Philippines would follow.

The nation's youth were making the military sacrifice, but the taxpayers were not asked to increase their contributions to the war effort. It was a business-as-usual war for us. President Johnson was under increasing pressure from critics on all sides. He tried everything to keep the country behind his war decisions.

As chairman of the nation's governors, I was one of six governors President Johnson invited to Washington to discuss the war effort. Our meeting with President Johnson was scheduled over a noon luncheon at the White House. We were seated at a rectangular table in a small dining room. The President sat at the head of the table, and the chairman of his Council of Economic Advisors sat at the opposite end. The governors faced each other across the table.

The President began talking immediately after we were seated. Waiters brought food and drink, and the President talked on. Amazingly he could talk nonstop while eating a substantial lunch at the same time. He spoke with his mouth full and with his mouth empty. He pulled polls and folded newspaper articles out of his pockets without laying down his fork. The main thrust of his talk was that we were winning the war and that we could have guns and butter without raising taxes. And besides, House Ways and Means

Committee Chairman Wilbur Mills never would allow a tax increase through his committee.

President Johnson asked no one present for his opinion, and there wasn't an opening between his nonstop eating and talking to voice an opinion.

I felt very strongly that if the war was justified in the national interest, we should all support it with higher taxes. We should not leave the total war effort on the shoulders of our sons and daughters, who were dying in Vietnam because those who lived would have to shoulder the unpaid war debt when the war was over. Later events proved that Congressman Wilbur Mills was an unstable alcoholic who represented the worst in decision-making responsibility. But the President wasn't looking for advice at that noon luncheon, and there had been no opportunity to offer any. A disillusioned group of governors left the White House that day, all wondering why they had been invited.

The Spy Ship *USS Pueblo*

President Johnson didn't like to take foreign policy advice from governors, but sometimes he took it.

In January 1968, politicians and editorial writers were outraged over North Korea's capture of the U.S. spy ship, *Pueblo*. Loud suggestions of "Send the Marines in to get it back," or "Bomb those North Koreans to teach them a lesson," were heard in the halls of Congress and among self-appointed super patriots. Any question of why our spy ship was so close to North Korean shores was muffled in righteous claims of our right to be in international waters. It was the kind of provocation on both sides that too often in history has led to needless death and destruction.

I wanted to assure President Johnson that there were people who believed we should swallow our pride and back off from a confrontation over the incident, so I sent him the following telegram:

> Dear Mr. President: History is cluttered with tragedy where men and nations placed pride above reason. In time, the crew of the *Pueblo* will come

home, and perhaps in time the North Koreans will have the job of scraping the barnacles off the *Pueblo* hull, and we can look back and wonder what the excitement was about. I strongly recommend that the *Pueblo* incident be reduced to proper perspective and that the United States take this golden opportunity to respond with a massive peace offensive in this world rather than rattling our sabers.

Respectfully,

William L. Guy
Governor of North Dakota

By sheer coincidence, I was in Washington, D.C., on state business several days after I sent the telegram. I checked in late at the Shoreham Hotel. About 5 o'clock in the morning, loud voices and the sound of automobiles in the parking lot below my window awakened me. Policemen had parked their motorcycles and were directing a steady stream of cars to parking places in the huge parking lot.

I wondered what all the early activity was about. Upon checking with a call to the desk, I discovered that a Presidential prayer breakfast, open to the public, was scheduled for seven o'clock, and President Johnson would be there.

I decided immediately to attend. When I bought my ticket, I was told to go to a certain room where special guests would get seating assignments. To my surprise, six other governors were present. Before we left for our assigned tables, a White House aide handed each of us a note inviting us to join the President at the White House at 9:30 after the breakfast. All of the governors had plans for the day, but we adjusted our schedules to accommodate the President's unusual invitation.

In the Oval Office, the President talked about the Vietnam War, now complicated by cries of revenge on North Korea for capturing the *Pueblo*. As was usual in meetings with President Johnson, he did all the talking, and we did all the listening. As I reached the door, the President grabbed my arm and said, "Governor, I want you to know that I do not intend to rattle any sabers over the *Pueblo* incident." He obviously was referring to the telegram I had sent him three days earlier. I wondered how my message to the President had survived the layers of White House bureaucracy to reach his eyes.

The Moon Walkers were Honored

I learned in 1969 that state dinners were not inevitably pleasant affairs.

It was an historic state occasion. President Nixon honored the first men to set foot on the moon—Neil Armstrong, Buzz Aldrin, and their orbiting teammate, Mike Collins.

The dinner was held in Los Angeles in the huge elegant Century Plaza Hotel.

By 4 o'clock on that historic Wednesday afternoon, August 13, 1969, police were guiding incoming traffic to the hotel. Each of the 1,600 invited guests had been issued a 5" x 5" orange card to stick to their auto windshield to get through police lines. The day honoring the astronauts had begun in early morning in New York City. Mayor John Lindsay had kicked it off with an official reception and medals after a ticker tape parade through downtown Manhattan. The next stop for the honored space travelers was Chicago.

The end of that exhausting day for the astronauts was Los Angeles.

That week, President Nixon was living at his nearby summer White House at San Clemente. He would make

The Presidents I Knew

the short hop from there to the Century Plaza parking lot by helicopter.

The Century Plaza Hotel is a massive, curved structure built on a section of the grounds of what was once the Twentieth Century Studio movie lot. The remaining movie stage sets could be seen from the hotel windows. The false fronts of the movie sets were part of the world of make-believe. It was difficult to fully comprehend that we would honor moon-walking men for exploits that exceeded even the most bizarre plots of the movie makers.

The dinner was set for 8:30 in the mammoth grand ballroom. The reception, beginning at 7 o'clock, was to precede the dinner.

By 4 o'clock, the tempo of activity around the hotel definitely had increased. Men were carrying tuxedoes carefully protected by plastic suitbags. Secret Service types were everywhere. They looked young and clean-cut.

Jean went to her 4:30 appointment in the hotel hairdressing salon. I picked up a newspaper to get the press' view of the big event.

In our room on the 17th floor, our balcony overlooked the sprawling terrace, the swimming pools, and two asphalt-covered parking lots, covering a city block. The largest parking lot had been sealed off from the public all day. Seven red fire trucks were spotted around its perimeter. A dozen or so police patrol cars were parked in a cluster. This was the landing area where the helicopters carrying the Presidential party and other VIPs would land.

Every few minutes, the peculiar shuddering clatter of a circling helicopter would blot out all other sounds. Far below and on a street adjacent to the heliport, but blocked from its view, wound a circling procession of antiwar demonstrators. They walked slowly and carried their signs in an orderly manner. I doubt that they knew or were concerned when the President was to arrive.

Printed instructions had been delivered to each room, warning its occupants not to step out on their balconies when the Presidential party was arriving or taking off. I was content to watch the panorama below from behind the sliding glass door that provided access to our room's narrow balcony. Hanging over the bar of a balcony 17 floors above the terrace below is not a pastime I would choose whether the President was arriving or not. Helicopters came and went. The passengers were guided quickly to a nearby string of limousines and cars that seemed to be replenished as soon as a copter load of passengers was driven off.

We could only guess when the VIPs were arriving by the response of the security forces in the parking lot below. Sometime in the late afternoon, the President's helicopter arrived. Black hoses had been strung from one fire truck. These hoses, manned by about 20 yellowhelmeted firemen, were of sufficient length to take care of watering down any copter crash that might happen in the parking lot.

A helicopter, probably carrying security people, staff or press, landed immediately behind the President's machine. I was told that the Presidential party entered the hotel through an obscure service entrance.

Dressing in formal clothes always presents minor crises. Our invitation had stated that dress would be formal for women and "black tie" for men. I assumed that "black tie" in southern California in August meant a white formal dinner jacket. I was jolted to learn from the office of the dinner coordinator that "the President would wear a black tuxedo, and you can take it from there." I had brought a white formal dinner jacket but had left my tuxedo at home. Many white coats will be worn, I assured myself as I mulled over the possibility of renting a tuxedo.

The huge ballroom was jammed with excited guests when the head table was seated. It was difficult to comprehend that these honored men had recently been standing on the moon, looking up at our tiny planet called Earth.

It had been a warm day, and the new hotel's air conditioning capacity was struggling to keep the temperature down to a comfortable level in the cavernous ballroom. To prevent an electrical system overload, the hotel management turned off all air conditioning in the kitchen. Designed to prepare food for 1,600 guests, the kitchen became intolerably hot as the last of the main course was served. Suddenly the heat set off the ceiling sprinklers in the kitchen. Waiters dived for cover. When the sprinklers were finally turned off, an inch or more of water stood on the floor. Chagrinned waiters clad in red coats and black trousers served the desserts to the tables in as dignified a manner as possible, hoping the guests would not notice the water that squished in their shoes at each step.

The Assassination of a President

Not all of the national ceremonies a governor attends are pleasant or humorous. Some are tragic.

In 1963, the Midwest Governors Conference was only two years old. I was in my second year as chairman of the conference, chosen because I had been the one who had called the 12 states together to see if working as a regional organization would be advantageous. The first conference of the governors had been held in Chicago after the fall election returns were in. That conference was marked by the bitterness of the defeated governors and the unwillingness of the newly elected governors to participate until they had been inaugurated. The new Midwest Governors Conference almost folded before it began.

Governor Frank Morrison of Nebraska, a great supporter of regional cooperation among states, had invited the Midwest Governors Conference to hold its second meeting in the fall of 1963 in Omaha.

The morning session of the conference on November 22 was filled with discussions of problems that plagued nearly every governor and state. The North American Air Defense Command, which had a large base just outside of Omaha, had arranged a special event. The governors were invited to board a bus before lunch to go out to the base, tour it, and be the luncheon guests of the base commander. As chairman of the conference, I stayed at the hotel to work on the agenda for that afternoon when the governors returned.

Shortly after noon, I decided I needed a bowl of soup and a sandwich to satisfy the gnawing pangs of hunger that were beginning to assert themselves. As I came to the head of the broad carpeted stairs leading from the mezzanine floor to the lobby, I became uncomfortably aware that something was wrong with the normally boisterous crowd in the lobby below. An eerie silence had settled over the ornate lobby, and people were gathered in groups talking quietly or standing, watching the large television set in one corner. As I stepped off the stairs, I overhead somebody say, "I think he is worse off than the commentators are admitting."

The unsmiling faces and anxious voices told me that something serious had happened to someone of great importance. And then the blow fell. President John Kennedy had been gunned down as he rode in his limousine in a caravan of cars in Dallas! Never had I been so stunned. I walked over to the television set and edged my way up to where I could see over the crowd and watch the commentators who were carrying on a minute-by-minute description of the tragic events that were unfolding in Texas. I hoped desperately that the President was only wounded, but somehow the words that were being said on television and those that weren't being said seemed to indicate that perhaps the President was dead.

My appetite had entirely disappeared.

Then the word was official. The President was dead, his handsome head shattered by a bullet from a cowardly assassin, yet unknown.

I walked in a trance back to the elevator to return to my room. I knew that the governors would cut short their visit to the air base and would want to meet briefly and conclude the conference so they could return to their states. When

I returned to my room, I sat on the edge of the bed, unable to think clearly. I realized that as chairman of the conference and in the absence of the other governors, reporters soon would ask for my reaction to this incredible tragedy.

I took a yellow pad and began to jot some thoughts. My fingers refused to function normally, and the words that I wrote were barely legible to me. As the shock subsided, my anger at this senseless violent act began to rise. There was a knock on the door. I opened it. There stood Mercer Cross, a reporter from the Minneapolis *Tribune* and Fletcher Knebel, the well-known author who had written *Seven Days in May*.

"Could we speak to you, Governor?" Mercer Cross asked after he had introduced the gentleman with him.

"About what?" I asked, feeling a growing sense of outrage that anyone, even a reporter, would have the right to come around in what seemed to be a ghoulish effort to measure the shock and grief that this stunning tragedy had on everyone. We talked for a few moments with the reporters standing at the door with pencils poised. But the words didn't flow into anything that made much sense. They left.

Several days later in the state capitol in Bismarck, I reread the thoughts that flooded from my mind onto that yellow legal pad in the hotel room in Omaha. This is what they said:

> The President of the United States was killed by the hatred of one man. He was the victim of a bullet, but at that moment, it was the nation which was the victim of an insidious growing thing which should be foreign to our national sense of honesty, fairness, and justice.
>
> For several years, we've witnessed this strange phenomenon in which vicious rumor, distorted facts, and a phony patriotism have, in a cold, calculated way, been used to arouse suspicion, hatred, and villification of those in public office. It has almost been fashionable,

in some quarters, to slander and question the patriotism of certain of our public officials. A calculated campaign to degrade the legislative branch of government, the executive branch of government, and the judicial branch of government has been under way in the United States for some time—made sharper than ever before by the new skills in mass persuasion through modern means of communication.

As the life of President Kennedy ebbed away, perhaps we as a nation have been shocked to our senses to the terrible devisiveness that has been weakening the strength of our democratic form of government. Perhaps we shall be shocked into realizing that there are wholesome limits of criticism of our public servants and their policies beyond which we go at the peril of the very existence of our democracy.

I had turned the sheet of yellow tablet paper over and had continued to write in a curious, almost illegible scrawl some other thoughts that came to me in that silent hotel room.

We cannot bring back President Kennedy, but we can nourish the memory of him. His visit to Grand Forks only two months ago was an historic event for our state of North Dakota. His reception, described by one national magazine as "cool," was in reality a warm, enthusiastic expression of admiration by more than 20 thousand persons gathered to see his youthful stride, his shock of hair, and his friendly smile. As he turned to board his plane that day, he said to me, "I am overwhelmed; I didn't expect a reception as fine as this!"

Obviously, thousands on either side of the political fence were cheering their President as a welcomed guest in North Dakota.

I continued to write in the tablet,

It will be up to the historians to decide the greatness of President Kennedy. But greatness is a relative thing.

Certainly in terms of the contributions that he might have made in the years he had a right to expect, he was prevented from achieving the full range of accomplishment toward which his youth and drive were carrying him. But President Kennedy's record has not been completed yet. We must wait to see how much of his program will yet be adopted by a congress which, up to now, has vacilated between stall and start.

The following morning, all of us felt the full impact of the impossible tragedy of the day before. The conference had been immediately concluded on the previous afternoon, and I stayed to tie up the many loose ends the abrupt change had caused in our plans. Several North Dakotans were with Jean and me at the conference to act as resource people and advisers on the subjects on the governors' agenda. One of those who was with me was Skip Meade, the Commissioner of Higher Education in North Dakota.

Early in the morning after the assassination, our North Dakota conference delegation was gathered in a hanger at the Omaha airport, waiting for our National Guard C-47, affectionately known as the "Minnie H" to be warmed up and made ready for flight. I was still undecided as to whether I should fly to Washington or return to North Dakota first and then go on to our nation's capitol. Skip Meade was concerned about why I was mulling over whether to go to Washington, D.C., or not.

"Governor, you must go," he said. "I have enough money here in my billfold to buy your ticket on a commercial flight to Washington from here and then back to North Dakota."

Skip had a very concerned look on his face, and I knew that his unusual offer had been made most sincerely.

"No, Skip," I said. "It isn't a matter of money; it's a matter of trying to anticipate how I should plan North Dakota's official response to this national tragedy." I mention Skip at this point because he was to figure in another tragedy that was just one of thousands to happen as a direct result of the assassination of the President.

I did fly to Washington, D.C., that day to officially convey the grief of our North Dakota people and their sympathy to the President's family.

When I landed at National Airport in Washington, it was easy to sense the shock and grief of the people, whoever they were. Even the massive limestone buildings, the park statues, and the gold dome of the nation's capitol building in the distance seemed to gloomily reflect that something was terribly wrong.

Heavy, dark, low clouds drifted slowly and ominously over the tip of the stark, pointed shaft, which is the Washington Monument. Two red warning lights, set in windows at its peak, blinked in alternating cadence, contrasting sharply with the leaden gray sky. Fine rain formed from the misty air and wet the leaves on the ground below the bare-limbed trees.

Washington, D.C., was in a state of shock. It could be seen everywhere. The President had been murdered less than 24 hours before. That day, his body lay in repose at the White House. Cars and buses, their tires smacking along on the wet pavement, moved in subdued lines. People walked with heads down, unseeing and unsmiling.

My mission, at that moment, seemed simple enough. I had only to express the sympathy and grief of all North Dakotans to the dead President's family. As my taxi cab approached the north side of the White House, moving sporadically in the line of traffic, I began to wonder about protocol. Much had been written about how to act in routine official situations, but how does one cope with a situation of gravity beyond comprehension? How do you pay last respects to a President?

Police in black raincoats held back the quiet, curious crowd gathered at the White House gate to watch the flow of visitors who were coming from foreign countries as well as from every state in the union. A police officer requested to see some identification. In my case, a Bell Telephone credit card seemed handiest and turned out to be adequate. We were waved on to join the slowly moving caravan of cars winding up the drive to the front entrance of the home of the nation's chief executive.

Military personnel seemed everywhere—at the entrance, in the halls, on the stairs—and all stood stiffly at attention. No one ushered or spoke. You just moved forward in the quiet and shadow of the halls.

Coming into a parlor made somber by the silence and fading light of the fall afternoon, I came face to face with two young women, standing alone. I recognized them as the sister and sister-in-law of the late President. Their eyes were tired and red-lined. Their faces were gray and drawn. I wondered how many times that afternoon they had heard the phrase, "I'm sorry." Nothing I could think of seemed appropriate to say. I said only, "I'm from North Dakota. I'm Governor Guy." They said nothing as they shook hands. I had never seen such bone-weary grief etched so deeply in a person's face as it was in the faces of those two young women. I hesitated for a moment, groping for words. They didn't come. I turned and walked to the entrance to the east ballroom.

My wife and I, only eight months before, had walked through that same entrance to the sparkling elegance and gaiety of a formal state dinner, hosted by President Kennedy and his wife. But this day, I was not to greet the President—I was to say goodbye.

The unopened casket, in the center of the cavernous, dimly lit ballroom, was draped completely with the stars and stripes. It rested on a platform which brought the top of the casket even with the chests of the four military men standing rigidly at attention facing inward a few feet from each corner. A fifth soldier stood at the head of the casket looking down its length and through anyone who chose to meet his gaze. About ten feet back from the foot of the draped casket were two simple wooden prayer stools where people, one or two at a time, knelt quietly with their thoughts. Large, tall candles flickered slowly at each corner of the casket.

The three huge sparkling chandeliers above had lost their charm. Today, they gleamed dully and seemed almost out of place. Their subdued glow brought out the crisp colors of the flag, but their light scarcely reached to the dark corners of the large, vacant room. Every other light in the chandeliers had been darkened, and those that were left were the only source of light. Black bunting draped the four stately fireplace mantles, and bunting was intertwined in the chandeliers, further muffling the subdued light.

One by one, people moved to the foot of the casket to stand for a lingering moment or kneel. Silence was complete except for the hollow sound of footsteps that echoed from the carpetless, hardwood floor. There was no winking back the tears. A friend had gone without warning. A smiling personality who had been the buoyant spirit of the nation was snuffed out.

Outside the rain quickened, but people seemed oblivious as they silently returned to their cars. The lights at the tip of the Washington Monument had disappeared in the mist.

How deeply scarred the people of this nation and of the civilized world were by that traumatic, outrageous, and imponderable tragedy will never be measured. But it is easy to point to some of the tragedies that were a part of the aftermath of that never-to-be-forgotton last week in November 1963.

One of those incidents occurred in North Dakota. Skip Meade, the Commissioner of Higher Education, who at the Omaha airport had been so concerned and so insistent that I go to Washington, D.C., to represent our state, had settled himself on the davenport in front of the television tube in the living room of his modest home in Bismarck to watch the funeral ceremonies that completely transfixed the nation that day. His wife was in the kitchen preparing lunch.

She later reported that she could hear him sobbing as he watched the ceremony. This was unusual as she had never heard her husband cry before. Suddenly, there was a dull thump in the living room as something heavy struck the floor. She rushed in to find her husband unconscious on the floor in front of the television set. Skip Meade never regained consciousness from the massive heart attack that his deep grief brought on, and he died a few hours later. One wonders how many heart attacks could be traced to the sight of the President's 3-year-old son, Jon, saluting as the President's body went by in the casket on the horsedrawn military caisson.

A Promising Leader Is Gone

Less than five years later, it was my grim duty to attend the funeral of John Kennedy's brother, Robert, who also was felled by an assassin's bullet.

The delegation of North Dakotans I invited to fly to New York City to pay our last respects to Senator Robert F. Kennedy consisted of men who were active in the affairs of the Senator's political party in our state. They were Larry Erickson, Minot, state chairman of the Democratic-NPL party; Rolland Redlin, Minot, former congressman; Dr. James Whittacker, Fargo, and Edwin Sjaastad, Bismarck, co-chairmen of the Robert Kennedy for President effort; Bernard Majors, Fargo, chairman of the Concerned Democrats; Gary McDaniel, Minot, chairman of the Hubert Humphrey for President organization; and Reverend Roger Grussing, Bismarck, western chairman of the Eugene McCarthy for President effort. Reverend Troy Keeling, chairman of the Eugene McCarthy for President organization, was invited but could not accept because of a funeral he was to conduct in Minot.

We boarded the North Dakota National Guard twin-engine C-47 at the Bismarck Airport at 8 a.m., June 7, 1968. We landed at Grissom Field, an air base near Peru, Indiana, at 2 p.m. for fuel. We had a quick lunch at the base and took off at 2:45 p.m.

Our flight had been uneventful and fairly smooth when the Atlantic Ocean came into view and indicated that our trip across half the continent was nearly over.

We landed at Floyd Bennet Field, a Naval air station at the top of Long Island, at 7:30 p.m., EDT.

Governor Nelson Rockefeller had placed two limousines at our disposal during our stay in New York. We were whisked into downtown Manhattan over a 30-mile freeway and toll tunnel route through a heavily suburbanized countryside in sight of Long Island Sound. The bridges and the skyscrapers of New York City formed an interesting backdrop to the passing scene. We went directly to the Abbey-Victoria Hotel, whose 22 stories were dwarfed by surrounding skyscrapers. We were quickly and courteously assigned to four rooms reserved for us.

Immediately after placing our luggage in our rooms, we returned to our two waiting limousines and headed for St. Patrick's Cathedral four blocks away. We hoped to be able to get into the Cathedral to join the hundreds of thousands whose presence would pay tribute to Senator Robert Kennedy.

We were fortunate to be riding in two officially licensed limousines. The streets and sidewalks around St. Patrick's Cathedral were barricaded by gray, sawhorse-like devices manned by hundreds of blue-uniformed policemen. The sight of our limousines, however, drew immediate response; and the police quickly moved barricades to permit us to enter a blocked-off street and park in a restricted area. I marveled that our drivers knew exactly where to go and which of many entrances to the church was the appropriate one.

A young New Yorker, who only weeks before had been in North Dakota as a Kennedy campaign advance man, met us on the sidewalk outside the door to a small waiting room. This was our first New York City contact with that marvelously efficient organization of young people who had worked so devotedly and so fervently for weeks in all of the states in the nation as they sought to acquire delegate commitments necessary to secure the Presidential nomination for Robert F. Kennedy. Now they had come back to New York City to carry out their final sad and bewildering volunteer assignment for their dead leader. They could be seen everywhere—seemingly tireless— handling the mountain of details that arose minute by minute as the sudden sad funeral preparations unfolded in hasty but carefully thought-out arrangements.

We signed our nine names and addresses in the guest book placed in the small waiting room.

Unknown to us, thousands of people still were standing a dozen abreast in a line that extended several blocks from the main entrance of the Cathedral, waiting patiently for a single moment beside the closed, flag-draped casket inside. The doors of the Cathedral had opened at 5:30 that Friday morning and were to close 24 hours later to permit final funeral arrangements. Thousands were turned away when the doors were closed early Saturday morning.

A Kennedy aide led us single file out of the waiting room through a door into the night air and by a circuitous route into the front of the huge Cathedral sanctuary. We followed along the side of the hushed chamber to the rear where a double line constantly was formed from the throng pressing through the arched doors of the Cathedral. These people, slowly moving down the center aisle of the church, had been waiting in line for five hours for their moment. We had flown 15 hundred miles for our moment.

Scaffolds of pipe and plank had been built on either side at the front of the sanctuary. Banks of hot television lights and several television cameras looked down on the scene from the scaffolds. The harsh television lights seemed out of place in the quiet shadows of the enormous, cavernous sanctuary. Heavy television cables were looped overhead from pillar to pillar. They clashed with the classic lines of the beautiful columns and stone work. The air was heavy with humidity and heat.

As we slowly approached the casket, some people left the line to slip into a pew to sit or kneel in thought or prayer. An honor guard of friends stood four on each side, facing one another as they pressed close to the mahogany casket. Every 15 or 20 minutes, one of the honor guard would step back to be replaced by another of a constantly replenishing group of friends waiting quietly in front pews.

As the double line moved slowly down the center aisle of the sanctuary, it parted to pass on either side of the casket. Some people paused to reach out to touch the casket. Others knelt for a moment of prayer or stooped to kiss the American flag which covered the casket. Bouquets wilted in the oppressive heat almost before they were placed on the floor along the bier. They had to be removed constantly. Touching the casket seemed to give people a sense of serenity and fulfillment that was apparent on their faces as they left the sanctuary.

We returned to our limousines to travel a dozen blocks or so to the Kennedy for President headquarters. Here the coveted tickets, which would admit their bearers to the funeral services tomorrow, were to be allocated. It was 9:30 p.m. We were told that ticket distribution would not start for half an hour.

We returned to our hotel to have our first meal since noon.

At 10:30, Edwin Sjaastad and James Whittacker returned to Kennedy headquarters, seeking tickets to admit us to the funeral. They were told that St. Patrick's Cathedral would accommodate only 2,000 people. Therefore, only the Governor and two others in our party could receive tickets. We were dismayed that all of our party could not be admitted, but knowing of the number of people from 50 states and many foreign countries who were seeking admittance, we understood.

Saturday, June 8, 1968, was a clear, warm day, which Governor Rockefeller had proclaimed as a day of mourning. Traffic in downtown New York City was relatively light. But nonetheless, the streets in every direction from St. Patrick's Cathedral were swarming with uniformed police and firemen, brought in from precincts all over the city.

We arrived by limousine in front of the Cathedral at 9 a.m. A steady stream of people moved up the steps between a double row of police, security people, and ushers. Barricades held back crowds of onlookers. Cameramen resembled blinking, one-eyed monsters as they madly photographed each one of the hundreds of nationally known people as he or she arrived.

We were asked to show our large admission cards every step of the way. The crowd was directed and seated in accordance with the color of their cards. My card was brown, and I was sent down the center aisle to a seat about one-third of the way back from the front of the sanctuary. Pierre Salinger was the usher who showed me to a seat. It was 9:10 a.m., 50 minutes until the start of the ceremony.

The air was oppressive, heavy, and warm. There was a noticeable overtone of hushed voices as people sought directions to their seats. The pews were without cushions, and the wood backs were uncomfortably straight up and down. The kneeling rail made the long wait awkward.

I became aware of the sad faces of many well-known people around me. In the pew ahead was singer Eartha Kitt. Behind me I could hear Walter Reuther conversing in low tones. Behind and to my right sat Sidney Poitier, and nearby was Cary Grant. Across the aisle sat Jack Paar. Economist John Galbraith towered above others in a nearby pew. Congressmen, cabinet members, athletes, entertainers, and business people of national repute made their way to seats.

The television lights glared at the front of the church but were mercifully turned away from the mourners seated in the subdued light that filtered through the large, intricate, stained-glass windows placed high in the towering sanctuary walls.

Now and then, a hymnal dropped or a chair collapsed to send a shock wave of apprehension through the tense audience. Violence seemed all too possible in these highly charged circumstances.

There was a flurry of whispers when sorrowing Vice President Humphrey and his wife came down the aisle trailed by several secret service agents.

A few minutes before 10, a Catholic bishop escorted President and Mrs. Johnson down the aisle. Secret servicemen guarded the President.

The service was beautiful. A choir bathed the sanctuary in music from the loft high above the entrance at the rear of the church. The golden tones of a string orchestra rose and fell in a mood of sorrow.

Senator Ted Kennedy walked resolutely to a lectern facing the TV lights and the seated crowd. He was magnificent. He talked of his dead brother. He kept a grip on his emotions. Many in the crowd could not control theirs.

The ritual and ceremonies so meaningless and burdensome to laymen at funerals of past years had been eliminated. Everything now had purpose and meaning. We should not make more of his brother in death than he was in life, Ted Kennedy said.

The archbishop announced that buses would leave for the funeral train from one of the side doors. Many in the crowd left their seats and moved to the center aisle, thinking the funeral was over. It was not. The most emotional part began. Andy Williams' voice filled the Cathedral as he sang the Battle Hymn of the Republic in slow cadence. Pallbearers moved the casket slowly down the center aisle toward the rear of the sanctuary. The large Kennedy family, proudly composed in their aching grief, followed slowly with chins held high. There were very few dry eyes among spectators. Slowly the crowd emptied the church into the warm sunlight.

The Presidents I Knew

With great efficiency and courtesy, the New York police dispersed the crowd. I did not wait for our limousine to come up. I welcomed the short walk back to the hotel.

That part of our delegation who had not been able to get into St. Patrick's Cathedral watched the proceedings on television screens just as hundreds inside the Cathedral who were seated behind the massive columns, which lined the sanctuary, watched the events at the front of the church on television screens set behind each pillar.

Within minutes after the funeral, our party had assembled and decided to leave immediately for Floyd Bennett Field and the long flight home. We were in the air at 2 p.m., EDT. Box lunches awaited us on board. We stopped at Truax Field in Madison, Wisconsin, to refuel. A storm system over Minnesota caused us to swing west into Iowa before turning north. We arrived at Bismarck airport at 11 Saturday night. It had been a long two days. But Senator Robert Kennedy deserved to have the people of all of our states represented at his funeral.

With John F. Kenndy at Gand Forks, September 1963.

Top: President and Mrs. Nixon present a North Dakota flag that traveled to the moon on Apollo, along with particles of lunar dust, to Jean and me and our daughters Debby, Nancy and Holly, at the White House, 1969.

Center: With Lyndon Johnson in the Oval Office, 1965.

Bottom. Jean and I with Senator Edward Kennedy at dedication of the Kennedy Center at State Democratic Headquarters in Bismarck.

7

Governing Can Be a Funny Job

There's No Place Like Home

As chief executive officer of North Dakota, I tried to meet the requests of the citizens, even when those requests were not of an earthshaking character.

Casmir Paluck, a huge burley man of swarthy features and twinkling eyes, had been badgering the State Game and Fish Department to do something about the antelope herd that had taken up residence on his small ranch south of Belfield. His pleas for help had fallen on sympathetic but unresponsive ears at the department that protects wildlife at all costs until they can be killed "humanely" by a bullet backed up by a bought-and-paid-for hunting license. Wildlife prefer it that way, I am told.

Casmir's neighbors had taken him to court, charging him with abusing his cattle by starving them on overgrazed pasture. But the rancher was adamant that it was the herd of state-protected antelope that was grazing his pasture down and forcing his cow herd to go hungry. In desperation, Casmir came to the governor's office as the court of last resort. I listened to Casmir spin his tale of woe. Why should one rancher raise a herd of antelope for the benefit of those macho hunters whose duty and pleasure it was to harvest the wildlife each fall. Casmir had a point, I decided.

A few days later, I called the Belfield rancher to tell him that Game and Fish Commissioner Russ Stuart and I would be out to see his situation early Friday morning. It was a beautiful day when Russ and I set out in the department's little four-seater Cessna airplane. Because of the one-hour time changes, we arrived in Belfield at about the same time we took off.

Casmir and his wife were surprised to see the local game warden's four-wheel drive pull into their yard before they had finished breakfast. But we were in time for a cup of very robust coffee.

"Get in my pickup," Casmir said, "and I'll show you what antelope will do." We drove toward a high hill that dominated the center of the ranch, with cropland on one side and rangeland on the other. The antelope had left paths in his wheat and flax fields. In places, they seemed to have used the fields to bed down in. "They must come across these fields to get water," Casmir mused, as he shook his head at the crop damage.

We continued until we stopped just below the brow of the hill. We left the pickup and climbed to the top to be confronted with a vast view to the west that went for miles to the distant buttes. "Count 'em," Casmir said, pointing to the cattle grazing below and handing me a pair of binoculars. Sure enough, acting as though they belonged there, 32 antelope could be seen peacefully grazing interspersed in Casmir's herd of about 75 cows.

"Can't you scare those antelope so bad they will leave for good?" I asked.

Casmir gave me a withering look. "I'll tell you how they scare. Back in June, my hired man and I got two shotguns and four boxes of shells. We got that herd of antelope running, and we chased them in our pickup about ten miles east across country. Every time they showed signs of slowing up, we would stop and get out and send a few shotgun blasts in their direction. We were lucky because there were very few fences to go through and no woven wire. Antelope don't jump fences; they crawl under. Finally we ran out of road, and they were still running east so far ahead of us we could hardly see them.

My hired man and I had chased those critters past South Heart. Feeling pretty good except for sore shoulders from firing the shotguns, we headed for home. As we drove through Belfield, we became aware of a sudden thirst for a glass of beer. I suppose telling our success story to every new patron who came into the bar took longer than we realized and before we knew it, it was supper time. We drove leisurely home and as we came by our big pasture, guess what we saw. We saw a herd of 32 antelope peacefully grazing with my cattle! They almost beat us back to Belfield!"

Casmir had made his point! I instructed Russ Stuart to devise some method of reducing or eliminating that herd of antelope during or before hunting season. Whether they were trapped and released elsewhere or whether they were reduced by hunters directed to their Casmir Paluck ranch hangout, I never knew. But something must have been done because I never heard Casmir Paluck's Polish brogue again.

How to Petition Your Government

Sometimes a citizen could get to me without knowing it. In 1967, our family headed east for a summer vacation in Minnesota. Taking advantage of one of our rare trips by car on the newly landscaped interstate, we stopped at one of our North Dakota Highway Department's heavily used rest areas. We wanted to inspect the restrooms to see how well they were being kept up. Our rest area restrooms were simple wood frame buildings without running water.

Everything appeared to be spic and span. But in the men's restroom, a very pointed message was written on the clean, gleaming white-painted wall. It said, "Any state that can afford to landscape its interstate highway can afford to have running water in its rest rooms." This statement, after being signed by its author, had been endorsed by a dozen other men in different handwritings from different states.

When I returned to Bismarck a week later, I marched into Highway Commissioner Walt Hjelle's office and said, "Do you know what, Walt?"

"No, what?" he replied.

"Any state that can afford to landscape its interstate highway can afford to have running water in its restrooms."

Walter swallowed and blinked and said, "Yes sir."

I thought the "on the wall" petition that reached the Governor in a roundabout way was one of the most effective and eloquent I had seen. In the following year, the restrooms at that rest stop and others along Interstate Highway 94 were rebuilt to contain the modern comforts of running water.

One Favor Deserves Another

Of course, legislators always carried their constituents' requests to me, and I did my best to fulfill them.

In my first three terms as Governor, there were no more diligent legislators than those who came from Richland County. Representative Tom Stallman always seemed to be calling me to say that I had to do something for him or for Richland County or he stood no chance of re-election.

One day he called me and, in an excited voice, said, "Bill, you know that great big hole next to the high school on the edge of Wyndmere where the highway department excavated dirt for the overpass."

I said, "Yes."

"Well," he said, "if we don't get that water and mosquito-infested pit filled up with dirt, I'll never get re-elected to the House of Representatives."

I said, "Tom, I certainly wouldn't want anything like that to happen. I'll see if I can get the highway department

Governing Can Be a Funny Job

to fill up that big borrow pit with dirt, and we'll hope that we get you back in the House of Representatives."

The highway department did fill up that borrow pit near Wyndmere, and Tom Stallman was re-elected. But two years later, he called me again and he said, "Bill, you remember that borrow pit that you filled with dirt near Wyndmere?"

I said, "Yes, I do."

"Well," he said, "it's just a weed-grown eyesore now and unless we can get it leveled off and planted to grass, I'll never get re-elected to the next session of the Legislature."

I said, "Tom, we wouldn't want anything like that to happen. I'll see what we can do." And so I had the highway department level off the fill at that borrow pit, and they seeded it down to grass. Tom was re-elected

Two years later Representative Tom Stallman called again. "You know Governor," Tom said, "that borrow pit that was filled, leveled and seeded to grass is right next to the Wyndmere high school. There's a lot of agitation around here to get that land deeded to the school as an addition to their athletic field. If I don't get that job done, I don't think I'll be re-elected."

Once again, I said, "Tom, I certainly wouldn't want anything like that to happen."

But I added with tongue in cheek, "If I get the highway department to deed that borrow pit over to the school, do you think you could get them to name it Guy Field?"

"Consider it done." Stallman said.

The land was deeded over to the school, and Stallman was re-elected.

When the legislature came to Bismarck in early January, I met Richland County Representative Treadwell Haugen in the great hall. "Tready," I said in a jocular mood, "how do the people like Guy Field over at Wyndmere?"

Tready's brow furrowed, trying to understand my question. Then he brightened and, laughing, said, "Oh,

I think you are referring to Stallman Stadium. It's doing great!"

What's in a Name?

One of my official duties was serving on the state pardon board, which met periodically in a tiled room with barred windows at the state penitentiary in Bismarck. As board chairman, I sat at the end of a long table with the four other members seated across from one another.

One by one, the convicts were brought in to sit in a seat at the opposite end of the long table. In this way, the convicts presented their pleas for one kind of consideration or another.

One prisoner who appeared before us interested me, especially because his last name was the same as mine. "There are not very many people around with the name Guy," I said. "Please tell me about your family. Perhaps we are related."

The prisoner fidgeted and looked at the floor, then finally spoke up. "My name is not really Guy," he said. "Years ago when I was barely 21, I was sent to prison. My name was Eidelhauser (ficticious). I was so ashamed of the dishonor I had brought to my family's name of Eidelhauser, that I chose the name of Guy."

"I am sure that all of us are impressed that you have protected the name of Eidelhauser from the dishonor of your long criminal record," I said, "all of us except one—that is. Thanks for nothing."

The Taste of New Industry

One of my major functions was to do whatever I could to promote North Dakota's economic growth and development. Few areas, if any, are more naturally endowed for raising sugar beets than the broad, fertile Red River Valley of the North.

Governing Can Be a Funny Job

It was not surprising when Holly Sugar Company announced in early 1968 that it was interested in signing up sufficient sugar beet acreage to warrant spending $25 million on a sugar refinery in either Minnesota or North Dakota. With that announcement, both states moved rapidly to woo Holly in hopes of capturing the new refinery.

I quickly lined up a trip to Holly Sugar Company headquarters in Colorado Springs. Fred Brandt, our Economic Development Commission director, and I arrived at the Colorado Springs Airport on a Monday morning at 10 o'clock. The president of Holly Sugar Company, Dennis O'Rourke, met us.

To our surprise and chagrin, we found that a second reception committee, headed by Holly Board Chairman, John Bunker, was also on hand to meet a Minnesota delegation who had arrived, unknown to us, on the same airplane.

Mr. O'Rourke seemed amused that Minnesota and North Dakota, in their haste to sell their states' advantages, should arrive on the same day on the same plane.

Both delegations were driven to the Holly Sugar Company's new headquarters building and were ushered together into the large reception lounge.

The Minnesotans eyed the North Dakotans with distrust, and the North Dakotans eyed the Minnesotans with suspicion.

Finally Dennis O'Rourke moved to ease the embarrassed tension. "I think it's only fair to tell you folks from Minnesota that North Dakota has the inside track," he said, "because Governor Guy had the foresight to name one of his daughters Holly."

For a moment the Minnesotans looked downcast. Then their leader, Wheelock Whitney, started to laugh. "Would it help Minnesota's chances, Mr. O'Rourke, it I told you that I call my wife, Sugar?"

This light repartee had broken the tension and the rest of the day was one of friendly competition, even though Holly Sugar didn't end up building a new plant anywhere!

Have You Got a Match?

The Garrison Diversion Irrigation Project, an important part of the Missouri River Basin Pick-Sloan Plan, had become a cause celebre in North Dakota. For years, we had been seeking the re-authorization and funding of the $225 million project that would bring Missouri River irrigation water to 250,000 prairie acres.

Scores of people had made many trips over the years to the nation's capitol, seeking support for the giant project. Suddenly it appeared to be within our grasp. President Lyndon Johnson had reaffirmed the approval given to the Garrison Diversion Unit by President John Kennedy shortly before his assassination.

A full-court press to get congressional approval of funding was mounted in 1965. About 30 North Dakotans descended on Washington, D.C. Teams of two were assigned lists of congressmen to contact. My wife and I operated as a team to contact the House and Senate leadership.

With some nervousness, we sought out House Speaker John McCormack. He was a tall, thin, old man with piercing eyes set in a craggy, colorless face, topped with shaggy, white hair.

"Come into my office, folks," he said. We followed him into the inner sanctum and were motioned to the chairs on either side of his big desk.

"Have a cigar, Governor," he said. I took it with misgiving because only six weeks before I had smoked my last cigarette—determined to break my chainsmoking habit. I peeled off the cellophane and stuffed the cigar between my teeth. It was incredibly dry, shattering at the slightest pressure.

"Got a match?" he asked quizzically. "No," I admitted, embarrassed because of my guilt feeling in accepting the dry cigar after having sworn off all tobacco.

The speaker reached over and pushed a button on his desk. An aide burst into the room. "Get me some matches," McCormack ordered. Soon there were plumes of smoke issuing from two dry cigars. I did not inhale.

Suddenly the phone rang. It was Senate Minority Leader Everett Dirksen, calling to inform the Majority Leader in the House that a Senate resolution lauding former President Herbert Hoover would be introduced. McCormack held the phone about 6 inches away from his ear. The deep, melodious tones of the Republican Senate Chief were clearly audible.

When Dirksen finished, McCormack, with eyes twinkling, said, "Everett, would you run that past me again? I'm just a poor little city boy, and you country boys are always trying to pull the wool over my eyes." To the obvious delight of the Massachusetss Democrat, the Illinois Republican went through his spiel again.

With the telephone conversation concluded, I was painfully aware that my cigar had gone out, and I had no matches. I cradled it in my hand to conceal the sad state of affairs.

John McCormack said, "You can be sure I will support your project, Governor. It has the okay of the chairman of the House Interior Committee, Wayne Aspinall. Wayne has a reputation of not turning projects out of his committee unless they are okay."

As we walked down the corridor from Speaker McCormack's office, I waited until we had turned the corner before I dropped the dead cigar into the nearest sand pail. What a governor has to go through to serve his state!

The Sweet Smell of Prosperity

Reuben Askanase, a wealthy former North Dakotan, gave North Dakota State University a large sum of money to build a theatre and arts building on the campus. At the April 11, 1967, groundbreaking ceremony, I was seated next to Mr. Askanase's son, who was a businessman in Ohio.

"I note that North Dakota is seeking new industry," the Ohioan said. "What kind of industry do you want?"

"Well, I know what we don't want," I said. "We don't want any of those industries with the belching smoke stacks which smell up the air and pollute the surroundings."

"By the way," I asked, "what work do you do in Ohio?"

"Oh," he said weakly, "I manage Dad's rubber plant in Akron."

I had a sneaking feeling that I had said the wrong thing.

Working on an antelope problem with Casmir Paluck.

8

A Governor Has to (try to) Relax, Too

Starting Can Be Easier Than Finishing

My official and unofficial duties put me in need of occasional recreation. Sometimes the "recreation" became the most taxing part of my duties!

In the early 1960s, the Kennedy family had stirred nationwide interest in physical fitness. Touch football and 50-mile hikes sparked conversations, and President Kennedy's physical fitness program was being pushed in every hamlet across the land.

A day was set aside to proclaim physical fitness for the nation and somehow or other, at age 42, I was drawn into putting on my sweat suit and getting out to jog on the capitol mall to help publicize the physical fitness movement.

A dozen or so joggers turned out that June morning. They included ardent jogging enthusiast Boston marathon runner Dr. Joe Cleary and a couple of St. Mary's High School girl students. The press corps and television cameramen turned out in high spirits to film this ludicrous spectacle.

As we started off from the steps of the capitol and swung along the west side of the mall, we were jogging downhill and the going was easy. Reporters following alongside with their pads and pencils were joking loudly back and forth. TV cameramen seemed to lampoon our efforts when they ran backward in front of us, filming our determined group.

We came around the bottom of the mall and started up the east side. We began to go up the long, gradual grade. The joking suddenly subsided. Huffing and puffing immediately replaced the banter. Cameramen mumbled something about the need to stop and reload film.

As we took the increased exertion going up the east side of the mall, veteran jogger Dr. Cleary glanced over at me and smilingly said, "This is the nitty-gritty side of the course. Have you noticed how it eliminates the men from the boys?" "Yes, and us cigarette smokers, too," I gasped.

I was getting to the point where I didn't have enough breath to carry on any unnecessary conversation, and I envied the cameramen who had resorted to the simple excuse of leaving the pack of joggers to reload their cameras. What business did the Kennedys have in getting the nation so physical fitness conscious anyway, I wondered. Couldn't they have suggested yoga or meditation!

Batter Up

Democratic softball, fortunately, was less demanding.

In the Spring of 1968, Art McKinney, my aide, called an organizational meeting of the softball team called the "Capitol Bombers," made up of over-aged, under-conditioned members of our Democratic-NonPartisan League administration with a few younger people thrown in for good measure.

McKinney explained the upcoming softball season and how the Capitol Bombers had a chance of winning the pennant that year. He suggested facetiously that maybe they should leave Bismarck early and go south for spring training.

John Kerian, highway department attorney, who was never one to pass up a caustic comment, observed, "Yes,

I think our Capitol Bomber softball team should go south and practice. Perhaps Lemmon, South Dakota, would be the place most fitting for our talent."

The organizational meeting, however, vetoed the idea of training in Lemmon, South Dakota, for fear the name might stick, and they settled instead for a training plan, which called for no more than two cigars per player per day.

Faint Praise for the Crew

Some of my recreation was reminiscent of my old naval days.

In July 1964, the Guy family rented a cottage on Madeline Island in Lake Superior, just three miles off the mainland from Bayport, Wisconsin. We were fortunate to have friends vacationing on the island at the same time. The Charles Conrad family was only two cottages away. The Frank Gokey family was down the beach a quarter of a mile in the cottage they owned.

Frank Gokey was an intrepid sailor. He had just purchased a beautiful 28-foot fiberglass sloop, complete with a towering mast and a small diesel engine. Frank Gokey was president of the Bayport Yacht Club that year. Frank invited Charles Conrad and me to act as his crew in a sailboat race the next Saturday afternoon.

When the big day came, we had recruited a Unitarian minister to fill out the crew. A brisk 30-knot wind was blowing down the strait between the island and the mainland. Twenty sailboats left the yacht basin but nine of them turned back because of the wind. Waves were running 4 to 6 feet high. We had never tested the jib sails on the new Gokey sailboat. As Charles and I clung to the bow, struggling with the new sails on the slippery deck, our going was very difficult because of the violent pitching and yawing. Our heavy sweat suits were soaked with cold water.

We ran up a racing jib sail that was larger than the main sail. The wind caught us and laid us on our side. I thought we would never right ourselves as we fought to lower the jib. We tried another jib sail somewhat smaller. This time the wind caught us and laid us over so that the sailboat just stayed in a shuddering position pitching up and down on the waves. We fought that sail down and brought up a third still smaller jib sail. Now the sailboat righted itself and appeared to handle well. By this time, we had drifted and blown far from the starting line of the race. We heard the starting gun in the distance, but by the time we reached the starting line, we were 17 minutes late.

The other sailboats were far ahead on their various courses and tacks. We tried valiantly to catch the other boats for an hour and a half as we tacked against the stiff wind coming down the strait. The other boats disappeared behind a large island around which we had to sail to enter the home stretch. As we finally came around the island with the wind astern, we raised the new spinnaker sail—but upside down. It was then that we noticed that all of our opponents were so far ahead that they were nowhere to be seen. Suddenly, the stiff wind coming in over the stern billowed out the right-side-up spinnaker, and we were on our way down the last leg of the race. Ahead of us, a sturdy little tug boat, pulling a raft of pulp logs that extended a quarter of a mile behind it, was making only about one-half knot. When we passed the tug, its crew waved and pointed, apparently telling us where our sailboat opponents had gone. There were some wry comments as we sailed past the tug. At least we had beaten one vessel in the race.

Only one other person aboard our boat wanted to win our race and get back to harbor sooner than Frank Gokey. That person was the Unitarian minister, who laid in a bunk as ballast during the entire journey, deathly ill from sea sickness. Finally, our boat arrived back in the yacht basin. The other skippers had already tied their boats up, and some were even on their second martini. Frank Gokey was a poor loser. It hurt him to listen to the conversation leveled in his direction. "But my crew was inexperienced," he was heard to say in his own defense.

The end of this story is that Frank Gokey did have an experienced crew the next weekend, Charles Corwin and Perry Clark of Fargo. His crew was so experienced that Frank Gokey, refusing to give way to a competitor, suffered a collision and his boat was stove in so badly that he had to send it back to the factory for repair! It was the crew's turn to wonder about the captain.

You Catch the Big Ones at the Tail Race

Fishing is supposed to be recreation, but I found a lot of frustration in it, too. One day, Jean noted, "Your son, Jimmy, will soon be out of high school, and there will be fewer chances to do things with him. Why don't you take him up to the Garrison Dam tail race this Saturday and do some fishing?"

I could see the truth in her statement. A governor's kids do get lost in the grinding schedule that comes with the office. But, I thought, how should I go about preparing to go fishing when it had been nearly ten years since I had tried to pin a worm on a fishhook?

Jim was agreeable to the fishing trip, but he informed me that worms were not what real fishermen used. I knew I could solve the fish lure problem by consulting my old friend, Jim Thompson, at Sioux Sporting Goods.

"Well I'll tell you what they are catching them on," Thompson said. "These cast iron plugs painted yellow with the tuft of yellow horsehair have the weight you need to get the plug on the concrete bottom of the tail race at Garrison Dam just between the wings. When the plug hits bottom, you start reeling in, and it will bounce up and down. That action has been getting some big ones," Jim promised. "I'll take two," I said, "one for my son and one for me."

When we arrived at the tail race that Saturday, it was crowded with fishermen. They stood shoulder to shoulder along the low mesh railing that allowed them to fish the entire length of the concrete wings. Jimmy and I found a small space near the end of one wing. Whispers, nudges, and sly pointing were running up and down the wings as the fishermen and fisherwomen became aware that the Governor and his son had joined their ranks.

I stooped down and nonchalantly opened the old tackle box I had inherited from my dad. I handed one yellow plug to Jimmy. I kept the other to snap on to the leader I had tied to the old cotton line on my dad's fishing rod. I was faintly aware that most fishermen had graduated to monofilament line and that the bunched cotton line on my reel should have signaled trouble ahead. Then, using my most practiced form, I swept the rod over my head, casting the heavy yellow plug out over the churning tail race water.

But the plug only sailed out about 15 feet where it stopped abruptly and dropped with a bang against the concrete wall five feet above the swiftly flowing water. I looked down at my reel; and, to my horror, I could see that the last one to borrow my fishing rod had left only 15 feet of all-cotton line on the reel. By that time, titters of laughter were breaking out among the fishermen on the wall. My son, Jimmy, vanished in utter humiliation. With embarrassed resignation, I reeled in my yellow plug whose horsehair tail seemed to be drooping. Putting my gear away, I trudged back to the car, wondering how I had gotten myself in such a predicament. Jimmy joined me from nowhere and suggested it was time to go home. All of a sudden, we were both laughing. How could you expect to catch the big ones when your fishing line didn't even reach the water?

Fish Can See But Can They Smell—Yes They Can

Then there was the time in 1962 when John Peterson of Bismarck invited me to again accompany him on a week-long sail on Lake Sakakawea. We planned to sail about 200 miles and planned our provisions accordingly.

John was an enthusiastic fisherman. He had gone to the Red Owl Store and bought a package of frozen smelt to use as bait for the big Northern Pike that were known to inhabit the reservoir.

Jean helped us carry our provisions from our station wagon down a long, steep bank to the dock at Sakakawea State Park where we loaded Peterson's 21-foot fiberglass sailing sloop. Our provisions included foul-weather gear, sleeping bags, extra clothing, food, emergency outboard engine fuel, and such items for comfort as a transistor radio, field glasses, fishing rods, and a tiny gas torch for heating coffee.

As we stowed provisions under the deck, our thoughts were running ahead to the thrill of the gliding movement of a sailboat on a sparkling lake. My wife called down from the station wagon that we had taken on all the provisions that we had brought. We waved goodbye and set sail.

On the second day out, a rather sweet, but objectionable smell became noticeable in the small, two-bunk cabin. We suspected that maybe the pump-operated toilet might be failing to operate properly. By the following day, the smell had grown almost overpowering. Again, we suspected the rather intricate mechanism of the shipboard toilet.

By nightfall, as we prepared to climb into our sleeping bags in the cabin bunks, I decided that something must be amiss and proposed that we unload the entire cargo of provisions and clean the boat from stem to stern. It was a job to get the extra sails out on the dock along with foul-weather gear, lines, anchors, fishing tackle boxes, and the rest.

Finally, in the bow of the boat, just forward of our sleeping quarters, we came across the cellophane-wrapped package of what had once been frozen smelt. It was now a rather mushy, foul-smelling mess. Very gingerly, I moved the aromatic glob through the cabin, up the ladder, and prepared to dispose of it overboard.

"No," John protested, "we can still use them for bait." And so he had me lay them tenderly on the transom at the stern of the boat.

That night, with the forward hatch open and the after-cabin entrance open, we were able to forget the smell as clean, fresh air flowed through our sleeping quarters.

The next day, we set sail again. Everything went fine until we turned to go with the wind. Then, every so often, we were bathed in the sickening aroma of rotting smelt. John did not agree that the smelt were no longer acceptable fish bait. So when John went down to the cabin for a nap in the afternoon, I caused myself to stumble in the stern of the sailboat, "accidentally" knocking the package of rotting smelt into the lake. It was not until John came up to relieve me at the helm that I "discovered" that the smelt were gone.

I am sure that if the smelt were attractive to those big Northern Pike lunkers, they were able to enjoy the smelt without fishing hooks in them.

Fish can be Selective

Following an Interstate Oil Compact Commission meeting in Miami in 1963, I accepted Florida Governor Farris Bryant's invitation to go deep-sea fishing.

I invited North Dakota Assistant Attorney General Gerry VandeWalle to accompany me. Governor Frank Morrison of Nebraska and his aide joined us.

We clambered aboard a Florida Conservation Department patrol boat. Our host provided two heavy deep-sea fishing rods and reels that we held in belted sockets while being strapped into swivel chairs, which, in turn, were bolted to the stern deck. We used frozen smelt as bait.

We cruised a couple of miles off Miami Beach. The high-rise hotels were clearly visible. The smelt drew no attention from our deep-sea quarry. Other deep-sea fishing boats were trolling back and forth with us.

The afternoon wore on. We watched with interest the huge tankers and cargo ships, which passed only a half mile away. I became stiff and thirsty.

"Take my rod while I have a Coke," I suggested to Gerry. He strapped himself down and took the fishing pole. I had just uncapped a cold Coke when Gerry cried out, "I've got one." We slowed to let him work a 21-pound dolphin aboard. Gerry was elated at having caught the first fish of the day as he returned the pole to me.

I settled down with a freshly baited hook and waited for my luck to change. After an hour of frustrated waiting, I was again tired of sitting and holding the heavy tackle. "Want to take my line again, Gerry?" I asked. Soon Gerry was again strapped in the deck chair while I moved around the deck to stretch my stiffened muscles.

Suddenly Gerry jerked back on his pole. "I've got one!" he shouted. We slowed again while Gerry worked a fighting 10-pound silver king mackeral to the boat.

Gerry, proud of his second success, handed the fishing tackle back to me. "Sorry about that, Governor," he said, "I guess I'm just irresistable!"

This time I couldn't even use the excuse that my line didn't reach the water!

Vacationing on Madeline Island, 1964.

Trout fishing with Walter Hjelle on Sweet Briar Lake west of Mandan, 1966.

9

At Governors' Conferences

Oh, By the Way

When I became Governor, I got involved with the Midwestern and National Governors Conferences. The meetings allowed the exchange of valuable ideas and important information. Sometimes they could be challenging and even a little frightening.

In March 1967, President Johnson invited all the governors and their wives to the White House for a conference on state and federal relations. I was chairman of the National Governors Conference at the time and looked forward to the event with some apprehension. I had attended a half-dozen White House luncheons, dinners, and conferences in the past, and I knew a certain amount of protocol had to be observed.

The conference was to open at 9 o'clock Saturday morning in the White House. Friday night, about dinner time, Marvin Watson, President Johnson's aide, called me at my hotel. "The President will open the conference in the morning," Marvin said, "and we would like to have you respond on behalf of the nation's governors. It need not be an elaborate response—maybe 15 or 20 minutes of speaking will do."

I swallowed a bit because 15 minutes of response to the President is not exactly small talk. I was grateful, however, that at least I had the evening to shape some thoughts.

The next morning we were bathed in a feeling of excitement. This came from entering the inner sanctum of the White House, which contained the President, who wielded more power than any other person in the world.

Forty-six governors were present. We were packed tightly in one of the small conference rooms off the President's office. The President came in and gave his opening speech on the importance of state/federal relations. I then rose and, speaking from the same lectern, responded to the President with about a 10-minute talk. My stomach had a knot because of the highly charged atmosphere. When this opening chore was finished, I sat down with a feeling of relief.

As the morning conference drew to an end, we prepared to move to the large White House dining room for the noon luncheon. As I walked down the long outside portico toward the central part of the White House, Former Governor Farris Bryant, aide to President Johnson, quickened his stride to catch up to me.

"The President will make a speech following the luncheon," he said, "and we would like to have you respond to the President's remarks. We will also ask Governor Love of Colorado to speak as a representative of the Republican governors." Once again, that knot in my stomach began to tighten as I wondered what I could say that would be meaningful.

All during the luncheon my mind seemed to churn. I was seated on the President's right at a small, round table containing places for ten. On my right was General Green, Commander of the Marine Corps. He was intent on explaining to me what a good weapon the M16 rifle was in Vietnam. I couldn't have been less interested at the moment as I groped for what I would say in response to the President.

Finally, the luncheon was over. The President rose, and a table lecturn was hurriedly brought forward. The President addressed the governors for about 10 minutes, then sat down amid their applause. The waiters moved quickly to carry the lectern away. I stood up and reached out to let them know that I had an assignment to take care of.

Speaking with what I hoped sounded like a voice of confidence, I again responded to the President. When my short talk was over, I had a feeling of satisfaction that it had been a good one, but by this time the knot in my stomach had another knot tied in it.

All afternoon, we toiled in our White House discussions on state/federal relations. That evening was to be the elegant banquet in the White House dining room. It was a formal banquet with all the dignity and graciousness that is unique to a White House formal dinner.

As I struggled with my tuxedo, the phone rang. My friend, Marvin Watson was calling again. "Bill," he said, "the conference is going great. Now, tonight the President will speak to the governors, their wives, and other guests. Following the President's speech, we would like to have you stand and offer a very brief statement, ending in a toast to the President."

Suddenly the excitement that had made the evening so inviting faded as a thick knot joined the two knots in my stomach. All during the formal dinner that evening, I tried to shape something that would be worthwhile. I am sure that the other guests at that round White House table, which seated ten persons, must have considered me to be somewhat antisocial as I struggled with my thoughts.

Finally, the dinner was over and the President stood and spoke. His words disclosed how concerned he was about the tragedy that was unfolding in Vietnam.

While the President concluded his talk and sat down amid a standing ovation, I knew it was my turn to end the dinner with a toast. Standing there while the applause subsided, I raised my wine goblet and said, "Ladies and gentlemen, may I propose a toast." Then I said, "To the person who has more to do with the future of all of the world's children than any other living being, our President of the United States, Lyndon Johnson."

Fortunately for me, the speaking ended at that point. I had just about exhausted my ability to produce remarks on demand.

I Had the Last Word

Sometimes governors conferences could get intensely partisan.

Just before the 1967 National Governors Conference, which left from New York on the cruise ship, *Independence*, several governors were invited to appear on the NBC "Today" show. As chairman of the conference, I was one. Colorado Governor John Love, a Republican, was another.

We arrived at 6 a.m., New York time, at Radio City in downtown New York. The streets were almost totally vacant except for an occasional garbage truck or newspaper delivery van on its early morning rounds.

When we walked into the empty ground floor lobby of Radio City, we wondered how we were going to find the studio where the "Today" show was being filmed. Suddenly the elevator doors opened, and a familiar-looking man, carrying a briefcase, walked rapidly toward us. "Are you looking for the NBC studio?" he asked. Immediately we recognized the voice and face of newsman Herb Kaplow.

He escorted us up to the correct floor on the elevator, and we soon were behind the scenes of the popular NBC show. Hugh Downs was all smiles behind his desk on one side of the studio. We were seated informally in a stage setting just 90 degrees to one side.

During a break for advertising, Hugh Downs walked swiftly over to be seated with us and in a moment, the show was on. He asked us about the cooperation between President Johnson and the governors. Governor Love spoke up and said that there was little communication between the President and the nation's governors.

I knew that Republican Governor Love was intentionally spreading it a little thick, so when he paused, I challenged him by citing three or four innovations in federal/state relations that could be credited to President Johnson.

I spoke of the special office the President had established, headed by former Tennessee Governor Buford Ellington, for maintaining liaison with the governors. I spoke of the President's approval of the use of the Civil Defense teletype system for sending special messages to the governors from their new National Governors Conference Office in Washington. And I spoke of the personal luncheon meetings that the President had hosted for the governors in Washington and how he had kept us briefed on the Vietnam War.

After the broadcast, when we were sitting in the makeup room removing brown powder that was designed to take the shine off our foreheads, Governor Love turned to me and said, "Bill, you trapped me on the President Johnson question."

I said, "I didn't trap you John, you trapped yourself by not giving a truthful answer." Governor Love scowled a little and said nothing. Governor Love and I have always been good friends, and that little incident didn't change things.

Ronald Reagan

John Love's partisanship was spirited, but honest. I wasn't so sure about Ronald Reagan's.

President Johnson, while appearing to be a man of great ego and self-confidence, had to be assured constantly that what he was doing was right and that it was in the best interest of the nation. He sought that assurance from colleagues, political opponents, other heads of state, editorials, and polls.

I am convinced that Lyndon Johnson got his hands stuck to the Vietnam War tar baby because he didn't know how to let go and still go down in history as a fighter against communism. The President was a walking file cabinet with news articles, editorials, and the latest polls tucked away in a half dozen pockets. To emphasize a point, he often would pull out a handful of clippings, thumb through them until he found the printed proof to back up his point of view.

President Johnson's need for assurance showed itself during the 1967 National Governors Conference. The governors accepted a novel invitation from the Governor of the Virgin Islands to hold their annual meeting aboard a Caribbean vacation cruise ship. That cruise meeting set the stage for a very revealing incident concerning a future president, Ronald Reagan, as well as President Johnson.

The annual Governors Conference is a time when clashing political philosophies can be attached to almost any subject on the agenda. Governors, by nature, are a contentious lot who got to their high office by articulating points of view and verbally jousting with their opponents. I knew when I was elected chairman of the 1967 Governors Conference that it would take some careful preparation on my part to keep the playing field level so that no governor could claim that the conference had been politically slanted against him. As I prepared my plans to chair the 5-day shipboard conference, I had no inkling that it would not be the level of the playing field that would affect the conduct of the governors and the course of events, but rather the slow rythmic tilting of the deck as we rode the waves would cause fire-eating orators to become meekly subdued.

The slight roll of the ship was enough to cause many of the governors to hold their tongues even when the subject ordinarily would provoke a fervent response. It was not unusual for a pasty-faced governor to get up from the big horseshoe-shaped conference table and head for the open

At Governors' Conferences

deck, fresh air, and a horizon. Fortunately for me, the ship's slight movement caused me no more harm than a slight headache, and I was able to move the day's agenda along in an orderly manner.

On the second evening after our departure from New York Harbor, a mailgram was radioed to our ship's mailroom from President Lyndon Johnson to his personal representative at the conference, former Texas Governor Price Daniels. But Daniels didn't receive the President's letter, which was pilfered out of the mail room that evening before it could be delivered.

The following morning when the conference came slowly to life in the bright sunlight that sparkled on a dappled sea, all tongues were wagging about a letter Governor Ronald Reagan had circulated in the early hours only to the Republican governors aboard. It was not an ordinary letter, nor was it a letter to or from Ronald Reagan; it was an undelivered official letter from the President of the United States addressed to his personal representative aboard our cruise ship.

Most of the Republican governors expressed dismay and some were downright angry that Ronald Reagan had implicated them in an unethical and probably illegal theft of U.S. mail.

The letter was a confidential message from Lyndon Johnson to his aide, Price Daniels, asking him to do all he could to generate positive statements from the governors in support of the United States' war efforts in Vietnam. President Johnson sought at least the appearance that the governors agreed with him. Ronald Reagan gleefully offered the letter as proof that the Democratic President was secretly attempting to influence the deliberations of the nation's governors.

The Democratic governors were immediately angry at the Californian's actions. Reagan's explanation that the letter was stuck to the bottom of correspondence delivered to him did not ring true. Why had Reagan not quietly returned the letter to the ship's post office if he had received it by accident? Or why had he not quietly sent it on to the addressee, Price Daniels? Why had Governor Reagan so cavalierly taken the misdelivered or stolen letter and photocopied it for distribution only to the Republican governors? Why did Ronald Reagan see nothing wrong in his actions? Why did Ronald Reagan believe that embarrassing the Democratic President justified such behavior? I became aware that with Ronald Reagan, the end result justified the means. Reagan's judgment of what was right and what was wrong was flawed.

The captain of the ship was furious that Reagan should be so casual about theft from the ship's mailroom—a felony crime anywhere. The captain came to me as the chairman of the conference for my advice on what action he should take. Should he prefer charges against Ronald Reagan and anyone else who might have been involved in the theft? I did not look at Ronald Reagan at that time as a man of Presidential timber, but rather as an easygoing movie actor and semi-celebrity whose skills at governing hardly went beyond the oneline cliches. I assured the captain that the governors did not want charges brought against Ronald Reagan. The contempt with which Democratic and some Republican governors held Reagan's actions seemed sufficient penalty at the time.

The ocean voyage conference continued, and the governors passed a resolution supporting President Johnson's efforts in South Vietnam's civil war.

Drama in the Sky over Illinois

One of the most frightening experiences Jean and I ever had involved my National Governors Conference obligation as chairman.

On Friday morning, November 17, 1967, the big four-engine North Dakota National Guard C-54, commanded by Colonel Marshall Johnson, flew Jean and me from Bismarck

At Governors' Conferences

to Springfield, Illinois. We arrived about 11:15 a.m., making good time because of strong tail winds.

My wife and I had been invited to be a part of the official welcoming party, which would greet Japan's Prime Minister Sato and his wife and about 18 Japanese officials when they stopped in Springfield for a final visit before returning to Japan. Former Illinois Congressman Gale Schisler, now Governor Otto Kerner's aide, met us and advised us over lunch of the elaborate preparations being made to receive the Prime Minister.

At 2:55, the silvery Japan Airline jet rolled to a stop, and the smiling, bare-headed Prime Minister Sato waved from the open door and then led his wife and the large delegation down the portable stairs. Governor Otto Kerner, with outstretched hand, headed the welcoming party. It was Jean's privilege to present a beautiful bouquet of flowers to the Prime Minister's wife. There were bows, smiles, and more bows. After the airport ceremony, which several hundred spectators viewed with a background of lively music from the University of Illinois band, we were whisked to the historic shrine, Lincoln's Tomb. Here the Japanese delegation with hats in hands paid their respects to the memory of Abraham Lincoln. We toured Lincoln's house, which is open to the public. Our guests were soaking up Americana.

That evening, Governor Kerner hosted a gala formal dinner at a large Springfield Hotel. Before the dinner, Jean and I were guests at a small reception for Prime Minister Sato and his wife at the Governor's residence. It was an evening to remember, but one of rather subdued pleasantries because of the need to translate conversations.

The Japanese boarded their waiting jet at 8 o'clock Saturday morning and began their race with the sun on their trip home.

Colonel Johnson had flown the C-54 back to Hector Field in Fargo so another crew could have the benefit of cross-country flight training on a return trip to Springfield.

Because the Air National Guard ferried some guardsmen to Minneapolis for a training course, the big four-engine plane did not arrive in Springfield until Saturday noon.

Gale Schisler escorted us to the airport, and we boarded the C-54 at 1 p.m. The airplane had seen a lot of service. I suspected that it might have been on the emergency coal supply run to Berlin during the historic Russian blockade of that city years before. Now the U.S. Air Force had turned it over to the N.D. Air National Guard to replace an even more ancient twin engine C-47, the "Minnie H," which had served the N. D. Air National Guard for many years and had been placed on the retirement list. Though I couldn't see any coal dust in the cracks along the bulkheads, there was plenty of evidence in the dents and scratches of the long life of hard service the ship had already seen. It was really a cargo plane or troop carrier which had been renovated to try to provide some passenger comfort in its latest role with the Guard.

The return flight commander was Lt. Colonel Alexander Macdonald. The copilot was Lt. Colonel Thornton Becklund. Sergeants Dale Ness and John Meyer completed the normal crew of four. Also flying with us for hours of flight time were Captain Jerry Cover and Lt. Jim Reimers. In the rear compartment, four young airmen occupied the uncomfortable troop carrier seats assigned to them as part of their in-flight training. They were Sgt. T. J. Sullivan, Airman 1st Class Ralph Kieffer, Airman 1st Class Norman Erickson, and Airman 2nd Class Gaylon Aronson.

The executive cabin was just back of the pilot's compartment and had recently been completed with airline seats and fold-away tables. Unlike the windowless rear compartment, there were airline-type windows, which looked out over the long silver wings. Each wing held the heavy weight of two big engines nestled under their burnished aluminum nacelle covers. The huge propellers stood stiff and still. I seated myself, facing forward on the aisle, and lowered the table to begin work on the brief case full of papers I had brought along. Jean also seated herself, facing forward, on the other side of the aisle. We were alone in the compartment.

One by one, the big engines coughed and gasped as they came to life and eased into a steady roar. We waved to our hosts as the big plane slowly turned from the ramp to head for the runway.

The take-off was normal, and we gradually eased up through the heavy overcast to burst out above into bright sunlight. Our cruising altitude, limited by the fact that it was not a pressurized airplane, was set at 8,000 feet. Jean tilted her seat back and prepared to catch a cat nap. I unsnapped my brief case and lifted out a stack of correspondence to study. The air was smooth.

Sometime between 1:45 and 2 p.m., the right inboard propeller suddenly began an acceleration that went from a roar to a high pitched scream. The straining throb of an engine and the runaway scream of a propeller out of control, making nearly twice its normal revolutions, is a frightening sound. I expected corrective action to be taken immediately to subdue that screaming propeller. But nothing happened to bring that engine under control. The noise went on and on.

Almost immediately a veil of black oil seeped out from under the nacelle ventilator flaps and spread back across the wing, splattering the side of the plane in the process. With the engine still wildly out of control, I saw the ventilator flaps slowly spread open around the engine cowling, and suddenly flames burst in the engine compartment.

I didn't know at the moment, but this harrowing episode was caused when a piece of steel broke from a rapidly rotating gear and, flying with explosive force, severed a major hydraulic fluid control line and burst through the wall of the lubricating oil casing. This made it impossible to feather the propeller to take the high-speed strain off the engine. Black lubricating oil poured out of the broken case into the nacelle and out onto the wing. A pressurized system kept feeding replacement oil to the engine as the oil pressure dropped. The out-of-control propeller lost its lubrication and in minutes the propeller shaft became so hot it had ignited the oil being fed into the broken oil casing.

Flames billowed out of the engine ventilator flap openings and up the side of the airplane and across the windows. Suddenly, the scream halted, and I could see the propeller stopped, its hot shaft frozen tight. But the flames showed no sign of subsiding. Then they went out. The co-pilot had fired an extinguisher inside the nacelle. But the flames no sooner subsided than again they burst forth.

The flames appeared to snuff out as a second extinguisher was fired into the engine compartment, but flames burst forth anew. I thought of the 16,000 gallons of gasoline carried on the airplane, much of it in big wing tanks snugged between the two engines. It might only be seconds before it exploded.

One of the two hitchhiking pilots, clad in a bright orange fighter pilot suit, came back to our compartment to gaze intently at the billowing flames. I could see by the white lines in his face that he knew we were on the edge. "The colonel will dive the plane to try to blow out the fire," he said, "be sure your seat belts are tight." He turned and was gone.

The big plane nosed over, and we dove for the cloud cover below. I turned to look at Jean. She looked concerned but not panic stricken. We reached out and held hands and smiled at one another. It would all be over in a few seconds. I didn't expect us to come out of the dive. When we shot into the cloud cover, the cabin was suddenly gray with the red glow of the fire outside dancing in the gloom.

We came out of the dive under the clouds close to the ground, but the fire still burned; and, by then, the aluminum shell around the engine compartment had completely burned or melted away. The flaming engine was stark and black behind the frozen propellor. All manner of tubes, pipes, and braces seemed to surround the engine like a jumble of spaghetti. Suddenly the huge engine fell forward and swung below the wing. Held by that jumble of spaghetti and buffeted by the wind, the engine swung loose and crashed against the underside of the wing. Like a giant hammer, it swung time and again up and back against the big doors to the compartment that held our right-side landing gear.

The engine made one last twirling, pounding thrust against the underside of the wing and broke loose, plummeting toward a large corn field below. The fire was out. And where flames had billowed, a space surrounded by blackened torn metal remained. It was a relief to have the fire out.

Colonel Macdonald came back to share our relief but to caution us that we still had problems. Our hydraulic system was damaged, and we had to depend more on our right outboard engine. We would land at Moline, Illinois, he said.

As we made our approach at Moline, we discovered at low altitude that the left landing gear came down and locked but that the right landing gear remained in its wing compartment behind the metal doors, which the swinging engine had smashed and riveted. Efforts were made to lower the gear manually, and hydraulic fluid was brought forward to compensate for fluid that had been lost. But the wheels could not break out of their smashed doors.

We circled the Moline air field with the dual wheels on the left down and the nose wheel down, but nothing down on the right. Radio contact with the ground spread the news of our critical situation. Saturday afternoon was a bad time for an emergency since experts were off duty. The air speed was cut to 120 mph, the maximum speed at which the lowered landing gear could be expected to withstand the wind pressure. And at that speed, close to stalling, with one landing gear up and one engine gone, the airplane gave an unstable and unresponsive feeling, and the flight was wobbly and uneven.

Again, Colonel Macdonald came back to brief us. He said that the Moline's volunteer fire department was no match for an airplane carrying 16,000 gallons of gasoline, and it had no foam to slick the runway for a landing on one wheel with one wing dragging.

He said we could not raise the landing gear to reduce the heavy vibration from the buffeting wind. We would try for Peoria about 90 miles away. We were maintaining altitude with three engines and slow speed but just barely. Our chances of getting down safely were not good. I thought of the rack of parachute packs that were carried on the old twin-engine C-47. I was sure that we would have had a better chance of survival using a parachute rather than cartwheeling down a runway on one wheel with a load of gasoline. But the C-54 had no parachutes.

The Peoria airport had done the best it could to prepare for our arrival. They used all their limited amount of foam on one side of the runway. From the air, the foam looked like a white postage stamp on a ribbon of concrete. Five firetrucks gathered.

Again, Colonel Macdonald came back to tell us of his decisions. Chanute Air Base had an Air Force fire fighting school and was about 80 miles away near Champaign, Illinois. By now we had been in the air over an hour since the fire had broken out. Our crew had made contact by radio with several sources of help. The fire had damaged our navigation equipment, and we relied on radar on the ground to keep us headed in the right direction. Two fighter planes at a distance seemed to be monitoring our progress.

When we arrived at Chanute Air Base, our right outboard engine was beginning to show the extra strain under which it had been placed, but we continued to circle the field to burn off as much gasoline as possible. The plane shuddered and lurched as we staggered around. Below we could see the long strip of foam being laid on the runway. Fire fighting equipment rolled into position, and ambulances parked near the runway.

At Governors' Conferences

The airplane seemed to be shaking apart. Then suddenly, without warning, the riveted doors holding the right landing gear opened and the dual wheels dropped down. Were they locked in the down position or would they collapse under weight? The electric indicating device for informing the pilot of the wheels' position was out of service.

The decision was made to come in for a landing with the expectation that the right-side landing gear would collapse and our right wing would skid along in the foam.

Our landing was smooth and normal. The landing gear held up, but soon after touchdown, the right wheels locked and skidded, pulling us off the runway into the grassy field. Emergency vehicles converged on us. Men in fire-retardant suits and veiled hats came running with ladders. Our cargo door opened, and we clambered rapidly one by one down the ladders. Jean and I were the first to reach the ground, and instinctively we ran to the safety of the nearest passenger vehicle. The crew abandoned the airplane immediately. After a short conference about returning to the plane, Colonel Macdonald directed the rescuers to remove the luggage and records.

General Demler, the base commander, was on hand in his Saturday afternoon civilian clothes to direct his personnel and to make sure our party was offered the hospitality of the base. Our first concern was to let our families back in North Dakota know that we were on the ground and safe after three harrowing hours.

When General Demler learned that we were having trouble getting commercial air reservations from nearby Champaign to Fargo and Bismarck, he assembled a full crew for his twin-engine training Convair stationed at the base.

Finally, at 6:30 p.m., we took off for Bismarck. We had had nothing to eat since noon, and there was no time to prepare food to take on the Convair. However, all of us seemed so relieved to have survived that we thought little of food. Our Convair crew did have some canned soup and spaghetti to warm up and topped it off with a cookie apiece. It seemed like a banquet.

Fighting northwest headwinds delayed our Bismarck arrival until 10:30 p.m. When we disembarked, we were overwhelmed by our reception, which included a uniformed National Guard honor guard. Our children, who, at one point in the afternoon, had been told by a Des Moines newspaper reporter that our plane had crashed, were the happiest to see their parents home again.

The Convair took off for Fargo and delivered the rest of our party to their home base and loved ones.

Six months later, Lt. Colonel Alexander Macdonald, Lt. Colonel Thornton Becklund, and technical Sargent Dale Ness stood before the National Guard troops at Camp Grafton, and each proudly received the Distinguished Service Medal. They deserved it.

Miami Beach Is a Far Cry From Wyoming

Governor's meetings were also lots of fun, in part, because governors can be a lot of fun—believe it or not.

Jack Gage was the very crusty and colorful elderly Governor of Wyoming in 1962 when we gathered at an Interstate Oil Compact Commission Meeting in Miami, Florida. A dozen or so governors from oil-producing states attended the meeting.

Miami was very promotion-conscious, and one of the local television stations decided to take advantage of the governors' visit to gain publicity. Several governors were invited to appear on an evening panel show.

We arrived at the television studio about 9:30, only to find that there had been a mistake and our show would not begin until 10:30. It was too late to do anything else, so we sat impatiently in the studio, grumbling about having been talked into spoiling our evening that way.

Finally the big moment came, and Governor Gage, Governor Jack Campbell of New Mexico, Governor Price

Daniels of Texas, and I were seated behind the table. Perhaps the wait had irritated Governor Gage. When the announcer set Governor Gage up for the first question, he asked, "How do you like Miami Beach, Governor?" Governor Gage scowled, looked into the camera, and replied, "How do I like Miami Beach? I'll tell you, this place is the damnedest fraud I have ever seen. These hotels are built on sand that is dug up out of the ocean, and there's nothing to this town but sand and neon lights."

The horrified announcer tried to smooth Governor Gage's ruffled feathers. "Why, Governor," he said, "what you've said just doesn't hold water."

Governor Gage rumbled back, "That shouldn't be strange to you because nothing holds water down here."

By this time, the announcer was so flabbergasted at the unexpected responses that he made sure the camera did not return to Governor Gage during the rest of the 30-minute telecast.

Your Order, Please

When governors get together, you are reminded that all is not always as it appears.

The 1967 Governors Conference was held aboard the cruise ship *Independence* on a cruise between New York and the Virgin Islands. After the day's work, the governors and their parties would gather in the ship's cocktail lounges.

One evening when Governor John King of New Hampshire came into a crowded lounge, he thought, "This is a perfect setup for a spoof of governors." So he borrowed a candy-striped, Eisenhower-type jacket, which was the uniform of the waiters, threw a white towel over his arm, adjusted his fake mustache and glasses, and started to wait tables.

As he worked his way through the crowd of people standing and those sitting at tables, he noticed Liz Carpenter, the press secretary to Mrs. Lyndon Johnson, seated at a table. As Governor King, in his candy-striped jacket, passed the table, he reached down and picked up Mrs. Carpenter's newly poured martini, raised it to his lips, and downed half of it before he set it down again and walked on. Mrs. Carpenter, not recognizing Governor King, rose from her seat and with a cry of outrage, said, "Did you see that waiter?"

Governor King walked to the table where Nelson Rockefeller was entertaining friends. Governor Rockefeller gave his order, and Governor King promptly asked him if he was eligible to sit in the Governor's Lounge. When Nelson Rockefeller said, "Yes," Governor King, still unrecognized in his waiter's uniform, said, "Do you have any proof of identity?" Obediently, but taken aback, Governor Rockefeller reached into his wallet and hauled out five or six credit cards and other means of identification. Finally, satisfied, Governor King took abject Governor Rockefeller's order.

John Bailey, the Democratic National Chairman, with his glasses perched characteristically high on his forehead, had just ordered a round of drinks. Governor King intercepted the waiter, taking the tray full of glasses to John Bailey's table. When Governor King delivered the glasses to Bailey's table, Bailey, absorbed in conversation, absent-mindedly placed a dollar bill tip on the tray.

Governor King, playing his waiter's role to the hilt, took the dollar bill disdainfully threw it to the table, and said, "A tip like that is hardly worth picking up." Whereupon the confused John Bailey reached into his billfold, took out a second dollar bill, and neatly placed it beside the first.

About 15 or 20 minutes later, the management led a smiling and triumphant Governor King to the bandstand microphone and explained that the ship had to apologize for the rudeness of one of its waiters, who just happened be Governor John King of New Hampshire behind a false mustache.

At Governors' Conferences

Governors Are a Sorry Lot

Rough cut and garrulous Jack Gage, the Governor of Wyoming, told about a trip he had made to a governors' meeting in Houston, Texas. He was driving the state Cadillac with the "#1" license plate on it and was alone in the car.

Governor Gage was a very informal person who rarely took the time to dress the part of a governor.

When he arrived at the conference hotel in Houston, he pulled up at the front entrance, went to the back of his Cadillac, opened the trunk, and started to lift out his luggage. One of his suitcases burst open, and clothing and other personal effects were rolling around on the pavement behind his car.

The uniformed doorman stood on the curb and remained aloof of the accident. Governor Gage looked up angrily and asked, "Could you give me a hand in collecting all these things?"

The doorman surveyed Gage coolly and said, "Do it yourself, man! What do you think the Governor pays you for anyway!"

If Governor King could look like a waiter, I guess Governor Gage could look like a chauffeur.

You Can't Judge a Book by its Cover

Then there was the time during an evening reception at the 1968 National Governors Conference winter meeting in Washington, D.C., when I noticed a quiet man standing alone away from the boisterous crowd talking and laughing in small groups around the long hors d'oeuvres table. I immediately felt sorry for this man, who others were ignoring and who seemed a bit uncomfortable in such a sophisticated crowd.

I introduced myself and asked him what his name was.

"Copeland," was his reply. "Lamar Copeland. I'm from Delaware."

"Do you work in state government?" I queried.

"Yes, I'm on Governor Terry's staff."

Knowing that governors' staffs could include people from speech writers to office managers to press people, I asked him what his duties were.

"Oh, I only work for Governor Terry part-time," he said almost apologetically.

"What is your work the rest of your time?"

"Well, the rest of the time," he said with a faint smile, "I'm president of the Dupont Corporation."

I was talking to modest Lamar Dupont Copeland who headed one of the largest corporations in America. You can't always judge a book by its cover!

Civil Disturbance

George Custer came into my mind more than once in those gubernatorial years.

In 1969, a funny incident, which I thought was a sign of the times, happened in my office. General Vernon Mock, the commander of the Fifth Army stationed at Fort Sheridan near Chicago, took a swing around the nine states in his command area to become acquainted with those states' governors.

General Mock, a rigid, spit-and-polish, no-foolishness-type of military officer, had just returned from a tour of duty in Korea.

He strode briskly into my office, followed by a colonel who was his aide. Accompanying them was North Dakota's National Guard adjutant general, LaClair Melhouse, and a major who was his aide.

I marveled at generals. They wouldn't venture out unless a colonel or a major was along to open doors and hang up their coats and hats for them.

At Governors' Conferences

General Mock said, "Governor, I know these are trying times. I know that we have had civil disturbances across this nation in recent months, and I am sure we will have them in the months ahead. The riots in Detroit and the burning of Watts are the kinds of unrest we cannot accept."

"I want you to know that the Fifth Army, with its headquarters in Chicago under my command, is highly trained to handle civil disturbances. We are poised to respond at a moment's notice if any governor requests our presence."

"Well, General Mock," I said, "I doubt that we will have the type of civil disturbance that would require the Fifth Army to respond. As a matter of fact, I have a dim view of calling in the military to settle these problems. The last time we called on the military to settle a civil disturbance, the outcome was highly unsatisfactory. We have never even received a report from the man in charge of the operation."

The General's eyebrows flew up, and his jaw stiffened, as he asked sharply, "Who was in command of that operation?"

I hesitated a moment, then answered, "General George Custer!"

The General's stern visage did not soften, but our National Guard officers seated behind him had to stifle their chuckles.

Do Something That Will Make Headlines!

At an annual Midwestern Governors Conference in Michigan, each governor was required to entertain the state dinner guests with a humorous story about his state.

"How many of you know that General George Custer was a Democrat?" I asked. There was a roar of laughter. "Really," I said, "it is historically true. Custer was so much a Democrat that James Gordon Bennet, the famous New York newspaper editor and Democratic Party kingmaker, called him back east. 'General, I can secure for you the

Democratic nomination for President of the United States,' Bennet announced. 'But you need to be better known. Go back to Dakota Territory, and do something that will make headlines!'"

When the laughter had subsided, I suggested that "you can overdo a thing, especially in politics. Legend has it that the Indians did General Custer in. But my experience with seven Republican legislatures in North Dakota raises a reasonable doubt in my mind."

Was General Custer Really a Democrat or a Republican?

My Republican friends in North Dakota got edgy when I reported the historical fact that General Custer was a Democrat. So to placate them I concocted this story to shed a bit of the General's fame on the Republican Party:

> General Custer was a delegate to the Dakota Territorial Republican Convention meeting in Mandan. During that Republican convention, he received his orders to march west against the marauding Sioux. Dutiful soldier that he was, the General returned to his post at Fort Lincoln and gathered his troops for the sortie to the west.
>
> While leading his troops away from Fort Lincoln, he rode through the streets of Mandan. As he came abreast the Territorial Republican Convention Hall, he stopped his horse in front of the open doors. Leaning over his saddle horn, he shouted, "Don't do anything till I come back!" He didn't, and they haven't.

Top: Accepting the chairmanship of the National Governors Conference in Los Angeles, 1966.

Bottom: Opening a meeting of the National Governors Conference with President Lyndon Johnson in the meeting room of the Oval Office. Ferris Bryant, aide to President Johnson, is at the podium. February, 1967.

10

Off to Vietnam

President Johnson Backed Down

My long tenure as chief executive of North Dakota and my chairmanship of the National Governors Conference resulted in my being asked to observe the presidential elections in South Vietnam. It was one of the most interesting experiences of my life.

Midway in August 1967, I received a telephone call from Marvin Watson, President Lyndon Johnson's chief aide. Marvin, in his soft Texas drawl, asked me if I would be willing to leave in 10 days with 21 other selected election observers to view the preparations and the actual election in which the people of South Vietnam would go to the polls to elect the first president in their history. He explained that because the United States was fighting to bring democracy to Vietnam, President Johnson thought it important that our country have credible and objective observers on the election scene to make sure that it was carried out honestly.

I was taken aback by this unexpected request. My first reaction was not favorable because I visualized a long, hard trip in the kind of heat and flies that I remembered from my Asian experiences in Uncle Sam's Navy during World War II.

"I need some time to think it over, Marvin," I stalled.

"How much time do you need?" he asked.

"I will have to talk with my wife and then I will call you back."

"Oh, one other thing," Marvin said, "since you are chairman of the National Governors Conference, would you pass the President's request on to Governor Richard Hughes of New Jersey, Governor James Rhodes of Ohio, and Governor Tom McCall of Oregon?"

This I agreed to do; and in a matter of hours, I had talked to those governors and found them a bit apprehensive but willing to go if the President requested.

My wife was out of town, but I expected her back that afternoon. As I thought about the opportunity that had come my way, I thought that I shouldn't pass up a chance to get another North Dakotan named election observer, too.

Watson had told me that some high-powered academic types, though not designated as observers, also would be included on the trip. This group, I learned, was led by Richard Scammon, the well-known political scientist.

I thought of my Director of Administration, Lloyd Omdahl, who was on the verge of leaving my office to assume new duties as a professor of political science at the University of North Dakota.

At 2 o'clock the same day, Marvin Watson called again. "Well, what do you think, Bill?" he asked. "Are you willing to accept the President's request?"

I still hadn't spoken with Jean and the thought of going to South Vietnam still did not appeal to me, but I said, "I will go if you will let me take along another North Dakotan. I can bring a man who understands practical politics and who would be excellent in analyzing this election for posterity." I had in mind Lloyd Omdahl, but I didn't mention his name.

Off to Vietnam

Watson resisted. He said, "The President has given no one the opportunity to take along an aide."

"But this man would not be my aide, Marvin," I protested. "This man would be pursuing the President's objective of watching and reporting on the election process."

"Does your going hinge on taking this man?" Marvin asked.

"Frankly I haven't made up my mind to go at all," I replied, "but I think I could tell you right now that if you would approve another North Dakotan, I would accept the President's request right here on the spot."

"Okay, it's a deal," Marvin said and hung up.

I was overjoyed because I knew that this was an opportunity that very few political scientists around the country would pass up. When I enthusiastically informed Lloyd Omdahl of his stroke of good luck, I was shaken by his reply that he wouldn't make the trip. "I'm moving my family from Bismarck to Grand Forks," he explained, "and I have a great amount of work that must be done in preparing the assignments for the courses I will be teaching in a few weeks."

I was disappointed, but only for a few moments. Walter Hjelle would be an ideal person, I thought, since he was experienced as a former legislator and a former Democratic State Central Committeeman. He, if anyone, would understand the practical politics and democratic process which we would observe in South Vietnam.

Since I had not identified the North Dakotan to Marvin Watson, I did not hesitate to invite Walter Hjelle to accompany me. Walter leaped at the opportunity; and, in a few hours, we were arranging for the shots that had to be taken, and getting our passports ready. I never had used a passport before, and it was no small trick to get everything in order in a few days.

The local hospitals, of course, did not have all of the shots that are required for such diseases as cholera, plague, and malaria. I was shaken a bit when the nurse who gave what shots were available informed me that some of them wouldn't even take effect until I had gone to South Vietnam and had returned home. But the law required that we go through the procedure.

It so happened that the Midwestern Governors Conference was meeting about the same time at Tan-Tara Resort in Missouri. We planned to fly to Tan-Tara in the highway department's twin-engine Beechcraft C-45.

Our Governors Conference stay would be cut short a day so we could get to Washington in time to board the big, sleek Boeing 707, dubbed Air Force II, and head for Vietnam. That plane was identical to and was used as backup for the President's plane, Air Force I.

As we flew south toward our Missouri destination in smooth air, our pilot, Kenny Kampa, suddenly turned his head and shouted through the cabin curtains that President Johnson wanted me to call him at our fuel stop in Sioux City, Iowa. I thought someone must surely be pulling my leg, but in about 20 minutes, we landed in Sioux City and rolled up to our fueling station.

An employee came rushing out to say that the President indeed wanted me to return a call to him in Washington. As I stood in the cramped little charter flying service office, I wondered if this was reality or was I dreaming? But I dialed the number; and, in a matter of seconds, I heard the soft Texas voice of Marvin Watson.

"Bill," he said, "the President has decided that it will not be possible for you to take another North Dakotan along. If he were to allow you to have an aide, he would have to allow all of the other 21 observers to take aides."

Just then a very familiar voice broke in with a Texas accent, saying, "Bill, I am sorry; the aide is out."

I recognized the voice of the President. I was startled to think that the President would involve himself in such a trivial matter, but here he was involving himself.

Off to Vietnam

"I am sorry to hear that, Mr. President," I said, "because I thought I had a firm agreement with Marvin Watson, and the man I had planned to take along is with me on this flight at the present time."

"Did you tell the Governor that, Marvin?" asked the President in our three-way conversation.

There was an embarrassed pause, and finally Marvin said, "He may have gotten that impression, Mr. President."

"Well," I said, "I certainly did get that impression, but if you want to renege on the promise I will still go as an observer."

"We are not reneging on anything," the President said. "It is just that we could never have made such an offer."

I said, "All right, I'll be in Washington day after tomorrow to leave on Air Force II."

I felt very dejected when I returned to our airplane to tell Walter Hjelle that his going on the trip to Vietnam had been cancelled but that he should go along with us to Tan-Tara and take in the Governors Conference.

It was a subdued flight from then on as I fumed about having been out maneuvered by Marvin Watson and the President.

When we arrived at the beautiful lodge at Tan-Tara Resort on Lake of the Ozarks, I found a message in my key box. "Call the White House," it said. So I placed a call to Marvin Watson, thinking that perhaps this message might be for the call that I had already answered at Sioux City.

"Bill," said the soft Texas voice, "I guess I have seen something I never expected to see."

"What's that?" I asked.

"I have seen the President change his mind, and this is a rare occurrence," he said. "The President has decided that you can take one of your North Dakota friends along on Air Force II."

"Thank you, Marvin," I said. "I knew that you would keep your word," and hung up, elated at the change in plans.

Two days later, Walter Hjelle and I were settling back in the spacious seats of Air Force II, winging our way west to an unforgettable adventure; and to this day, it is hard for me to believe that President Johnson did change his mind or even took the time to be involved.

Most Mayors Were Army Officers

In South Vietnam, many of the officials spoke French and, in some cases, spoke English quite fluently.

Our 1967 election observer team arrived in war-torn Da Nang under the protective guidance of a squad of heavily armed Marines. One of our stops was a visit with the mayor, an appointed official who wore the uniform of a colonel in the South Vietnamese Army.

Our party was escorted into his large official conference room where we settled ourselves in comfortable but low chairs. Tea was brought and placed on the low tea tables around the room.

The mayor had his official interpreter seated beside him. We very carefully selected the wording of our questions to the mayor so there would be less chance of their being misunderstood as they were translated to him.

All went harmoniously until the time came for the meeting to be opened to questions from a half-dozen newspapermen who had accompanied us. One of the newsmen directed a question to the mayor's interpreter. "Ask the mayor," the newsman said, "why the corruption that we see everywhere in South Vietnam is so prevalent in his city."

As the reporter finished his sentence, the young mayor's eyes blazed, and he didn't wait for an interpretation. In perfect English and with a voice heavy with anger, the mayor snapped back, "There is no corruption in Da Nang. Your observation is typical of biased United States news reporting!" And he slammed his fist on the table.

Off to Vietnam

Suddenly we were all aware that the young mayor of Da Nang had not needed the interpreter, through whom we had been feeding questions, but spoke English as fluently as any of us in the room.

Apparently the interpreter had been used to build a protective wall to give the mayor time to reflect on his answer or perhaps to misunderstand the question.

Generals Are a Close-knit Group

The South Vietnam governmental palace, still a new building when I visited it as an election observer, had a huge, carpeted reception room where many official functions took place.

Premier Thieu held an official reception for all the election observers from foreign countries. The Vice Premier, General Ky, was also present. These two men looked trim and sharp in their highly styled and correctly tailored western clothes.

General Thieu, a proper, no foolishness-type of person, was a relatively young and capable administrator.

His Vice Premier, General Ky, was quite different. Ky, slender and flamboyant, reminded me of what the dashing hero in a Southeast Asia mystery plot should look like. He spoke English well but, in speaking, used the hipshooting style, which often left embarrassing statements for reporters to print.

I asked the smiling Vice Premier if the coming election would change the command of the South Vietnam armed forces if he and General Thieu were not elected vice president and president, respectively.

Ky laughed in that careless sort of manner and said cryptically, "It would make no difference because we generals are a close-knit group, you know."

He seemed to be saying that it made little difference whom the people elected to head their country because the military was strong enough to work its will wherever and whenever it wanted.

Last-Minute Campaigning—South Vietnam Style

It was the night before the South Vietnamese Sunday general election. The election was to take place under the staggering handicap of Viet Cong terrorist activity and the fact that every village, hamlet, and city seemed to be part of the front lines.

I had flown to Saigon that morning from Da Nang stopping briefly at Na Trang. The food or the water had disagreed with my system, and I felt weak and dizzy. After dinner, many of the election observers went downtown to watch the 11 candidates for president make their last appeals at election rallies, which were being televised. But I felt too sick to want to leave my quarters in the old United States legation building.

At 10:45 that evening, I popped a sleeping pill into my mouth and lay down in my darkened room on the second floor. Only a faint light shone through the cracks in the slatted steel, bulletproof shade that had been lowered over the outside of my bedroom window.

As I was drifting off to sleep, the sound of a violent explosion outside the building jolted me upright in the darkness. The explosion was followed by the sound of running feet outside my door and the the sharp crack of rifle fire outdoors. Soon I could hear in the distance the wailing sirens of emergency vehicles that seemed to be converging toward our part of the city.

My first thought was that something was wrong and that I had no weapon with which to defend myself. My state department guide was billeted down the street a few blocks, and he carried the .45 we shared in his brief case.

I got out of bed, guided by the light coming from under my door. I moved through the darkness to the door leading to the hall where a young, plainclothed Marine was stationed 24 hours a day as a second-floor security guard. I asked the young man sitting at his table, with automatic pistol out and with walkie talkie radio set crackling, what had happened. He said, "I don't know, but there has been an explosion in front of the building."

I was sleepy from the effects of the sleeping pill, so I told him I would lie down for a few minutes and would check again when he had more information. I fell asleep immediately and slept until the alarm went off at 5 o'clock the next morning.

As I stared up at the ceiling trying to get fully awake, I wondered if I had dreamed about an explosion the night before. I stepped out in the hall and asked the Marine if I had dreamed of an explosion.

"No," he said. "A Viet Cong terrorist on a small motorcycle came down the blockaded street in front of the legation. Two Army MPs in a jeep moved out from the curb to intercept him. When the terrorist saw he was being cut off, he threw a grenade at the jeep, blowing it up just below the windows of the legation."

Strangely enough, the two MPs in the jeep were not injured. They calmly stepped from their disabled vehicle and used their rifles to bring down their adversary. They immediately radioed for an ambulance and other security vehicles. That accounted for the explosions, rifle fire, and sirens I had heard and reassured me that I had not been dreaming.

I went downstairs to breakfast. Governor Tom McCall of Oregon, who was also staying in the building, had already arrived at the breakfast table and was reading the morning paper.

"There sure is a lot of destruction and killing around this city," Tom said. "Doesn't it make you nervous?"

I was trying to transport some slippery apple jelly to my toast when I answered, "No, I don't think I feel nervous." At that moment the slippery jelly left my knife and landed on the tablecloth.

Tom smiled and said, "I suppose you always drop your jelly on the tablecloth in the morning."

I got the point. Perhaps I was a little nervous.

Bill Guy Remembers

Election Day in South Vietnam

At 6:45 in the morning of a bright, hot day, Senator George Murphy, three guides, a free-lance reporter, and I lifted off the Saigon airport runway in a small Air Force executive jet and headed for Tuy Hoa, about 200 miles north along the coast.

I had not been successful in getting a Bismarck TV reporter, Jess Cooper, who just happened to be in Saigon, aboard our executive jet. Jess had called the night before, seeking to follow me on my itinerary. The Air Force said it would accommodate Jess and Ron Cross from the Minneapolis *Tribune* on a propeller plane, which it would put in the air earlier than our jet.

Dan Leady, senior U.S. aid officer, met us at the Tuy Hoa airport. There was little traffic that Sunday morning, and no armed security was in sight. Cooper and Cross had not arrived. I asked to have a vehicle wait at the airport for them, while we went to the headquarters of Province Chief Colonel Ba. On our 15-mile trip from the airport to Colonel Ba's headquarters, we drove through several hamlets, crowding the one-lane road. We bumped over temporary repairs on a bridge that the Viet Cong had blown up a few days before.

Colonel Ba was a sharp-looking, ageless man who spoke English. We were drinking tea on an open veranda, waiting for Jess Cooper and the other newsmen to arrive, when a distant blast rolled across the city that stretched out below our vantage point. The Colonel stopped talking in mid-sentence. In about five minutes, an aide approached Colonel Ba, saying that a bomb had exploded at a polling place. The Colonel looked at his watch. "That is the polling place you were supposed to be at now if you were not waiting for your newspaper reporters."

The bomb blast dampened our host's mood for light conversation, and we left. Dan Leady took us to his house. I protested the lack of security. Leady explained that the

Off to Vietnam

State Department wanted no armed U.S. security people visible on election day, lest foreign observers would think the United States was forcing its will on the election process. I pointed out that Mr. Swan, our 29-year-old Vietnamese driver, certainly could be armed without exciting adverse comment. Senator Murphy and I decided to sit tight until more security was provided and until the reporters arrived. After all, we said, the reporters are the ones who are the most valuable objective observers of this election, and if we don't wait for them, they might not be able to catch up to us.

Jess Cooper and reporter Dave Dyhe finally arrived at Leady's home at 11 o'clock. By that time, our security had been beefed up. A truck and two jeeps with four armed Army personnel in civilian dress had been added. Mr. Swan had a pearl-handled revolver in a belt holster, and an M16 rifle was shoved between the front seats. Our guide had a .45 automatic. We began to feel that we could respond if we ran into trouble.

The polls opened at 9 o'clock and closed at 4 o'clock. Each polling place had an air of patriotic competition. They seemed to try to outdo one another. South Vietnam's colors of yellow and red were painted on the two-foot-square ballot boxes, and yellow-and-red bunting was draped everywhere. That first presidential election was a festive affair that reflected the hungry pride with which the South Vietnamese viewed democracy.

Polling place officials and workers were unpaid. At least twice as many people manned the polls as in our country. Poll watchers representing individual presidential candidates took their work seriously. Many young women were part of the polling place team. They did not like to shake hands, but their male counterparts shook our hands warmly, often grasping our hands with both of theirs. The flow of traffic was important in the polling places. You entered at a specific door and left from another. Arrows painted on the floor emphasized that you stay in line. When the voter entered, his or her name was checked off the precinct register list. If a would-be voter's name was not registered, that person was turned away. I saw a platoon of 20 soldiers in uniform turned away because they were not registered in that precinct.

Each voter received 11 ballots containing the names of the 11 teams of presidential and vice presidential candidates. Each ballot also had a symbol identified with the candidate so the many voters who couldn't read could make a choice. The voter chose one ballot and slipped it into a small envelope. The ballot envelope was raised high above the voter's head so all could see it and follow it as it was ceremoniously lowered and tucked into the ballot box.

After a voter had voted for president and vice president, he or she was given 48 ballots containing 48 slates of 10 candidates for the national senate. The voter selected 6 ballots and, in effect, voted for 60 candidates. Again, the ballots were placed in an envelope, raised high, and slipped into a ballot box. Unused ballots were unceremoniously dumped on the polling place floor. As each voter left, he or she again had to produce their identification and voter qualification card, which were stamped and from which a corner and part of the stamp mark were cut off. The small triangular corner from the card was strung on a wire as documentation of the number of voters casting ballots.

We visited the polling place, which would have been our first stop that morning had Jess Cooper's late arrival not delayed us. A time bomb in a brief case placed beside the polling place had gone off at the precise time that a mimeographed itinerary had said we would be there. A second satchel bomb placed just outside the door had failed to explode. Three people in the polling place had been killed, and about 60 people had been wounded. The polling place was closed for an hour while they cleaned up the wreckage and then was re-opened. When we arrived, a large crowd was patiently waiting to vote, most of them hunkered down in the 100 degree heat in the dusty courtyard that still showed traces of dried blood. I was impressed. I wondered

Off to Vietnam

how many polling places in the United States would remain open after people, trying to disrupt an election, had blown out a wall. I also wondered who was behind mimeographing our itinerary and distributing it—and why did we have an itinerary?

We visited a half-dozen polling places of our choosing that day and neither saw nor heard evidence of election fraud. The noticeable civic pride among election officials and voters was underlined when we learned that 85 percent of the country's eligible voters had cast their ballots in that first election. Why had so many voted? Were they pressured or rewarded for voting? Our Vietnamese driver said it best when I asked him why he had voted. He looked at me with some surprise in his eyes. "Because I'm a citizen," he replied quietly.

With California Senator George Murphy (l) and Admiral Kenneth Veth (c), a native of Minot and chief of naval operations in South Vietnam, 1966.

11

Foreign Customs Abroad and at Home!

A Fish Tale

Secretary of Agriculture Orville Freeman asked Jean and me to represent him at a huge food fair in Tokyo. While we were busy selling North Dakota pasta products, sunflower seeds and wheat, our Japanese hosts were preparing a banquet which contained nothing I was used to eating.

I attended that official dinner hosted by a Japanese governor of a state that included part of the city of Tokyo. We were seated on the floor in stocking feet. Our legs were crossed under tables barely eight inches from the floor or were tucked up uncomfortably under our chins. The flat pillow on which we sat did little to ease the hardness of the floor beneath.

This was a state dinner served in high Japanese style. Waitresses brought on the courses while a geisha girl dressed in a kimono sat at each official guest's side to make conversation or to refill the tiny saki cup.

Everything went well until the raw fish course was placed before me. I have always taken a dim view of eating any meat raw, and raw fish was not appealing. I knew that

I must not insult my Japanese host if I could avoid it. So I drew on my powers of self-hypnosis. I imagined that I was a United States Navy flier whose plane had gone down in the ocean in the South Pacific. I had been floating in my rubber raft for 12 days without anything to eat. Suddenly a small flying fish popped over the side of the raft into my lap. I looked at the flying fish as my only hope of living a few more days.

And so, carefully convincing myself that I was a starving Navy pilot eating raw fish at sea, I picked up the raw fish set before me at this elegant state dinner, and I was able to force down my serving of the piscatorial delicacy.

Our Japanese host was watching me curiously. He must have noticed the look of determination on my face as I tackled the raw fish. He smiled and nodded his head, very pleased.

For a few moments, I feared that perhaps the geisha girl assigned to me would suggest that I take a second helping. She did not, and from that day until now, I have avoided being shot down in the South Pacific and having to eat raw fish.

The Japanese Checked the Lay of the Land

Another time we had the Japanese governors on our home grounds or so I thought.

The executive committee of the National Governors Conference hosted a 1967 reception in Des Moines, Iowa, for eight visiting Japanese governors and their wives. As chairman of the National Governors Conference, my wife and I were first in line to meet them as they stepped off their chartered jet aircraft.

There were many smiles and much bowing. Language was a definite communications barrier. Fortunately they had brought along their own interpreters.

After several hours of rest, the guests arrived at the reception room before the state dinner. I watched carefully

Foreign Customs Abroad and at Home!

to observe their reactions to the elaborate preparations that had been made in the hotel room to underline our hospitality.

A large supply of saki, the Japanese rice wine, had been laid in and was prominently displayed on the bar. As each Japanese governor gave his order to the bartender, he drew on his limited command of the English language and instead of saying "saki," in every instance, the order was "scotch." The saki went begging.

When the formal dinner was finished, it was time for speeches. As chairman, I stood up to give my short welcoming speech. I would stop after each sentence to let the interpreter translate my words into Japanese. I was alarmed to find the interpreter speaking a dozen sentences in Japanese for each sentence I spoke in English. Was he adding more thoughts than I was speaking or does the Japanese language require more speaking to convey a thought? I never found out.

When the leader of the Japanese governors arose to give his response, his lovely wife, dressed in a beautiful Japanese kimono, stood and turned solemnly toward him and with hands pressed together in a prayerful gesture, bowed slowly and sat down. With this traditional sign of subservient support from his wife, the speaker launched into his response with confidence.

That night as I tried to sleep, I was conscious of the city noise. The clatter of air hammers and the throaty roar of heavy trucks made sleeping difficult. Night work on an urban renewal project was in progress.

At breakfast the next morning, I asked the Japanese governors how they had slept. They smiled and answered emphatically in Japanese. The interpreter smiled, "Des Moines is so much more quiet than Tokyo; we slept very well!"

That morning, eight United States governors sat with their Japanese counterparts around a huge doughnut-shaped table. We all wore earphones so that we could enjoy simultaneous translation as we spoke to each other. It worked well.

The Japanese had chosen the subject of the conference, the shift of population from rural areas to cities and what the United States was doing to bring about a rural-urban population balance. This was a major problem in Japan.

We were embarrassed to have to admit that the United States was doing very little, if anything. As a matter of fact, Americans had not yet admitted that they had a population distribution problem. On the other hand, if our cities were that much quieter than Tokyo, maybe we didn't have much to worry about yet.

A Visit to Canada to Celebrate the Canadian Centennial

Canada is not as exotic to Americans as is Japan. But with their British heritage, the Canadians tend to do some things differently.

In the early Spring of 1967, Premier Duff Roblin of Manitoba invited the Guy family to officially represent North Dakota at the opening of the Pan American Games. That olympic-type sporting event would be held in new facilites in Winnipeg as part of the Centennial observations of Canada's federation of provinces. Thirty countries from the western hemisphere sent athletic teams to participate.

We accepted Premier Roblin's invitation because we believed it was our official duty to help to celebrate Canada's Centennial, especially since Manitoba had entertained Jean and me and our North Dakota Legislature at a Peace Garden reception on the occasion of our 1961 Dakota Territory Centennial celebration. But I also was interested in this invitation because I would have a chance to scout the possibility of establishing an international tourist loop with Saskatchewan, Manitoba, Minnesota, and North Dakota, similar to the five-state "Old West Trail" tourist loop I had pioneered for North Dakota, South Dakota, Nebraska, Wyoming, and Montana in 1962.

Foreign Customs Abroad and at Home!

We set forth from Bismarck on July 16, driving the state's blue Cadillac with its "#1" license plate. We took six days, exploring some of the spots that might comprise an international tourist loop.

Our arrival in Winnipeg was an event to remember. It was 5 p.m. when I stopped our car on the hot pavement in front of the City Center Motel. While I checked our reservations, I left the car running to maintain its air-conditioning. Suddenly a cloud of steam poured out from under the car, accompanied by a loud hissing noise. My family tumbled out of hastily opened doors, perplexed at the sudden turn of events. I raced to the car and stepped through a widening puddle of hot water as I reached in to shut off the engine. The hissing and steaming gradually subsided.

I guess a passerby must have read the look of consternation on my face because he stepped forward, handed me his card, and announced that he represented the one and only Cadillac garage in that city of more than a half million people.

Could he be of assistance? He sure could, and in 15 minutes a tow truck had raised our rear wheels off the pavement and was pulling us to the garage. Our problem was a ruptured radiator hose. But they had no replacment hose, so they fashioned an L-shaped hose, held apart at the bend by a stiff piece of screen door spring inserted inside. What a relief to find an ingenious mechanic on duty on a Saturday afternoon!

Sunday was the opening of the Pan American Games, for which all Manitoba had prepared for years. But rain threatened. Premier Roblin sent a government car and a military driver to pick us up in time to arrive at the newly built stadium at 2 o'clock.

As we drove through the heavy traffic, we were greeted by ominous raindrops, which soon forced us to use our windshield wipers. Our driver let us off at the pass gate.

We had to dodge puddles as we walked along with the spirited crowd.

Our seat location was the best. We were seated in molded fiberglass chairs in the Premier's box next to the oval track. The stadium was full of people who had paid $12 each to see this historic event. Canadian Prime Minister Lester Pearson was a guest in the box in which we were seated. Security personnel were seated or stationed discreetly about because Prince Phillip, consort to Queen Elizabeth, would review the marching athletic teams from this box.

We seated Holly and Nancy in reserved seats behind us and halfway up the stadium. We helped them make a shelter out of our blankets because light rain was coming down with little sign of subsiding.

Jean and I each wore a raincoat, and Jean wore a plastic hood to protect her hair. I was hatless. The rain collected, drop by drop, in my crewcut and then begin trickling down my face and neck. We soon found that our raincoats were rain repellent but far from waterproof.

Holly and Nancy finally gave up, their wet hair plastered to their heads. With teeth chattering, they pleaded to return to the motel. We sent them back with our driver.

Things perked up when the convertible carrying the Prince entered the stadium. He sat on the top of the backseat, waving and smiling to the crowd as the light rain fell on his bare head. His car stopped in front of our box, and he was escorted to a position of honor from which he would stand for the next hour, reviewing uniformed teams of athletes who marched by.

Appropriate opening ceremonies featured raising the new red-and-white maple leaf Canadian flag and the Pan American Games banner. A runner burst into the stadium bearing a lighted torch. His route took him up the aisle to the top of the stadium where he was to kindle the flame, which would signal the opening of the games. Because of the continuing rain, the officials had taken no chances with a sodden wick. The flame was already lit when the runner arrived to symbolically dip his lighted torch to the already dancing flame.

The rain continued. The crowd began to diminish, and vacated seats appeared. Prince Phillip stood erect, gamely smiling and waving in a rather reserved way as each contingent of athletes splashed by. The raindrops glistened in his thinning hair, combed straight back. He refused a hat or an umbrella. Two Scotland Yard-type security agents stood on either side, but slightly ahead, of the Prince at a level about three feet lower than the raised dias that supported him. They looked glum and soaked.

By the time a third of the teams had marched by, I was wet to the skin. The people in the chairs ahead of us had raised their umbrellas. The water dripped off their umbrellas onto our laps. The people seated behind us had raised their umbrellas. The water dripped off their umbrellas and ran down our necks. I looked down at the bucketseat chairs in which we were sitting. The water had filled them level full so that they sloshed over when we shifted our weight. I felt like a lump of sugar in a saucer of coffee. It gave us little comfort to watch Prime Minister Lester Pearson as he sat bolt upright, letting the rain pelt down on his homburg hat. When the hat brim filled to spill-over level, the dignified chief executive of all Canada would lean forward to allow the accumulated water to cascade from his hat to the floor.

The marching athletic teams were resplendent in colorful uniforms. Only the huge contingent of 400 athletes from the United States was equipped with rubberized blue rain capes. All teams sloshed through the puddles that had formed on the cinder track.

The teams were of different numbers. The Cuban delegation nearly stole the show. They wore white slacks or white skirts, topped by smartly tailored red blazers and red tams. When the smiling Cubans marched abreast of Prince Phillip, they reached into their red blazers and almost as one drew small Canadian maple leaf flags. These they waved to the obvious pleasure of their Canadian hosts.

As one very cute, young Cuban girl came opposite the Prince, she slipped back the front of her blazer and reached for a small object attached to her waist. Her action was so swift that it was all over before we realized that she had just snapped a picture of the Prince with a small camera attached to her belt. Her triumphant, smiling face was in sharp contrast to the anxious faces of the two security agents assigned to guard the Prince. His Royal Highness, however, returned the girl's smile with a genuine smile of admiration for her ingenuity.

When the last team had filed past our reviewing stand, I felt so uncomfortably cold and wet that I hated to move. I helped Jean to her feet. As she walked to the exit, her hand-knit wool skirt weighted with water, stretched and lowered with each step. By the time we reached our car, her skirt had stretched nearly to her ankles. We felt so miserable we could only laugh and admit that we would never forget this day.

There was barely time for me to take a hot bath and get ready for a formal black-tie stag dinner at Leftenant Governor Knowles' government house. In the Canadian goverment, the Leftenant Governor represents the Queen of England. His function is largely ceremonial, and his residence is a bit of Britain. This stag dinner was to honor Prince Phillip, who was to return to England by commercial jet later that evening.

About 40 men had been invited to the dinner. The Prince took his receiving line station promptly at 7:30 p.m. I joined the ranks of the slowly moving line, feeling very uncomfortable in my black tuxedo on this muggy July evening. As I came closer to the Prince, I was suddenly panic stricken, having had no experience addressing royalty by their proper titles. The humorous anecdote, which had Mayor Cermack of Chicago greeting King George of England with a "Hi, King!" flashed through my mind. In desperation, I turned to the Episcopal minister who was next behind me in line. I quickly told him my problem. The

Foreign Customs Abroad and at Home!

greeting was not, "Hi, Prin!" I was told, but rather "Your Highness." I barely had time to get a firm grip on this greeting before I was shaking hands with Prince Phillip.

He was a very genial, sincere man with a quick smile and a firm hand clasp.

We were seated at a single, long narrow banquet table. The Leftenant Governor sat across the table from the Prince. I sat to the right of the Governor and within easy conversational reach of the royal guest. I was surprised that I was the only person from the United States present. Most of the guests were Canadians, though I did meet a general from Mexico.

The Prince kept up a rapid conversation with those around him. His eating habits were strictly European and lay somewhere between the gluttony of King Arthur's court and the Canadian practice of eating peas with a knife. I marveled that the Prince could keep his slender athletic figure with such a prodigious appetite.

"Your state capitol is Bismarck, is it not?" the Prince asked. I was amazed that he would know the capitol of North Dakota. I said, "Yes, it is."

"Why did your founding fathers choose a German name rather than one of those romantic Indian names?" was his next question.

I was not sure that I knew the correct answer. "A relatively large part of North Dakota's population is of German extraction," I explained. "Perhaps a German immigrant in a position to name this frontier town chose a name from his country of origin." I realized that Prince Phillip, though married to the Queen of England, was himself a descendant of German royalty.

I mulled over the events of the evening as I returned to the motel. I wondered how the husband of the Queen of England had known that Bismarck was the capitol of North Dakota. However he did it, a politician could admire that kind of ability even though that politician didn't know where his state capitol's name came from.

Powder Puffs to Cigar Puffs

Sometimes I found our own customs pretty strange.

In 1966, my wife and I were among 150 guests at a state dinner hosted by President and Mrs. Johnson in the White House. The guest of honor was German Chancellor Ludwig Erhardt.

As usual at White House dinners, the guests were seated at round tables that accommodated 10 people. A woman prominent in Washington, D.C., social life acted as hostess at each table.

I was seated next to our table's hostess, the wife of the nationally known attorney, Abe Fortas, who later would be appointed to the U.S. Supreme Court. Mrs. Fortas was a tiny, feminine person in her 60s.

After the elegant dinner, Mrs. Fortas reached down and picked up her purse from the floor. Opening it, she took out a slender tin box which contained four cigars. I marveled at how thoughtful she was to bring cigars for the male guests at her table.

But my assumption was wrong. She took a large cigar out, jerked off the cellophane wrapper, and popped the cigar between her lips. I reached for the matches, but lacking in the sophistication required to light women's cigars, I fumbled the job badly. A member of the German diplomatic delegation seated on the other side of Mrs. Fortas came to her rescue and lighted the stogie.

Fifteen minutes later, uniformed servants carried ornate boxes full of cigars to all of the tables as after-dinner gifts from the President. I declined the proffered gift because I had given up smoking. But Mrs. Fortas, knowing a good cigar when she saw one, reached into the President's cigar box and neatly extracted three of them.

Tea Time

In December 1966 at the Greenbrier resort hotel in West Virginia, the National Governors Conference convened the first of what would become annual winter meetings. I was chairman of the conference.

The Greenbrier Hotel was one of the largest and most stately resort hotels in the world and did things in an elegant and dignified way. In the morning, at a white clothed table, supporting a sparkling silver coffee service, coffee was served to all who wished it. In the afternoon, those who wanted took tea at the lobby tea table.

I approached the tea table and asked for a cup of tea, more as a novelty than in any fit of desire, as I seldom drank tea. The primly dressed waitress behind the tea table asked me if I wanted lemon in my tea. I said, "Yes, plenty of it, please, and put in some cream, too."

She gasped a little at my instructions and said stiffly, "Sir, you do not use cream and lemon together in tea."

Who was she to tell me how I liked my tea, I asked myself.

So I said bravely, "Well, I do." And so she went ahead and added a liberal squeezing of lemon and some very thick cream.

I picked up my cup and saucer, and acting as worldly as I could, I began to drink. Almost immediately, I noticed that the cream was forming a very thick curd in my cup. The waitress was watching me closely, and I had to admit inwardly that it was indeed an embarrassing situation to be so wrong and unsophisticated.

With carefully planned steps, I maneuvered myself behind a large potted plant in the lobby and hastily put down my cup full of curds. Then looking as satisfied as I could, I beat a hasty retreat from this experience of taking tea in the afternoon.

I could handle coffee in Amenia, but this tea in West Virginia was just too much!

Top: A joint meeting of Japanese and American governors with simultaneous translation in Des Moines, 1967.

Bottom: Speaking to the Manitoba legislature from a balcony overlooking their chamber as Governor and Mrs. Frank Farrar of South Dakota look on, 1969.

12

Famous North Dakotans

Stuck With the Sausage

As Governor and First Lady, Jean and I became acquainted with a number of famous North Dakotans. That was pleasurable for us because North Dakotans are proud of their accomplished sons and daughters and because our famous natives are loyal to the state. One of our favorite native North Dakotans is Lawrence Welk.

Jean was thrilled to learn that Lawrence would be staying with us at the Governor's residence when he returned to North Dakota in the summer of 1961 to receive the first Theodore Roosevelt Rough Rider Award, our state's highest official honor.

"I will have a breakfast for Lawrence and some friends," Jean said. "I will cook the kind of breakfast that will bring back memories of his years as a boy on the farm." Our maid, Mrs. Wald, of German-Russian descent, suggested delicious, juicy, spicy, fried German-Russian sausages. "Just the thing," Jean thought, and she ordered 20 pounds from a meat market at Glen Ullin.

Finally, the great day—or really the great evening—arrived. Lawrence Welk and his Irish tenor, Joe Feeney, came on the 10 o'clock flight. They were dog tired from a full day of entertaining in South Dakota. As soon as they settled on our front-room couch, Jean asked if they would like some coffee and a cookie before bed. This suited Joe fine. But Lawrence raised his hand and said, "Please, only a glass of milk."

When he had been served, he reached into his jacket pocket and drew out a small envelope, containing a powder that he sprinkled into his milk. "What's that?" I asked.

"Don't you watch my TV program?" Lawrence laughed. "Those are vitamins. I've been on a diet for 26 years."

I glanced at Jean. She looked concerned. "Are there some foods you don't eat?" I asked.

"I never eat fried foods."

By now Jean's jaw had dropped. "I imagine you would make an exception for those delicious German-Russian sausages," Jean asked hopefully.

Lawrence slapped his knee, reared back and laughed. "Boy, that stuff would kill me," he exclaimed. Jean was crushed.

Do I need to explain that we had a supply of German-Russian sausage for three months after that episode?

What Goes Up Must Come Down

Perhaps we assumed Lawrence was a sausage-eater because we knew what North Dakotans would go through to get good sausage.

For a number of legislative sessions, Secretary of State Ben Meier and Senator Gail Hernett hosted an evening sausage feed in the banquet room on the roof of the Patterson Hotel. From 6 o'clock until 9 o'clock, the hotel lobby swarmed with legislators, lobbyists, media people, state bureaucrats, and friends of the hosts. A rickety elevator, run by a gnarled little old man, was the only transportation to the sausage feed. The elevator was an antique, cage-like device that moved slowly, shuddering suddenly when the knot in its rope went over the pulley. You could watch the peeling walls, greasy cables, and weights pass by as the elevator went up or down. Slowly the elevator raised the crowd to the noisy gathering where the aproned hosts doled out plate after plate of hot juicy sausage.

The crowd was so great that people had to leave continually to make room for new arrivals. The departing guests, full of sausage and beer, crowded around the single elevator door. When the door opened and the elevator disgorged its passengers, there was a crush of those seeking to enter to get down to the ground floor. Walter and Norma Fiedler had missed a chance to board the rickety elevator cage. When it returned to the top, Norma was carried by the pressing crowd into the elevator. Turning, she saw the door close with Walter still trying to enter.

"Oh, Walter, we're going down without you," she said in a loud wailing voice. "Quiet lady," the little old elevator operator said. "This isn't the Titanic, you know!"

Get a Firm Grip on Your Club

Lawrence Welk couldn't eat sausage, but he and his family certainly had a taste for good food.

In 1967, Lawrence returned for his annual visit with his mother, brothers, and sisters who lived in and around Strasburg. Welk was an enthusiastic golfer. If the weather was right, he would play golf every day he was in North Dakota.

We made a date to meet at Bismarck's Apple Creek Country Club one late August morning. Welk had already played nine holes when I arrived.

A shapeless mass enclosed in aluminum foil had been placed in the tray at the front of his golf cart. He reached down and opened it gently. "Have a piece of kuchen, Bill," he said. "My sister made it fresh in Strasburg last night."

I had never tasted kuchen before and did not know what I was getting into. I discovered that it was something like an open-faced fruit pie with a soft, sticky, cake-like bottom crust.

After working the delicious piece of kuchen into my mouth, I discovered that it left a residue of stickiness on my hands like I had never experienced before. All through the nine holes, I noticed that I was gripping my clubs better. I do not know whether I can credit the sticky kuchen for the firmer grip, but on that round I did lop a few strokes off my score.

Lawrence Welk Wunnerful, Wunnerful

The date was September 28, 1971, and the hour was 3:30 p.m., Pacific Standard Time. We entered the rear entrance of the old ABC TV-filming studio in Los Angeles to watch a dress rehearsal for an historic TV show.

Lawrence Welk was making a comeback on his own "Lawrence Welk Network" of some 200-plus TV stations across the United States. ABC had not renewed the Champagne Music Makers' contract for the coming 1971-72 winter season and Lawrence Welk was not about to let a little thing like the loss of a network contract slow him up. He was making a TV show based on his recently released autobiography, *Wunnerful, Wunnerful*.

The passageways leading from one part of the building to another were narrow, so people moved back and forth in a single file. But somewhere in the heart of this battered old building, a suite of rooms still retained a sense of elegance. These were the rooms that contained the dressing and relaxing facilities for the stars who had used this television studio over the years.

Lawrence Welk, a lont-time friend of the Eisenhowers, had just returned from Washington, D.C., where he had been one of the featured guests the night before at Mamie Eisenhower's birthday party.

Because there were no windows and because all light came from electric or fluorescent bulbs, we soon lost track of the time of the day as we became immersed in the unreal world of costumes, makeup, and stage props.

The large room that served as Welk's off-stage office and reception room was full of talking and laughing people. Most of them were part of his business staff, but others were members of his family or well-wishers like ourselves. Coffee and cookies were available, and a dozen conversations were going on in all parts of the room.

Welk moved around, chatting with this group or that. He was relaxed and fit looking under his golf-course tan. His rigorous work schedule did not seem to bother him at all.

The only way you could find complete quiet was to slip into his private dressing room and close the door. His dressing room was exceptionally neat and spotlessly clean, not like the messy movie version of the stage dressing room.

His private barber had come to give a few minutes of attention to Welk's hairstyle, which had not changed in years. A wardrobe attendant was standing by with his change of clothes for the performance later that evening.

Big George Cates, the enthusiastic musical director who had been with Welk for more than 20 years, took us down the narrow passageways and up a narrow flight of stairs to the long booth that overlooked the stage below. But the booth was not the typical glassed-in balcony that is part of many studios. It looked like a small model of the military situation room at the North American Air Defense Command in Colorado. A dozen small TV screens in a curving console dominated the mass of small levers and buttons that controlled lights, cameras, sound, and colors. Intense operators, all wearing headsets for conversing among themselves and crew members on the stage below, shifted sound volume, lights, and shades of color as the cameras recorded the show.

Bill Guy Remembers

The dress rehearsal was on the chaotic side. People seemed to take their jobs lightly with considerable laughter and bantering off stage. The smooth-flowing television show that you see on your home TV set misses much of the interesting action that those in the studio witness.

Performers tore off their costumes and squirmed into new ones, fixing their makeup in the process, to come dancing into view of the camera as though they had been preparing for this moment for several hours.

The huge cameras on their little rubber wheels moved back and forth soundlessly across the smooth floor, their heavy cables snaking out behind for performers to trip over or avoid as they ran from one scene to the next.

Jean and I were invited to appear briefly on the show and converse with Welk. In the dress rehearsal, this seemed like a very relaxed assignment, but during the filming of the show, the tension mounted to an almost unbearable level as we waited to step forward into the glaring lights in front of the little staring eyes of the television cameras.

The director stood to one side of the camera, and started and directed the action with a sweep of his arm. There was no stopping because the show was being filmed continuously for one hour. Timing had to be observed carefully.

During the final filming, Lawrence Welk was his usual somewhat intense self before the cameras. Welk was never able to relax fully in front of the camera in quite the warm and wonderful way he did before a live audience or with his friends.

He didn't trust his memory or extemporaneous speech and stuck closely to what he called ''idiot cards,'' which were 18" x 18" with his script printed on them in marking pencil. An assistant quickly shifted the cards into their position just over the camera lens as Welk read the message he had to give in commercials or in his banter between numbers.

That program was historic because it was based on Lawrence Welk's autobiography, *Wunnerful, Wunnerful.* About one-third of the show's hour-long action stemmed from his experiences in North Dakota. There was a scene of Welk playing the old organ in the living room of his parents' farm home near Strasburg. That rather sedate scene shifted to the rousing two-man show that Welk and George T. Kelly performed in one-night stands in the little North Dakota towns.

The Champagne Music Makers played and sang a song about North Dakota while scenes from films by Fargo photographer Bill Snyder shifted from waving wheat to sunsets on Lake Sakakawea. North Dakotans couldn't help but have a catch in their throats at these scenes, which Welk's music so beautifully highlighted.

While all of these acts were flowing by, the audience, seated in theatre chairs in the back of the huge hayloft-like studio, could see the show live before them or they could monitor it on a large television screen on either side of the room.

The ceiling of that cavernous studio was a jumble of hundreds of spotlights of all sizes and colors. They came on and went off or changed intensity as the sensitive color filming required.

The scenery moved silently up and down on ropes as the back of the stage became an elegant ballroom with lighted chandeliers at one moment and a church sanctuary at the next moment.

Performers would finish one scene, rush off camera, circle around behind it, and come on-scene on the other side of the stage without the television camera's picking them up.

To the live audience in the studio, it was a humorous display in which we all held our breath hoping that no one would trip or lose his hat in his flight from one side of the stage to the other.

As the show came to a close with the bouncy Champagne Music Maker theme song, we all left our theatre seats to dance for a few moments to the remaining strains of music, and then the show was over. The director was elated. "We are only 20 seconds over," he smiled, "and there were no flaws in the entire production."

Lawrence Welk was a perfectionist. He gently demanded perfection from his performers and got it. His performers were more than just members of the Champagne Music Makers, they were individual stars whom Welk was able to shape by his genius and his encouragement.

There was no question but that Lawrence Welk was pleased with the show in more ways than one. In a way, he was saying in a subtle manner that it doesn't make any difference how humble your origin, a person has a chance to make it big if he is willing to work hard and has the God-given talent to go with it. Welk was the living example.

Do You Have Proof You Are a Guest?

Early in 1974, Jean and I received an invitation from Lawrence and Fern Welk to visit them at their BelAir home in the foothills on the edge of Santa Monica, California. We were gearing up for the start of my campaign to gain a seat in the U.S. Senate. The vacation invitation from the Welks was a happy diversion from campaign planning for what we knew would be an exhausting political battle with Senator Milton Young.

The view from the Welk's beautiful home was spectacular at night. It looked out over the sea of lights that was Los Angeles and that extended forever, it seemed. An indoor swimming pool and an outdoor putting green made their home appear to be the celebrity's palace it was. One somber note was struck, however, when Lawrence grabbed my arm to prevent me from opening a door to a small balcony. "All doors and windows have electrical security devices installed in them," he explained. "We can only use the doors for which I have turned off the alarm." I discovered that many people in the cities of California are virtual prisoners in their own homes—so great is the threat of crime.

Jean and I did not stay in Welk's BelAir home but were given the key to the beautiful Welk apartment in the new building in Santa Monica adjacent to the huge new office building, which the Welks owned and which contained offices of the Welk organization, a bank, and Southwest Bell Telephone Company.

"On your way back to North Dakota," Lawrence said, "I want you to stop at our new winter home at the Indian Wells Country Club, just a few miles south of Palm Springs here in California. We're proud of that home, and it has a nice outdoor swimming pool."

"The house has 24-hour security, and all windows and doors are electrically secured," Welk said. "When you get to our house, go to the back door with this key. You will notice a small red light glowing above the lock. When you turn this key in the slot under the light, it will go off indicating that you can use the same key to unlock the back door. But," he cautioned, "when you close the back door, it will automatically lock, and the electric security will be activated again. And," he added, "remember, too, that there is an alarm sensor under the rug in the hallway." His hallway warning seemed of little significance because we could use the back entrance at all times, and we would stay out of the hallway.

When we drove through the closely guarded gate into the grounds surrounding the Indian Wells Country Club, we seemed to have entered paradise. Winding streets passed between manicured lawns, exotic shrubs and small trees, blazing flower beds, and palm trees of all sizes. The golf course lay up against the craggy rocks of a mountain, and huge new expensive homes lined the fairways. Lawrence Welk's home had a back yard adjoining the golf course. A large swimming pool lay next to his house.

We had no trouble finding the little red warning light at the back door, and the key turned it off and let us in the door to the kitchen. It was a large new house with a vaulted ceiling and much Mexican decorative tile in its construction.

The next morning Jean and I slept late in the guest room of Lawrence Welk's winter vacation home. We were alone in the house and in total silence. I lay in bed and reviewed in my mind the fascinating two weeks of travel to new places we had enjoyed. I thought of the irregular meal hours we had been forced into and the snacks that always tasted good at the time, but caused a guilt feeling if not gas pains soon after. "I'm sure I've gained 5 pounds on this trip," I groaned.

"Why don't you go down to the master bedroom and check your weight on Lawrence's scale," Jean suggested. "I'm sure there will be one there because when he is here, he checks his weight daily."

I slid out of bed and into my clogs. The hallway from the guest room to the master bedroom was long and passed by the big arch leading to one end of the living room.

As I padded along the hallway, I had almost reached the master bedroom door when all at once pandemonium broke loose. A buzzer rattled the windows, and a piercing shriek seared my eardrums. And through it all, I heard the telephone ring. All noise stopped when I picked up the receiver.

A stern voice said, "Identify yourself please." I hardly got my name out before the voice snapped, "Stay where you are, a patrolman is on his way." I put down the phone and raced back to the guest room. "We're going to have company," I warned. I pulled my slacks over my clogs. Before I could tuck my night shirt into my trousers, the front doorbell rang.

I clop, clop, clopped in my clogs over the tile floor in the dining room to the hallway carpet at the front entrance. Wasn't this the hallway rug that was supposed to be bugged? I asked myself.

When I swung the big door open, there stood a beefy patrolman behind dark glasses and dressed in a natty tan uniform with gun holstered on his hip.

"You live here?" he asked.

"No, we're just guests," I said weakly. I knew that, having just gotten out of bed and still being in my nightshirt, I looked like I had just arrived on a slow-moving freight.

"Is the owner home?"

"No, he is in Santa Monica."

"Do you have proof you are guests?" was his next unsmiling question.

My flustered mind wouldn't function. Then suddenly I remember that in our suitcase was Welk's letter which we received two months back inviting us to visit them in Santa Monica.

"Wait a minute," I said. "I'll try to dig up some proof."

The security man read the letter carefully.

"Can I see your driver's license?"

He looked at me, and then the license and then back to the letter. "Okay," he said, "but please be careful about tripping the alarm again."

As I closed the door, still trembling, I pondered how confining this strange need for security was for those who live in the fast lane.

If You Can Get a Project to Drain my Quarter

Sometimes one could run into accomplished North Dakotans by accident. After all - they're all over the world. I remember the time *Life* magazine devoted one entire issue to the exposure of pork barrel projects the U.S. Congress was supporting. Although it didn't come right out and say so, I thought *Life* magazine was condemning the work of the Bureau of Reclamation and was coming much too close in its criticism of the Garrison Diversion Irrigation Project, which North Dakota was seeking.

I wrote a letter to the editor of *Life* magazine, protesting that all water resource development projects were not pork barrel as it inferred. As a matter of fact, the water users on irrigated farms and the hydroelectric power users in the river basin where the water resources were being developed would repay the cost for a Bureau project like the Garrison Diversion Irrigation Unit.

I received a rather facetious reply from the managing editor of *Life*, Edward Thompson.

> Dear Governor Guy:
>
> If you can figure out how we can develop a water resource project that can drain the water off of some low, swampy land I own in Walsh County, North Dakota, I might be persuaded to go along with your defense of some of these pork barrel projects.

This was the first inkling I had that North Dakota could claim a distinguished member of the news magazine profession as its own. Ed Thompson turned out to be a man with a remarkable sense of humor and a great feeling of loyalty to his native state. In 1968, he received the Theodore Roosevelt Rough Rider Award, the highest recognition North Dakota can give. After leaving *Life* magazine, Ed Thompson founded and was editor of the *Smithsonian Magazine*.

A Contact Lens

One thing I learned was that you can take the people out of North Dakota, but you can't take that great North Dakota compassion, decency, and downright friendliness out of the people.

In the fall of 1967, Jean and I journeyed to New York City to spend several days planning the opening of the National Governors Conference, of which I was chairman.

While in New York City, Ivan Dmitri, a former North Dakotan who won the Theodore Roosevelt Rough Rider Award in 1962 because of his prominence in etching and

Famous North Dakotans

color photography, arranged a luncheon with some interesting people. I was seated at a long table in the elegant old Plaza Hotel with TV commentator Eric Sevareid on one side and *Life* editor Edward Thompson on the other. Also present were several North Dakotans and prominent members of the New York business world.

As our pleasant luncheon drew to a close, my wife suddenly began glancing at her napkin, then her lap, and then the carpet around her chair. "I have lost one of my contact lenses," she said. This was a new experience for me because Jean had been wearing contact lenses only about a month.

Nearly everyone at our table moved their chairs and got down on their hands and knees and combed the carpet inch by inch. Waiters stopped their work and put down their trays to try to find the tiny bubble of glass, apparently hidden against the very ornate, patterned carpeting. Diners at nearby tables patted their mouths with white napkins and clucked sympathetically. If I hadn't known the price of one of those contact lenses, I would have sneaked out of the huge dining room on my hands and knees just to avoid the embarrassment.

After moving chairs and table without avail, we finally sorrowfully told the head waiter where we were staying in case the tiny lens was found. As we were leaving the elegant lobby, my wife decided to stop in the powder room. Suddenly, after a 10-minute wait, the powder room door burst open, and my wife came charging out, almost shouting, "Bill, I found it; I found it."

I said, "You found what?"

"I found my contact lens," she said.

"Was it in the hem of your skirt?" I asked.

"No, it was down in the corner of my eye!"

All that effort of these famous North Dakota natives served no purpose—except, that is, for showing the kind of people they were.

Top: With Eric Sevareid in Minot, 1964.

Bottom: With Pat (Mrs. Roger) Maris at the State Capitol, 1971.

Jean and I with Lawrence Welk on the set of his show, 1971.

13

Representing North Dakota

North Dakota — Cleaner and Greener

One of my jobs as Governor was representing North Dakota to the nation and the world. I always tried to give a positive imiage to people who knew little about our state.

Ever since radio began covering national political conventions, the delegates have attempted to use whatever means possible to publicize their states. It was not unusual to hear a delegate answer roll call by saying something like, ''The great and wonderful Garden State of XYZ casts its votes for John Doe.''

I wondered how I could give North Dakota a little positive publicity when, as leader of our state's delegation at the 1968 Democratic Convention in Chicago, I answered the roll call vote to adopt the Democratic Party platform.

As I mulled over all of the short, terse compliments I might say about my state, I remembered a conversation with our capitol guide, Ernie Ames. He had told me of a tourist who signed our capitol guest book with the remark that North Dakota was cleaner and greener than any other state. Why not use this, I thought, and maybe add a little to take the edge off our cold winters.

So, when the voice of the woman secretary of the convention called through the echoing amplifier system for North Dakota's vote, I stood up at our delegation's microphone, and, reading my message off a scrap of wrapping paper, I said, "North Dakota—the state which humbly admits to being cleaner and greener than any other state in the summer and whiter and brighter than any other state in the winter—casts 24 votes in favor of the platform."

It wasn't an earth-shaking announcement, of course, but I felt satisfied that I had said a lot in a few words, and I wouldn't get any challenges from any other state.

I didn't impress everyone because Norman Mailer, in his book about that historic 1968 Democratic Convention, told of this brief theft of precious convention time when North Dakota announced its balloting for adoption of the platform.

The self-congratulating slogan stuck and later it was even stenciled on the green trash barrels at North Dakota's interstate highway rest areas.

What Was That You Say?

Political conventions can enhance your state's image, but that's not inevitable.

At that same 1968 Democratic convention, North Dakota was one of the states, which tried to divide its votes somewhat along the lines of the support shown for Senator Hubert Humphrey and Senator Eugene McCarthy at the state convention. McCarthy had been allotted six delegates, who were pledged to vote for him on the first ballot, and Humphrey had 18 delegates, who were pledged to vote for him.

Though our delegates were pledged to vote for certain candidates, there was no legal reason why they must vote for anyone in particular.

When the moment arrived at the Chicago National Convention to begin the first ballot to nominate a President, the tension was high. The gigantic convention hall, teeming with people from the uppermost shadows near the rafters down to the crowded sections on the floors, amplified the electric atmosphere that actions of primary battles in many states and intraparty struggles had precipitated.

As leader of the North Dakota delegates seated behind our sign under one of the balconies, I had ballots passed out to the other 23 delegates. They wrote their votes on slips of paper and placed them in a hat that had been commandeered for the occasion. I heaved a sigh of relief when the ballots counted out to 18 for Humphrey and 6 for McCarthy.

To give recognition to our state chairman, Larry Erickson, I invited him to stand at the microphone and call out North Dakota's vote when our turn came. Finally the moment arrived, and the secretary called out over the cavernous convention hall, "North Dakota." Larry glanced nervously at the torn piece of brown paper sack that I had scribbled the vote on and then, with great confidence, called out, "Six votes for Eugene McCarthy and 24 votes for Hubert Humphrey."

Almost immediately, the voice of the woman secretary shot back over the amplifying system in the convention hall, "North Dakota, you do not have that many votes." Larry was plainly disturbed. He glanced over at me and mumbled something about, "We must have two alternates in our section," and started over again by calling out through the public address system, "Six votes for Eugene McCarthy and 22 votes for Hubert Humphrey."

Again the familiar voice thundered through the convention hall, "North Dakota, you do not have that many votes." Larry's face had turned pale, and he looked over at me and said, "My God, what's wrong?"

I, too, was shaken because he was reading my handwriting. Suddenly I realized that instead of writing down 18 votes for Humphrey, I had inadvertently put down the delegation's total of 24. In a flash, both Larry and I realized what was wrong, and for the third time Larry's voice boomed out, a little less certain perhaps, over the public address system, "Six votes for Eugene McCarthy and 18 votes for Hubert Humphrey."

"Thank you," droned the voice of the convention secretary, but she was drowned out by the waves of laughter from delegates who thought it funny that little North Dakota was having trouble tabulating 24 votes at the National Democratic Convention.

King Olav V of Norway

One of my interesting tasks was to welcome distinguished visitors to the state.

Since North Dakota never had officially received a king before, this was an entirely new experience for my wife and me. We had been involved with the limited protocol that is observed among congressmen, ambassadors, prime ministers and the like, but we never had played host to a king with all of the protocol that surrounds royalty.

The sun was shining brightly, and a whispering breeze barely moved the crisp spring air at Fargo's Hector Airport that May 5, 1968, morning, as three small executive jets swooped in to land. The first jet rolled to a stop, and the advance staff of security men and newspaper reporters scrambled out. The jet carrying Norway's King Olav V rolled up a few minutes later.

What would the King look like? The first man down the step smiled; he was not the King! He did not indicate how the King would make his appearance. I don't know what I expected, but it seemed as though ruffles and flourishes from drums and bugles should always accompany the appearance of kings.

Suddenly, a smiling, tanned man appeared at the doorway in what appeared to be a rather battered felt hat. He almost bounded down the short steps to the ground. Instinctively, I reached out my hand to greet him, but groped for a moment for the correct words. If he were really the King, I knew that he must be addressed as "Your Majesty." He had a firm grip. A rather high voice clipped his fluent English in a manner that reminded me of an Englishman rather than a Norwegian.

He was dressed in a gray business suit with wide, wing-tipped lapels. He wore a gray-silver tie. He moved quickly down the rather informal reception committee line, shaking hands, smiling, and laughing a bubbling laugh that always seemed to break forth from just beneath the surface.

A crowd of 200 people strained against the airport fence, snapping pictures as he strode toward them. But rather than go up to that crowd and shake hands as most politicians would, the King moved directly to the Governor's blue Cadillac, which was flying a flag of Norway and an American flag on opposite fenders.

Ambassador Gunneng and Consul General Seyersted were senior members of the King's staff of about 15 people. Representatives of the United States Department of State and the Secret Service were on hand to smooth the way for the monarch and to protect him.

The reception committee, which included Senator Quentin Burdick and Fargo Mayor Herschel Lashkowitz, as well as other prominent North Dakotans, took their places in cars in the caravan that would take the King to his first public appearance in Island Park. My wife and I were seated in the back seat of the Governor's car with the King. He sat on the right side so that those standing along the curb could see him easily. Chester Serkland, the Norwegian Vice Consul in Fargo, and a Secret Service officer rode in the front seat. The Governor's chauffeur, Walter Dockter, drove.

The El Zagal patrol, in their brightly colored uniforms, provided an honorary escort with their flashy motorcycles. A Fargo police car led the caravan.

All along the road, people craned their necks and moved to the curb, seeking a glimpse of the King of Norway as the cars moved down the streets. There were shouts of "There he is!" and from the children, "Hi, King!" People along the curb waved many small Norwegian flags as well as American flags. The crowds increased as we approached downtown Fargo. Considering that it was nearly lunchtime on a quiet Sunday in Fargo, a surprisingly large number of people were observing the caravan.

The police car led the caravan up the brick paving in Island Park, leading to the statue of Henrik Wergeland, a Norwegian poet and champion of persecuted Jews. This statue which had been standing almost unnoticed in Fargo's Island Park for many years, suddenly became the focal point of King Olav V's visit to North Dakota.

Snow fences kept a crowd of about 2000 people back from the area in front of the statue and the speaker's stand. Behind the statue sat the Lakota High School band, the Governor's Band of 1968. A dozen large banners, looking like painted sails of viking ships, proclaimed the various chapters or "Lags" of the Sons of Norway. Women and children were dressed in traditional Norwegian costumes with their long skirts and brightly colored jackets and caps. A dozen Indians stood near the speaker's stand in full Indian regalia.

King Olav obviously was pleased with this huge turnout and the warmth he could feel from the crowd. He stood at the speaker's lectern and told the crowd of his visit as a Crown Prince in 1939. He also reminded them that in 1914, Governor L. B. Hanna had led a delegation of Norwegian-Americans back to Oslo to present the Norwegian people with a large bust of Abraham Lincoln, which still stands in an Oslo Park.

As I listened to the King speak of this group of Norwegian-Americans who returned to their native land in 1914 for the bust unveiling, I recalled that my own grandparents, Ole and Marget Leet of Webster, North Dakota, had been with the group who accompanied Governor Hanna to Oslo. My grandparents had emigrated from Telemark and Tonset, Norway, to North Dakota in the 1870s and had homesteaded on what was to become their family farm near Devils Lake.

It was obvious listening to the King's talk that he was a liberal and democratic monarch. He spoke of the needs of the people. He spoke of the discrimination against the Jews in his country in years past.

When the King had finished speaking, I presented him with a gift on behalf of the people of North Dakota. The gift, manufactured in North Dakota, was a small branding iron with the King's brand on it. I told the King that this would remind him of his visit to the rugged western country to which so many of his countrymen had emigrated over the years. He was pleased.

Representatives of the Four Indian Reservations moved forward and made King Olav a member of their tribes. He was given the Indian name, "Chief of the Northern Lights." The tribal chairmen from the four Indian reservations were present. They included Reginald Brien of the Turtle Mountain Chippewa, Lewis Goodhouse of the Fort Totten Sioux, Aljoe Agard of the Standing Rock Sioux, and August Little Soldier of the Fort Berthold Three Affiliated Tribes.

I was apprehensive lest the King might not understand the sincerity and the seriousness of the Indian ceremony. But King Olav looked every bit the monarch as he stood ramrod straight and received the Indian war bonnet that ruffled gently in the breeze. After he had received the bonnet, the Indian dancers—to the unique strains of Indian singing and beating of a drum—gave a short sample of their colorful dancing. At the close of the dancing, Senator Quentin Burdick, on behalf of the United Tribes, presented the King with the official certificate stating that King Olav had now become a member. Senator Burdick was the only member of the North Dakota congressional delegation present for the day's events.

Following the ceremonies in Island Park, the King was driven slowly along the snow fence, which kept the crowd back, so that they could get a close look at him as he smiled and waved from the open window. The Secret Service man in the front seat warned people against reaching out to shake hands with the King as the car moved slowly along.

A luncheon had been prepared at the Fargo Elks Club with a brief reception for the King just before the luncheon. Champagne was served, and the King shook hands with any person fortunate enough to be invited to that event. A crowd of 300 people was being seated in the next room. The walls of the Elks Lodge ballroom were decorated with paintings by North Dakota artists.

The King and the reception committee took their places at the head table on a raised platform along one side of the room. In front of the King on the table was a small replica of a Viking ship. A steel statue sculptured by Terrence Larson, a North Dakota artist, was presented to the King at the luncheon. It was called "Loki" from Norse mythology and is a person who spreads mischief and disorder and when confronted with his misdeeds, is able to change himself into a raven to escape. The small statue had the leg of a bird on one side and the leg of a man on the other. One arm was the wing of a bird, and the other was the flared cloak of a man.

Toasts were exchanged with red wine at the close of the luncheon. I stood and thanked the King for visiting our state and for generating in the hearts of so many North Dakotans a pride in their ancestry, which reached back to the King's country of Norway. I said, "To His Majesty Olav V, King of Norway." The crowd, who were holding their wine goblets in a toasting gesture seldom seen in North Dakota, drank their toast in respect to the King.

King Olav stood and said, in a manner which is considered a proper response for a visiting monarch, "To the President of the United States." Once again, the standing crowd raised their wine goblets to their lips.

The King and his party left the banquet ahead of the other guests to meet the tight schedule in which he would appear as the speaker at the commencement exercises at Concordia College in Moorhead. Once again, my wife and I rode with the King in the Governor's car under escort to the Concordia College fieldhouse.

As we drove through Moorhead, he spoke of the unrest in the minds of the youth today. He told how he relaxed through sailboating or skiing. He remarked that the area from which my grandparents had come, Telemark, was one of the rustic and beautiful sections of Norway. "There are many small skiing resorts in Telemark which combine the rural atmosphere with the beautiful scenery of snow and pines and mountains."

I realized how difficult it was for royalty to move around the world because of the protocol, security, and occasional political overtones when royalty visits another country. I could understand how a King might feel, confined to his own country unless he was invited to visit another. President Johnson had invited him to visit the United States, and, of course, I, as Governor of North Dakota, and Mayor Lashkowitz, as Mayor of Fargo, had invited him to our state.

The reception at Concordia was one of sustained applause and obvious warmth from 6,000 people. King Olav spoke from a prepared text for about 10 minutes. He then left to meet his tight schedule, which required him to be in Duluth, Minnesota, that evening.

As we returned from Concordia College to Hector Airport, the King seemed to relax, with his royal duties in Fargo and Moorhead now behind him. He smoked an occasional cigarette, planting it firmly in the middle of his mouth and inhaling deeply. I asked him what brand of cigarettes he liked, and perhaps by instinct, the King avoided endorsing any product. "I smoke a great number of brands," he laughed and let it go at that.

The three executive jets on loan from Minneapolis and St. Paul based corporations were standing ready when our caravan arrived at Hector Airport. The King left in a different jet from the one in which he had arrived. I wondered if this was a device to give each plane and each crew the distinction of having flown King Olav on one leg of his triangular flight among Minneapolis, Fargo, Duluth, and back to Minneapolis.

Our reception committee shook hands with the King as he prepared to leave. "Thank you so much," he said. "You have been so very kind to me." Then he bounded up the steps of the plane, turned and waved to the crowd, and ducked inside the door. As his plane slowly turned to taxi away, he waved again from his window.

King Olav had returned to North Dakota as King 30 years after he first visited us as the Crown Prince of Norway.

The 19-Gun Salute

The greeting process didn't always operate as smoothly as it did with the King of Norway.

It was 1961 and a great day for Bismarck. Stewart Udall, the new Secretary of the Interior, was coming to town. We wanted to go all out to welcome him, for he was the cabinet officer who would do most for us in securing the Garrison Diversion Irrigation Project for North Dakota. After all, John Kennedy had promised Missouri River Basin water resource development in an historic campaign speech in Billings, Montana.

Elaborate plans had been laid for the welcoming festivities. Only one problem existed for me. I had promised months before to speak at the County Commissioners State Convention in Dickinson the same day. By flying in our highway department twin-engine Beechcraft, I could return from Dickinson in time to be at the Bismarck Airport when Udall's commercial flight arrived.

The returning flight from Dickinson seemed to take forever. As the long, crooked valley of the Missouri River came into view, I knew it would be touch and go if my airplane beat Udall's plane to the airport apron.

In the distance, at the end of the runway, I saw a puff of blue smoke rise slowly into the air. Our plane's radio crackled into action. "Northwest Airlines Flight 87, this is the Bismarck Tower. There is a cannon near the end of the runway. . . ."

"There's a what?" radioed the Flight 87 pilot in disbelief.

"There's a cannon near the end of the runway practicing a 19-gun salute for one of your passengers, Secretary Udall."

"Oh, I see," the airline pilot growled. "Well, tell them to keep the dang thing pointed the right way."

The big Northwest Airlines Electra settled down through puffs of blue haze and touched its wheels to the runway. We followed. The last thunderous volley pealed out as I stepped from the highway department plane.

I was a minute or so late but not too late to join the enthusiastic crowd as it greeted a smiling Secretary Udall on his first visit to North Dakota. And the National Guard's saluting canon had fired its last cabinet-officer salute for decades to come—if ever again!

Vice Presidents Are Always Welcome!

We had a steady stream of national politicians, some who came to visit, some who came to campaign, and most who did a little of both! The year of 1967 was our seventh year in the Governor's residence. No other North Dakota governor had served more than six. Some friends decided that this new record of years in service as Governor called for a recognition affair, which was to be held at the Fargo Civic Auditorium on May 13. A bipartisan committee of Republicans and Democrats who were our good friends was formed to promote the affair.

Vice President Hubert Humphrey agreed to attend as the main speaker. When WDAY heard that Humphrey would be on hand the day of their traditional WDAY High School Band Festival, they asked the committee to invite the Vice President to be the honorary parade marshal. He agreed to arrive in Fargo early to participate in the parade.

This was not an election year, but political jealousy in some Republican officeholders and party officials began to mount. Devious means were planned to minimize the success of the event. Too many Democrats were in the limelight.

First, Republican members of the bipartisan committee were pressured to resign. They refused. Then a large public service corporation was pressured to demand that one of their vice presidents serving on the committee resign. The corporation buckled and reluctantly ordered their vice president to resign from the committee or be fired. He resigned in anger, telling the rest of the committee why he was being forced to do so and who was behind it all. Democrats were infuriated.

Next, WDAY, which had invited the Vice President to be its band festival parade marshal, abruptly cancelled its annual band festival of many years because they had discovered a week before the bands were to arrive that their new TV station at Devils Lake would "keep them too busy to follow through on the festival." Since the TV station at Devils Lake was merely an extension of WDAY and would not require more than two or three new employees, it was apparent to close observers that WDAY had caved in to political pressure. The WDAY band festival, with more than 100 units already registered, had been an annual affair for 20 years.

Now independents, as well as Democrats and a goodly number of Republicans, were indignant. What had been a recognition banquet that would have passed unnoticed outside our circle of friends now became a topic of conversation everywhere. The success of the banquet was assured.

A few days before the banquet, a resolution was introduced in the Fargo City Commission to welcome the

Vice President of the United States to Fargo. It passed three to two!

Finally, the big evening arrived. It was a gala event. Seventeen hundred people overtaxed the auditorium capacity to be seated at the banquet.

When it was time for me to acknowledge the joy that the event was giving Jean and me, I addressed Hubert Humphrey.

"Mr. Vice President, I welcome you to North Dakota. And I want you to know that you are also welcome in the city of Fargo. This was made official a few days ago when a city commission resolution was passed 3-to-2 to welcome you." The crowd roared with laughter.

"And, Mr. Vice President, lest you think that a 3-to-2 vote is not a compliment, I want you to know that no Democrat has ever gotten a 60 percent vote of approval in Fargo before."

By now the Vice President was laughing so hard with the crowd that tears came to his eyes.

It was a smashing success—that banquet. The behind-the-scenes sabotage had raised it to a cause celebre and brought notice and people to the event far beyond its sponsors' expectations.

Robert Kennedy

Robert Kennedy visited North Dakota during his 1968 presidential campaign. But deciding to become a candidate had not been easy for a man who had already lost a brother to an assassin's bullet.

Jean and I were invited to Des Moines, Iowa, to attend a Democratic banquet to honor our friend Governor Harold Hughes, who had announced his candidacy for the United States Senate. Senator Robert Kennedy was the featured speaker.

When the evening's applause had died away and the huge auditorium emptied, several of us, including Governor

Robert Docking of Kansas, were invited to visit with Governor Hughes, Senator Kennedy, and a handful of others in Hughes' hotel suite.

The subject of discussion changed from time to time but always returned to the question of whether or not Robert Kennedy should declare himself a candidate for his party's nomination for President of the United States.

Eight years before, I had been fully committed to Senator John Fitzgerald Kennedy, but now I was less enthusiastic about his brother Robert.

I counseled him not to seek the nomination. Above all, I believed Hubert Humphrey was the best-qualified candidate on any ticket, and I was solidly committed to him. I told Kennedy that our party had too many problems and that he shouldn't needlessly squander his political capital in the upcoming race.

I pointed to the unpopular Vietnam War and the candidacy of Senator Eugene McCarthy as two very divisive elements that could destroy the chances of the Democratic party in the fall election. I tried to point to Kennedy's youth and the probability that another year would be better in which to seek the Presidency. I told him that some day, perhaps, I could support his seeking the nomination but that in the upcoming Democratic Convention, I would support Hubert Humphrey.

Senator Kennedy had ardent supporters in the room, but he did not indicate at that point whether he would announce his candidacy. However, a week or so later, Robert Kennedy did announce his candidacy.

I made my public position clear as a supporter of Hubert Humphrey; but at the same time, I urged North Dakota Democrats to follow their own personal preferences and be prepared to battle for their Presidential candidate in our state convention.

Senator Kennedy visited our state in late spring. I met him at Hector Airport in Fargo. We got into an open convertible with the Senator perched on the back of the seat like a homecoming queen. The airport crowd was large, young, and enthusiastic. They pressed in to touch him. Two security men in front of the car parted the crowd with difficulty so the car could inch forward. I was sure that in the press of the shouting, teeming crowd, there would be injuries, especially to feet forced under the slowly moving vehicle.

We proceeded down Fargo streets, a caravan of slowly moving cars through the gathering dusk. I held one of the Senator's ankles lightly. I was sure that sooner or later someone would reach up to shake Kennedy's hand and would not release it as the car moved on, thus jerking the Senator to the pavement. It did not happen that evening, but it did in Indiana a week later.

As we passed down the parade route, I had never seen such a large turnout of Fargoans along the curb sides. Nor had I ever experienced the outpouring of warm rapport and excited enthusiasm that I saw and felt that night as the young Senator passed by, waving slowly and smiling.

Senator Kennedy was exhausted as he stood at the lecturn to talk to a capacity crowd in the Fargo Civic Auditorium. His trembling hands and his rumpled clothing were telltale clues of the many events in which he already had participated that day.

But he had those magical Kennedy qualities—the flat eastern accent, the unruly shock of hair, and a sense of humor close to the surface.

"I want to thank Governor Guy for meeting me at the airport tonight," Kennedy said. "I know, however, that his heart belongs to another."

"But," the Senator quipped, "he did open the car door for me tonight, and who knows what a little gesture like that could develop into!"

President Nixon Visited Fargo in 1970

I was seated at the horseshoe-shaped table at the Midwestern Governors Conference in Columbus, Ohio, when a messenger leaned over my shoulder and said, "There is a call for you from the White House."

I examined the messenger's face carefully to see if it might betray someone's gag, but he seemed serious.

I went to one of the phones reserved for governors and, sure enough, it was a call from a White House aide. "The President is planning a visit to Fargo, North Dakota, in 10 days," he said, "to discuss rural-urban population imbalance with you, four other governors, mayors, and public officials from five Upper Midwest states. Will you be able to be present?"

I assured the aide that I would adjust my schedule to be present. "We will want you to name a mayor and one of your top officials." the aide said. I gave him the name of Mayor Lashkowitz of Fargo and Ralph Dewing, the head of the Department of Accounts and Purchases in our state government.

"We will want Mayor Lashkowitz and Mr. Dewing to come to Columbus to meet with us tomorrow morning," the aide stated. I protested that this would be difficult on such short notice but said I would do what I could.

I called Mayor Lashkowitz and Ralph Dewing immediately and explained the invitation to them. I suggested to Ralph Dewing that should he not be able to find air transportation to Columbus, Walter Christensen, my administrative assistant, was present and could sit in at the meeting the next morning.

As the Nixon visit approached, there was some conjecture as to whether it was a legitimate official function or if it was a visit set up purely for political reasons. The difference was important. If it was an official visit, the President should have an official greeting from my wife and me as Governor and First Lady of the state. If it was a political visit, then my wife and I should stay in the background, and Republican officials should represent the state. I was assured most definitely that the visit was official with no political overtones.

One day before the President was to arrive, I received a call from Republican legislator Warner Litten, who was the Fargo chairman of the planning committee. "You and the other governors from Minnesota, Iowa, Nebraska, and South Dakota will meet the President at the Public Library in downtown Fargo," he said.

"But," I protested, "I must be on hand at the airport to greet the President lest the public think I am snubbing him."

"No," Litten replied, "the White House aides are arranging this. It is out of my hands, and those are their orders."

"I am sorry," I said firmly, "but I will have to countermand their orders. I feel I must be on the apron of the airport when the President alights from his airplane."

"What are my wife's responsibilities?" I asked.

"I will have to find that out and call you back," Litten said.

At 7:30 the night before the President's arrival, I received a call from Mrs. Nixon's advance man, who was headquartered in Fargo. "Mr. Litten has informed me," the advance man said, "that your wife wonders what her role will be tomorrow. She has no part in the ceremony. Mrs. Nixon will come to the Town House Motel just before noon to view a 4-H Club style show. Your wife can meet her there, but beyond that, there is nothing for your wife to concern herself about."

Later, at 9 that evening, another aide to the President, who was acting as an advance man, called to say he had just arrived in Fargo from Utah and had reviewed the preparations. It would be all right, he said, for my wife to accompany me to the airport to greet the President and his wife if I insisted on being at the airport.

The following morning we arrived in Fargo an hour ahead of the Presidential party. The sky was blue, and the day was beautiful, though warm in the sun.

The planning was obviously designed around the President while the incoming governors were ignored. Litten and his committee had provided no greeting party to take care of people who came with the visiting governors. Television cameramen who had accompanied the governor of Nebraska were left stranded on the concrete airport apron without even a taxi in sight to get their equipment to the downtown press conference location.

Fortunately, I had alerted five units of our highway patrol to be on hand to make certain the governors had transportation even though the local planning committee a few days before had refused the patrolmen's assistance.

The airport crowd was large and enthusiastic. Cars were lined up on both sides of the streets, leading to the airport. Traffic moved slowly.

I was told that we should come over to a large bus that had been placed near the portable airport unloading stairs so that the reception committee could be briefed just before the President's arrival.

The bus was cool and comfortable and provided welcomed protection from the sun.

Republican Congressman and Mrs. Clark McGregor of Minnesota were already seated as were Congressman and Mrs. Mark Andrews and Congressman and Mrs. Tom Kleppe.

The advance man in charge of the whole operation stepped into the bus. He called for silence and said, "Now, this is the plan. When the aircraft rolls to a stop, the portable stairs will be moved up to the plane, and the President and his party will alight facing east. A row of television cameras will be along the south edge of the apron, and the reception committee will line up from the base of the portable stairs facing toward the television cameras. In this way, no one will come between the cameras and the President and his party. The first persons at the bottom of the ladder will be Governor Guy and his wife."

Representing North Dakota

"What?" Congressman McGregor exploded. "That is not the way it was planned last night at the White House."

The aide ignored him and said, "And following Governor Guy and his wife will be Congressman Andrews and Mrs. Andrews."

Clark McGregor was very irritated! He fumbled frantically in his pocket and pulled out a crumpled piece of copy paper and shouted, "Look, I was at the meeting in the White House last night, and here is the plan for meeting the President, and it doesn't have the Governor listed at all!"

I smiled inwardly because Congressman McGregor didn't realize that my wife and I were seated several seats ahead of him in the bus, and we were the only Democrats present.

"I demand to have this checked," McGregor shouted.

The aide stepped out of the bus for about two minutes and returned and looked at McGregor rather sternly and said, "The Governor will be at the bottom of the stairs, Congressman."

By this time, McGregor was deflated and said, "When was that decision made?"

The aide looked at me and said, "Right now."

The question then arose as to what role the congressmen's wives would play. "Just a moment," the chief planner said. "I will get Mrs. Nixon's advance man in here to tell you."

In a moment, the advance man for the President's wife was standing in the front of the bus. "This is the plan," he said. "Mrs. Nixon will be taken up to the Town House Motel where she will view a 4-H Club style show. Everybody is welcome to be present for that function. But I am sure there will be some of you who won't care to go because it is really no big deal with those kids, you know.

"Present at the Town House will be Governor Guy's wife. However, Mrs. Nixon will be accompanied by no one except her escort when she leaves the Town House. She will meet Congressman and Mrs. Andrews at the Cereal Lab at NDSU, where we will get our campaign pictures of Congressman and Mrs. Andrews with Mrs. Nixon.

"Then the President's wife will view the Indian training program at NDSU where Congressman and Mrs. Kleppe will be waiting to have their campaign pictures taken with her.

"Mrs. Nixon will then be driven to *Moorhead State College* where Congressman McGregor and Mrs. McGregor will meet her at a project having to do with the aging. Here, the McGregors will get their campaign pictures. Governor Guy's wife will not be present at any time after the 4-H style show."

I smiled to myself as I listened to the advance man expose all of the political campaign plans for the "official visit." Having the President arrive on Air Force 1 under the guise of an official visit was to allow him to campaign subtly at taxpayers' expense.

As Jean and I got out of the bus, still not recognized by Mrs. Nixon's aide, Mark Andrews, who had been seated near us, was outraged at how crudely the aides had handled the affair. "I hope you have a few stupid people in your party, too," Mark grumbled. "I wouldn't believe that these people could surround a President."

In a few minutes, the President's plane arrived, and the reception committee waited patiently at the foot of the stairs. I could see that Congressman McGregor was steaming inwardly because the original plan had called for the three Republican congressmen to bound up the stairs into the airplane and spend a suitable period of time in private conference with the President before they emerged triumphantly, beaming and waving to the crowd. Things just weren't working out for McGregor.

The President walked smiling down the line of people who made up his reception committee. Cameras popped, newsreel cameras whirred, and the people cheered. The

President walked along the snow fence, reaching out to shake hands or touch the eager people who had waited so long.

Mrs. Nixon, in her quiet, charming way, waved greetings to people from a point somewhat removed from the crowd who jammed around her husband. I stood back because, having been in politics for awhile, I knew that the Republican congressmen were anxious to be close to their President for the picture publicity that would come from the event.

My wife and I left the receiving line and got into the state Cadillac and followed the caravan of cars taking the President and his party toward the new Public Library Building in downtown Fargo. When we arrived at the Library, the President crossed the street to shake hands with the throng of people, who had been waiting.

I made my way to the Library to see if all was ready for the meeting, which would be held in a large, second-floor inside room with no windows but several doors. A large square table had been set up with a lectern at the west end of the table. Governors and the cabinet officers who had accompanied the President sat around the table. The President sat at the south side of the table; and, as host Governor, I sat at his right. His staff and the mayors and state officials occupied chairs around the outer edge of the room. It was an ideal place to meet from the standpoint of size, security, and congeniality for concentrated work.

For two hours, the President led the discussion on population growth and urban and rural imbalance. He solicited comments from everyone present. Unlike President Johnson, President Nixon had the capacity to listen. One by one, he would call his aides or cabinet officials to give short statements from the lectern at the end of the table.

While this was going on, I realized that my wife would be waiting for me since her role started when the President and Mrs. Nixon came down the steps from their airplane and ended when Mrs. Nixon left the Town House en route to NDSU.

I later agreed that Jean made the best of what was for her a disagreeable situation by catching up on some knitting in the state car.

On the campaign trail with Hubert Humphrey in Bismarck, 1964.

14

Politics and Politicians

The Hat Trick

A governor is never far away from politics; and, under our system, he or she shouldn't be. During my years in office, I had a running battle with the opposite party—sometimes serious and sometimes amusing, but always interesting.

In the Spring of 1962, my second year as Governor, I was invited to speak at the Indian Rodeo Cowboy Reunion at Halliday near the Fort Berthold Indian Reservation. About 800 people gathered in the school auditorium for the great event.

About half of the audience were Native Americans, and they were obvious admirers of Indian rodeo performers Joe Chase and Pete Fredericks seated on the stage. With them in their short western jackets and leg-hugging trousers were other North Dakota cowboys, Alvin Nelson, Duane Howard, and Jim Tescher. They were the new breed of rodeo cowboy—lean, wiry and tough, but quiet and courteous.

It was a colorful sight, and enthusiasm ran high. My Indian friend, Nathan Little Soldier, was a master of ceremonies and in fine fettle. The crowd roared at his jokes.

"Ladies and gentlemen," Nathan said, "in soliciting money to stage this affair today, I had occasion to stop in to see former Republican Lieutenant Governor Ray Schnell at his livestock sales ring in Dickinson."

"Here's $25, Nathan," he said, "but don't go out and spend it foolishly."

"Well," Nathan continued with an impish grin on his face, "with that mandate not to spend Ray's $25 foolishly, I went out and bought our Democrat Governor Bill Guy a new hat!"

With that, he pulled a box from under the lectern and extracted a beautiful, new, silver-beige Stetson hat and ceremoniously placed it on my head. The hat fit perfectly.

Schnell, also seated on stage, in good humor, rose to the occasion. "I'm glad you were so careful with my money, Nathan," he boomed over the microphone. "I think highly of my friend Bill Guy; he's the greatest governor this state has had—since 1961!" Eighteen months was slightly better than no compliment at all, I thought.

When it Rains, It Pours

Another time, clothing got me into trouble with the Republicans.

Bill Stern and Jack Williams were two prominent American legionnaires. Bill Stern was also the Republican national committeeman. Jack Williams was prominent in Republican Party kingmaking, but his real job was adjutant of the North Dakota American Legion.

Jack had invited me to ride in the American Legion parade at its annual convention in Minot. The lead cars containing the guests stopped at the reviewing stand so that their passengers could get out to stand and watch the colorful Legion parade units go by.

It had been a beautiful morning, with a blue sky and a sparkling sun, and spirits were high. But we had hardly mounted the reviewing stand when we noticed that the sky had turned ominously black in the northwest and that the weather was changing rapidly. Suddenly, huge drops of water were splashing down, and then the deluge hit.

I stood my ground bravely on the reviewing stand because the marching legionnaires seemed only to gather new determination as the rain pelted them. My green polyester-wool suit was saturated with water. I glanced down at the meshed cloth tops of my summer shoes and watched with interest as water squished up through the mesh when I shifted my weight.

The parade units continued down the street bravely—the water pouring off the snare drums, and white shirts plastered to the marchers' bodies.

Suddenly I was aware that Bill Stern was tugging at my trouser leg from the sidewalk in back of the reviewing stand. He was handing me a raincoat. I thankfully accepted his offer and put the raincoat on only to find it was three sizes too small and way too late.

After the parade was over and we were walking away in our cold and clammy clothes, Bill Stern said, "Just keep the coat. I went into the store behind the reviewing stand and bought it for you when I saw how wet you were getting."

I knew his heart was in the right place, so I kept the coat rather than to embarrass him by telling him it was far too small for me to wear.

Several years later, this incident came back in the shape of a charge from one of my Williston political detractors who publicly accused me of improperly accepting a gift from the Republican national committeeman, Bill Stern. He didn't mention I had given the too-small raincoat to the Salvation Army.

Dog Days on the Campaign Trail

Any candidate can tell you that some funny things happen during a campaign.

Charles Tighe was running for the office of Attorney General on the Democratic-NPL ticket in the fall of 1962. His Republican opponent was Helgi Johanneson.

We were campaigning in Wahpeton in the residential district, going door to door to meet people and to distribute our political literature. Charles would go down one side of the block and I would go down the other. We would then drive on several blocks and repeat the procedure.

I returned to our car to find Charles already seated, surveying a torn pants leg, a sock that was in ribbons, and some scratches around his ankles. He said:

> "Boy, oh boy, that was something! I came up to this house and punched the door bell. Just then this little long-haired terrier came running out of the bushes and grabbed my pants leg. Then the door opened and a mean looking lady stood there looking through the screen. The dog had given up on my pants leg and was working my sock and ankle over!"
>
> "He won't hurt you," she said. But the pain I was feeling told me other wise. I tried to smile and say something nice, but finally that snarling little cur got the best of my composure. I turned and booted him yelping back into the bushes. The lady scowled at me through the screen. "You can keep your political junk," she snapped, "I wouldn't vote for you if you were the only one running!" I bowed and said, "I'm just out soliciting your vote for Attorney General, mam. Please remember my name; it's Helgi Johanneson!"

Do Bird Watchers Vote?

Charles Tighe was again on our Democratic-NPL ticket in 1964 when he successfully campaigned for the office of Lieutenant Governor. Charles' campaign tour took him to the North Dakota Badlands country. Upon wearily stopping at a Medora hotel, he found that a North Dakota bird

Politics and Politicians

watcher society was in town, planning a bird-watching hike in the Theodore Roosevelt National Park early the next morning.

Charles Tighe never had been a bird watcher. In fact, he was an ardent hunter of wild waterfowl and upland birds. But he saw an opportunity to make some new friends and do a little subtle campaigning by joining the birdwatchers' hike the next morning.

So, armed with a pair of borrowed binoculars, he set out eagerly with the large group of nature lovers. Suddenly he stopped with binoculars poised. "There is a cardinal," he said excitedly. The park ranger raised his binoculars and gazed intently at the object of Charlie's attention.

"No, Mr. Tighe," the ranger said gently, "that is not a cardinal; it's a robin."

This announcement provoked a wave of chuckles among the bird watchers. Charles felt put down and subdued.

Later, their hike took them down along the Little Missouri River. Suddenly a waterfowl burst out from along the shoreline. "That," Charles shouted confidently, "is a blue-winged teal. I know because I have shot hundreds of them."

He could almost feel the wave of indignation that swept through the bird watchers. The idea of someone bragging about killing birds! Once again Charlie realized that he had said the wrong thing.

Some days are like that on the campaign trail—you lose more votes than you win!

Whatever You Say May be Used Against You

Sometimes you can get into trouble with your own party. That's bad enough when it's your fault, but when you're blameless, it's really irritating!

In 1964, I was invited to speak to the Mississippi Valley Association in New Orleans. After my talk, which was designed to generate downstream support for the Garrison

Diversion Irrigation Project, a local newspaper reporter questioned me.

After the questions about water resource development were answered, the reporter drifted to the subject of politics. He assumed, I later found out, that since North Dakota was historically a Republican state, he must surely be talking to a Republican Governor.

He asked me who I thought was the strongest candidate the Republicans could nominate for President. I said, "I think the strongest candidate the Republicans could nominate for President is Mark Hatfield."

"Who is he?' the surprised reporter asked.

"He is the young and very able and attractive Governor of Oregon," I replied. I then listed some of the attributes that Mark Hatfield had that would make him a good candidate.

The next morning I was dumbfounded to see a headline on a front-page story in the New Orleans *Times Picayune*: "Governor Guy is Number One Hatfield for President Fan." I read the article, which sounded as though I was a Republican Governor beating the drums for Republican Mark Hatfield. I was embarrassed that the reporter had cast me in the role of a Republican rather than a Democrat, but I thought surely this story will not go beyond Louisiana.

A month or so later, I was in Washington, D.C., to urge President Lyndon Johnson to publicly endorse the Garrison Diversion Irrigation Project. As I sat in the Oval Office waiting room, Cliff Carter, one of the President's closest advisers, came in and sat down to chat. We talked for several minutes, and suddenly Cliff asked sharply, "How is your Hatfield for President Club coming?"

My heart sank because I could see that the New Orleans newspaper story had indeed reached the White House. I made a full explanation of the incident to Carter, and he seemed relieved that no Democratic Governor was going around endorsing possible opponents for President Lyndon Johnson's job.

A mistake like that doesn't do a politician much good. But then, I don't suppose my "endorsement" helped Mark Hatfield much among his fellow Republicans either!

For Want of a Nominator the Nomination Could Be Lost

Sometimes people get the idea that politicians are something more or less than human. For example, to most uninitiated observers, political conventions are carefully laid-out affairs in which a machine organization has greased the skids for everything that takes place. Such is not the case. Dozens of details are left undone, and many inadvertent actions take place, which are typical of politics in a rural state that depends on citizen political delegates and volunteer workers rather than paid political machine employees. There is very little grease for the skids.

At the Democratic-NPL Convention in 1962, I intended to again seek my party's nomination for Governor as the incumbent. The day before the nominations were to be made, I suddenly realized I had not made any preparation to have my name submitted to the convention.

I hurriedly wrote out a short biography at home and typed it up myself to give to a delegate so he or she would have correct information to use in a nominating speech for me on the floor of the convention the following day. I made six copies, using carbon paper that was nearly worn out. The original text was quite readable, but the carbon copies left much to be desired. The carbons were to be available to hand to any reporters who might want my biography.

I sought out Ray Vendsel, a prominent Democrat, to make my nominating speech. Ray was pleased to be asked. I breathed a sigh of relief, knowing that everything now was taken care of. That night, tragedy struck the Vendsel family. Ray's father was badly injured when his pickup truck left a Ward County road. Ray was called to a hospital in Minot and remained there into the following day.

When I learned of that sad news, I suddenly realized that nominations were to start in about 30 minutes and the man whom I had asked to nominate me would not be present.

I was panic stricken, trying to think of a delegate who would be well known to the general public and willing, on short notice, to place my name in nomination. To make matters worse, the nominating speech and all but the last carbon copy was in the hands of Ray Vendsel in Minot, 120 miles away.

I caught Senator Clark Van Horn as he entered the convention hall. Senator Van Horn had a commanding, booming voice. Quickly I told him my embarrassing problem. He agreed to place my name in nomination and took the faint, hardly legible carbon copy of Vendsel's nominating information with him as he hurried toward his delegate seat.

A few minutes later, Clark Van Horn marched resolutely to the speaker's rostrum to place my name in nomination. Senator Van Horn was wearing trifocals, and he desperately tested all distances trying to read the faint and blurred print of the nominating information that I had handed to him. As he misread dates, places, and names in a halting voice, my heart sank. With this kind of lack of preparation going out over the air, what on earth would the listening public thing of me, the nominee?

Finally the nominating speech was over, and Senator Clark Van Horn shot me a glance of helpless resignation as he jammed the piece of paper containing the nomination speech into his pocket.

I have always been indebted to Senator Van Horn for taking on this difficult assignment at the last minute; and the speech was apparently good enough, because I was renominated and then re-elected in 1962.

Politics and Politicians

Wild Plums at Dickinson

Then there was the time during the fall of 1968 that the loop road in the south unit of the Theodore Roosevelt National Memorial Park was dedicated. Senator Quentin Burdick had come from Washington for the occasion. We enjoyed a beautiful afternoon under a blue sky and bright sun. The speaker's stand and chairs were set out on the brown grass of a Badlands hillside. The Bismarck Mounted Patrol added a bit of Western color to the proceedings. The loop was opened, and traffic flowed slowly uphill, down dale, around buttes, into draws, and among the cedars on a smooth, winding asphalt surface that brought animals from prairie dogs to buffalo within a stone's throw of the cars.

On our return to Bismarck, our highway-patrolman driver kept the speed right at the maximum legal limit because Senator Burdick was trying to catch a commercial flight back to Washington that afternoon.

As the Senator reminisced about his boyhood, he recounted his love for wild plums. "Say, I know a place where there are some plums," the highway patrolman said, "and it's right off the interstate."

"Do you think we have time to stop and get some?" the Senator asked excitedly.

"I think we can just make it," the patrolman said. And in a matter of a few minutes, we made a sharp turn off the interstate onto the highway that goes north from Dickinson. In only a few hundred yards, we came to an old shelterbelt that was furnishing a little wind protection to a dozen or more trailer homes temporarily situated just off the road.

Our highway patrol car bounced into the driveway alongside the trailer court and came to a quick stop in a cloud of dust. Senator Burdick's door swung open, and he raced toward the plum bushes that the patrolman had pointed out. The patrolman quickly unbuckled his seatbelt and slipped out the other side of the car running after Burdick.

It was a funny sight. Suddenly I thought how serious it might be should the gawking residents of the trailer court think that the highway patrolman was chasing down an escaping prisoner and they should throw something at him or do even worse. Soon patrolman and senator were side by side reaching here and there in the branches of the plum trees.

In a few minutes, Senator Burdick was back with his pockets bulging with the tart, sweet, red, wild plums from the shelterbelt.

"Boy," he said with a happy smile on his face as we roared off for Bismarck, "these plums have made the whole trip back from Washington worthwhile."

Politicians are people, no better or worse than anybody else, but I do have the sneaking suspicion that they have more fun! I know Jean and I did.

Sharing a joke with Senator Burdick, 1969.

Conclusion

The anecdotes and vignettes I've recounted may cause a reader to think that the lives of a Governor and First Lady were only one humorous incident and social function after another. That conclusion would miss the mark. North Dakota's governor and first lady work as a team. The days start early and end late, and weekends are jammed with official functions and political appearances.

A typical day began with decision making and ended with decision making. Those decisions had to be made quickly as the subject matter changed rapidly, like shifting gears every 10 to 15 minutes. One minute, my focus might be on economic development, and next it might be on highway construction. Then it was on to air quality, to vocational education, to rail service, to fine arts funding, to school redistricting, to oil well spacing, to interstate tourism, to wetland conservation, to student loans, to selling Dakota Maid flour, to restoring a fort, to opening a park, to sending National Guard units to a flood or tornado, to planning drought relief, to setting a hunting season, to vetoing a bill, to paroling a felon, to preparing testimony for Congress, to signing a proclamation, to reviewing mountains of reports on such things as retired employees' pensions, Bank of North Dakota industrial loans, higher education enrollments, Pick/Sloan Missouri River Basin development.....

And then the governor had boards and commissions to chair and hearings to hold. Sandwiched in between, I hastily composed press releases and jotted down outlines of speeches that, when given, necessarily bordered on the spontaneous for lack of time. Not once did I ever resort to a speech writer to prepare my speeches.

I can't do justice to the pressure my wife was under to be mother to our five children and at the same time to be a heavily scheduled First Lady and confidant to the Governor. Too often she had to present a smiling appearance when she was bone weary or when she was crying inside. Imagine the frustration she felt when she had to be silent in the face of what she knew to be unwarranted or untrue political attacks against her husband, her family, or the Guy Administration.

The memories, anecdotes, and stories I've recorded here are necessarily deficient because they dwell too much on what happened to me in my youth and when I was Governor while equally interesting happenings to my wife and children go untold.

When people ask what I think was the most important accomplishment of the Guy Administration, it is easy for me to answer. My election in 1960 finally ushered in a true two-party political system in North Dakota—so necessary if democracy is to work. I was able to open the door for a host of immensely talented people from my side of the political spectrum to serve in state government and in politics. It is precarious, I know, to try to remember all of the standout people with whom we worked so long ago, but some were very special. I wish they had received the recognition they deserved in the anecdotes and stories, but such was not the purpose of those accounts.

I think of Lloyd Omdahl, Agnes Geelan, Walter Hjelle, Gordon and Mary Gray, Norma and Walter Fiedler, Jan and Art McKinney, Eugene Rich, Lee Fraase, Larry Erickson,

Conclusion

Austin Engle, Ralph Dewing, Bruce and Sylvia Hagen, Abner Larson, Jim Fine, Art Link, Bill Murray, Fred Brandt, Byron Dorgan, Bob Huey, Ray Vendsel, Quentin Burdick, Charles Tighe, Richard and Diane Ista, John Maher, Myron Bright, Rolland Redlin, Herb Thorndal, George Sinner, Charles and Joyce Conrad, Jim Grahl, Dick and Lu Dunn, Russ Stuart, LaClair Melhouse, Henry Steinberger, Mylo Hoisveen, Irv Redman, Ralph Wood, Oscar Berg, Roy Amos, Bob Bradley, Joe Satrom, Lloyd Everson, Howard Dahl, Herbert Carbone, Howard Snortland, Bill Lanier, Cameron Clemens, Bob Hansen, Walter Dockter, Dick Weber, Walter Christensen, and Woody Gagnon. You couldn't find a more selfless, dedicated group of people.

The decade of the 1960s was important, interesting, and unique. The little slices of life recorded here will give historians a glimpse of life as we lived it. There were more smiles than tears—it was a good time to live.

Office of Vice President
for University Advancement
North Dakota State University
P. O. Box 5753
Fargo, ND 58105